NEVER OUT OF REACH

Never Out of Reach
Growing up in Tallinn, Riga, and Moscow

Eugene Dubnov

CLEMSON
UNIVERSITY
PRESS

To the memory of my brother, Vladimir Benjamin Dubnov (1937–1960)

Works published by Clemson University at the Center
for Electronic and Digital Publishing (CEDP), including
The South Carolina Review and its themed series "Virginia Woolf
International," "Ireland in the Arts and Humanities," and
"James Dickey Revisited," may be found at our website:
http://www.clemson.edu/cedp/press.

Published by Clemson University Press at the Center for
Electronic and Digital Publishing, Clemson University,
Clemson, South Carolina.

Typeset in Adobe Garamond Pro by Carnegie Book Production.
Printed and bound in Poland by BooksFactory.co.uk.

Front cover photo (left to right): Adele, Vladimir, and Eugene
Dubnov (early 1950s). From the author's personal archive.
Back cover photo: Leonid Dubnov (late 1930s). From the author's
personal archive.

CONTENTS

ACKNOWLEDGMENTS

I am indebted to the late John Heath-Stubbs for his encouragement and close reading of the first draft of Chapters 2–7, to Justin Lumley for his painstaking editorial efforts throughout the work, and to John Hunt for his generous literary counsel. Special thanks to Anne Stevenson for her comments.

Grateful acknowledgments are due to *The South Carolina Review* and *North Dakota Quarterly,* where several chapters of this book have first appeared.

The names and identifying details of a few individuals and some place names have been changed to protect the privacy of those involved.

Chapter 1: "I Needed a Woman"

"**W**hat could I do?" my father shrugged his shoulders thirty-five years later, an old man speaking to his middle-aged son, man to man, in a Jerusalem park. "I needed a woman."

My parents, in their mid- and late eighties, were sitting at the table at my sister Lena's birthday. There were about a dozen more relatives and guests present. By way of wishing her daughter a happy birthday, my mother gave a lengthy and abstruse cabbalistic discourse, which was only tenuously connected with the event. She was obviously showing off, especially in front of her former husband, a man who'd left her for another woman. In spite of all that, I couldn't but feel proud of her: a half-educated woman who'd only done four years of elementary school, she'd mastered Hebrew to perfection when already in her early sixties, and had since been studying religious philosophy and Jewish mysticism with great zeal and success. Then my father spoke. "My dearest daughter," he said, "I love you very much." That was all he had to say.

Mother burst into derisive laughter. "Do we really have to repeat the same cliché on every occasion? Can't we come up with something less trite, for a change?"

Father didn't say a word; he only slumped slightly and put his hand up to his chest, on the left; he had a weak heart. I felt an enormous respect for him then, for showing quiet and dignified restraint, for not giving as good as he got.

Sister Milla: Father had always loved Mother very much. She did everything to destroy that love. He wrote her beautiful romantic letters from the front lines. And do you know that he even tried to drown himself after they'd quarreled? Our granny—his mother—told me about it. It happened quite soon after their wedding, in Gomel. She said: "It's dangerous, you don't know my son, he can do anything to himself." Now, you may say it shows weakness of character, but it surely shows a great love! All right, so he had mistresses, but who didn't during the war? And I wouldn't rush to credit those words she likes to quote about everybody womanizing but his depravity being worse than anybody else's.

Sister Lena: I could well believe it. The war may be a mitigating factor, but even so, libertinism and debauchery and all that filth is most certainly unforgivable!

(Milla was her father's daughter and Lena her mother's; I'd like to hope I was the son of both, able to be objective about each of my parents.)

Mother: I married your father when I was a silly young girl and he was a dashing naval officer in uniform. I wish to God I hadn't. I don't know where you got that absurd idea from—that I ran away from home to a farm to drive a tractor and ride a horse. Must be his lies again. It's no trouble for him to make up florid untruths, he specializes in this. He was proud of my looks and loved to put me on display. He was happy to spend all the money he was earning on my clothes rather than on his own children. But he's a weak and shallow man, easily influenced. The Party gave him his orders right from the start and he's never questioned them. My older brother referred to him as "that atheist-communist." He warned his religious comrades-in-arms, practicing their religion underground, not to speak openly of it in your father's presence. It was only years and years later, after his death, that I discovered my own brother had been studying in an underground Talmudic school. Neither he nor our parents, who knew, would tell me, because of your father the communist. Once your father said, in my father's presence: "All priests and rabbis are thieves." And my father asked him, ever so politely, "And what exactly did they steal from you, my dear son-in-law?" In the nineteen thirties, when your father was the editor of a newspaper, his secretary, a young girl, came to him all in tears. "Fire me," she said, "my dad has been arrested as an enemy of the people." How could he have turned a blind eye to the horrors that were happening all around him? Every religious person, Jewish or Christian, saw through the regime, lots of atheists did too, but somehow he didn't! Only fools and scoundrels remained loyal to the thugs in power, all those Lenins and Stalins.

Father: What could I have done, under Stalin? I had to fire that girl, otherwise I'd have lost my own job—or even worse, been sent to a labor camp—and she would have still been fired. When in 1956 the Party opened our eyes to Stalin's crimes, we all breathed more freely. As for Lenin, don't you dare touch Lenin! Your mother's full of falsehoods. She married me partly, perhaps, for love, but mostly to gain freedom from her suffocating religious family. And she did gain it, but her family, in the person of her older brother Meir, kept pulling her back. She always obeyed everything he said. Can you imagine being married to a woman whose loyalties are to somebody with a worldview opposite to yours? Still, she was quite happy in our marriage, which gave her vanity many opportunities to shine in high society, to be admired for her beauty and wit by my educated friends and colleagues. Yes, she was happy until our son died. She saw that as divine punishment for her having failed to perform the due ceremonies at his birth—he was our firstborn, you see—and generally for not raising an observant family. Because of her brother's influence, her marriage to an atheist had always been suspect in her eyes, but now she also held me responsible for her own compromises. Books, theater, classical music—that's what has always given my life its meaning—and she had no interest in any of those. All right, I admit I sometimes also fell for pop songs all of you considered rubbishy, but I regularly went to classical concerts and instilled love for music in my children, you included. As for books, at night, when you all slept, I'd sometimes read on the stairs, so as not quarrel with the other families in the flat over using electricity in the communal kitchen.

Mother: Once I saw him crying over *Anna Karenina*. I said: "Why don't you take better care of your own family instead of shedding tears over books? Your eldest daughter is still unmarried; your other daughter's been bitten by a dog in another city; your son brings up his breakfast before school and he has no proper desk to do his homework because there's no place to put it, because you wouldn't lift a finger to ask your Party for a better flat. And all you do is weep for characters that never existed, snivel and whimper over a piece of fiction?

Several images connected with my father's departure from the family still remain fixed in my mind's eye. I was fourteen or fifteen at the time. Mother had raised the alarm a few weeks before, when a family friend reported seeing Father walking arm in arm with a woman in Riga's central park in the middle of the day. She threw his shaving things in his face and called him names. She accused him of preventing their eldest daughter, Milla, from finding a husband because of her father's public displays of infidelity, to say nothing of his family's loss of status in the community. Milla was Father's favorite child, still immature at the age at twenty-eight or twenty-nine. That day she could come up with only one rather sheepish pronouncement, "I don't like lies." Days later, Father started putting a few of his things into an old and quite small suitcase. Mother rushed to Milla who was in the other room: "Your father's leaving!" she cried. Milla confronted him. "My dear daughter," he said, "I hope you aren't condemning me?" The only thing she said was the already familiar "I don't like lies."

A few minutes later, Father called me out to the hall and said that, considering Mother's treatment of him, he had no choice but to leave home and rent a room, at least for a while. He said he hoped I understood and was on his side. "Of course," I agreed, having witnessed the razor and heavy tray thrown at him together with Mother's abuse, "but you will come back when things calm down, won't you?"

I still clearly see him looking away and hesitating. I was puzzled by that uncertain pause. "Yes," he said at last, "I will." He opened the front door and was gone.

After a couple of weeks, a letter came from his father, my granddad Abraham, who was living in Leningrad. "Dear children," he wrote in his child-scribble, "go and take Dad back. He'll be agreeable."

Mother quite rightly decided that he'd never have written this without consulting his son first and getting his consent. But her pride had once again done her a disservice. Instead of letting us do what our granddad had suggested, she persuaded me to write him a reply. That, I realized later, was a sly move. First, she discussed the matter with me and instilled in me anger at my grandfather's very idea of us begging our father to come back. After that it was easy for me, a teenager, to imagine it was my own thoughts and words that I put down on paper.

"Dear Granddad," I wrote, "how are we supposed to take our Dad back? Shall we kneel and beg him to return? Perhaps we should ask his forgiveness? No, Granddad, it is those who leave home that should ask forgiveness—and even then they aren't always forgiven!" And in that vein it went on over a couple of pages.

Again my mother had overdone things. I began to dislike this long and repetitious letter with its melodramatic and overblown rhetoric. It wasn't really my style at all. But still, I obediently put it in an envelope, glued a stamp on, and went out to post it.

Then, as fate would have it, I bumped into Milla climbing up the stairs. "Where are you going?" she asked. "To post this letter," I said, "the reply to Granddad. But I don't really like it. I think it's too long and fussy and grumpy and laboring the point. It's too full of particulars and too undignified. I wanted it to be laconic and spartan, but Mom disagreed and thought it should spell out our position in a detailed manner and with a lot of irony. She likes the result, but I'm not happy with it. I'd rather not send it." "All right," she said. "Want to read it to me?"

So I opened it and read it to her there and then, and she agreed with my criticisms. We both returned to the apartment, and the letter was never posted. Mother was furious, but there was nothing she could do. We never went to bring Father back, and Mother would never forget the role my sister had played. Many, many years later she'd sometimes say to me: "The way she came across you that day on the stairs—as if it had to be—and you were stupid enough to ask her advice! Your mother had vetted the letter, but it wasn't enough for you—you had to have the opinion of somebody who hadn't the foggiest idea about life and people and her own position as an unmarried and no longer young woman whose father had left the family for a whore! If only you had posted the letter, Grand-dad would have surely come here without delay and he would have brought his son back himself—or would at least have acted as an intermediary to make peace in the family. Whichever it would have been, it was you who stood to gain the most: you'd have had a father! But you had to listen to your bird-brained sister!"

Memory voyages to "The Road Not Taken" (Robert Frost) are perilous but all too human. Some four decades have passed since then. Several times throughout them my sister would raise the subject and attempt to justify herself by saying that the only way we could have made Father return was for Mother herself to bring him back—and she was far too proud for that.

Recently I had a conversation with an older friend, a psychotherapist with decades of professional experience. I recalled that fateful encounter on the staircase, curious for his opinion. "How old was your sister at the time?" he asked. "Nearly thirty," I said. "A mature woman, then, not a fresher," he mused, sadly shaking his head.

Still, after that I talked to my other sister, Lena, and we both decided that the letter would have ultimately made no difference. Even if Father had come back home, the only way to keep him in the family would have been for Mother to completely change her attitude toward him, a hundred and eighty degrees, and not just temporarily but perma-nently. Of that, we both agreed, she would have been totally incapable.

After the images of my father in the hall with his modest suitcase, and of my sister on the stairs, comes that of my schoolteacher visiting us at our home. She was pretty and must have been no older than her mid-twenties. My sexual awakening had erupted very powerfully a year or two before (following my first wet dream, I'd gone to the public library and read all the relevant articles in the *Complete Medical Encyclopedia*), and I was very attracted to this young woman who often gave me long looks and deep sighs. But I was far too shy. My mother had invited her over to discuss what she called "the frail little boy's criminal abandonment by his father." My teacher and I sat together on the sofa, our thighs touching, while Mother fulminated against her absent husband and suggested somebody should bring him back home to his sweet delicate child, all forlorn after his father had discarded him like some piece of waste or worse. For the sake of the said child she would even go as far as provide the father's current address.

Alas, her eloquence had little practical result. "You know," said the teacher, sighing and looking at me, "there's this film that has recently come out, *The Wild Dog Dingo*, about Tanya and her mother and Tanya's father arriving with his foster son Kolya and new wife, and also about Kolya and Tanya's pure first love."

That was the end of the visit. "Stupid fool," Mother snapped the moment the teacher was gone, "we're talking about restoring a father to a son, and she starts blabbing about new wives and pure loves—not to mention the dogs!"

At first, Father did in fact rent lodgings—perhaps, as Grandfather Abraham hinted, he hadn't completely made up his mind and was prepared to go either way—but after a while he moved in with "the whore," who lived just a few streets away from us. Her full title was "the KGB whore" because her whole life she'd been working as a German translator or interpreter for the Soviet secret police.

Soon after moving into her flat, Father filed for divorce, which Mother didn't contest and which was quickly granted. (I saw Father's second wife only a few years later, when Mother dragged me to their home to kick up a ruckus and force him to give me his written paternal leave to emigrate, which Soviet bureaucracy required. The woman was supposed to be a few years younger than him, but looked older and was quite ugly, even making allowances for her horrible black horn-rimmed glasses—and even taking into account my antipathy to anybody working for the KGB, in whatever role. My mother was already in her late fifties, but her beauty seemed to light up their entire place. But of that encounter, more later.)

Another image flashes up from a year later. I'm coming out of school, and my father's waiting for me. I, coached thoroughly by Mother, give him the cold shoulder. He walks with me and almost begs: "An affectionate calf sucks two mothers!" For the first time, coming back home, I begin to doubt the legitimacy of Mother's instructions.

"Coming to see you after school!" she parodies my words. "Big deal! A real father would come every day to try and see the son he's abandoned!"

I find enough presence of mind to parry: "It's you he abandoned, not me!"

But she's the stronger of the two of us: "All right, let's say he abandoned his wife—but shouldn't he show much more affection for you, his only remaining son, a boy who needs a father? All our family friends—Nina Solomonovna, Frieda Zelikovna, Vsevolod who's courting Milla—they all say with one voice: "How cruel he must be who leaves and then forgets his charming little boy whose health is so delicate!"

My health wasn't delicate at all; I was no athlete, but in no worse health than the average teenager.

The final image is the most powerful, and it affected my whole life. I'd come back home to Riga from the University of Moscow to apply for my exit visa, which could only be done at one's place of permanent residence. I was nineteen, and by now my relationship with Father had become considerably warmer. He'd helped me in my struggle against the unfair disqualification of my candidature by the admissions board of the university; he visited me during a business trip to Moscow and took me out to the theater; since leaving the family, he'd been supporting me financially. Without that help I wouldn't have been able to study, as the miserly scholarship was nowhere enough and students with no outside help had either to work nights or go half-starved. When I returned to Riga, Mother began to insist that I ask Father to raise my maintenance allowance: "Instead of giving all his money to that old hag, that KGB whore, he should spend it on his own son!" I raised the subject with Father on the phone, and he agreed in principle. But Mother had her own plans. "Don't meet him to discuss the raise on your own: he'll cheat you out of your due and give you only a little bit more—just what that whore would have told him to give his own son, and not a penny more! If you want more money—to which you are fully entitled—take me with you."

I discussed this with Father over the phone. He wouldn't agree to it: "What do we need your mother for? I don't want to see her."

"Make it a condition," Mother said. "You see how afraid of me he is: he knows I won't let him get away with ruses and subterfuges. Without me he's bound to fool and cheat you out of your own money."

I made her presence a condition of our meeting, and Father finally relented, very unwillingly.

We met at Strēlnieku Park nearby. Mother came along all dressed up in her holiday best. In addition to being beautiful, she had excellent taste in clothes. After the terms were settled (Father accepted the sharp raise she'd insisted on), the negotiations took an unexpected turn.

"So you left your son—and your whole family—for that old hag?" Mother shook her head pityingly.

"She's younger than you," Father retorted.

"My dear," Mother said with the utmost degree of seemingly heart-felt compassion, "you're forgetting you married me when I was a pure, untouched girl of twenty-one, while you took her when she was already a dried up old bag."

At these words Father began to run, blindly bumping into tree trunks, stumbling, miraculously managing to keep his balance and still running without stopping, until he was out of sight.

Father's second wife may have been all that—unattractive, getting on in years, even dried up—but she gave him what Mother had never done: respect. To justify himself, at one point he even showed Milla a letter from her, which began with the words "My dear husband." The letter, she said, had demonstrated fondness and appreciation.

"And why shouldn't she appreciate him, pray tell?" Mother asked with a contemptuous shrug. "Who else would have picked her up, old toe rag that she was?"

In the mid- to late 1490s, Mother's ancestors are settling in Stamboul (Istanbul), where they have fled after being expelled from Spain by an edict of Ferdinand and Isabella. They will remain there for close to three centuries. That's where, according to family tradition, Mother's birth name, Stambler, came from; some southern swarthiness in the facial makeup of many in the family may likewise be attributed to Spain and Turkey.

In 1605, in Prague, the Maharal (known to the world as the Magician of Prague), Simon Dubnov's ancestor, is busy creating his Golem, using all his encyclopedic knowledge of both the theoretical and the practical Kabala.

The distinguished (if not yet, at forty-three, renowned) historian and writer Professor Simon Dubnov is visiting his distant relatives in Gomel. The year is 1903. He gets the warmest of welcomes from my young, illiterate grandfather, Abraham the cabinetmaker (the likeness between the two is amazing), and the whole family; greatly touched by the warmth and admiration of these simple, poor folks, he autographs a few of his publications for them.

Unlike the Stamblers, the Dubnovs are typical Ashkenazi Jews looking, if anything, rather like northern Slavs. There are two strands among them, carpentry-cum-cabinet-making on the one hand, and philosophy-cum-theology on the other. The family tradition explains how they got their surname, which means "new oak" in Russian. The family roots are in the town of Mstislaw, in Mogilev Province of Belarus. The place is surrounded by dense forests, so quite naturally many of its dwellers were carpenters and cabinetmakers. Toward the end of the eighteenth century, competition between them was becoming more and more fierce. Until then, furniture had been made mostly from pine, linden, beech, maple, birch, ash, and aspen, i.e. mostly soft wood. One man decided, in order to escape the rivalry and price war, to try something totally new—hard oak. So he came to be called New Oak. (I personally feel quite proud to carry such a down-to-earth-and-nature name rather than, say, New Philosopher or, God forbid, New Theologian.)

I'm sixteen, pacing nervously up and down the small room, waiting for Mother to finish complaining about me to one of my friends. She's gone on for close to an hour now. She's standing by the window—and, oh, what luck!—a couple of pigeons have alighted on the window ledge clamoring for food. Mother, deep down a kind and compassionate woman ("Here's food for your sweet kittens," she'd say to me, half a century later, dying of cancer), apologizes to her interlocutor and goes to bring them breadcrumbs. I grab the opportunity and say it's just as well, as we should be on our way. My friend is politely saying goodbye to her, and now, already, we are both bounding down the stairs, full of the blessed insouciance of adolescence.

Chapter 2: It Could Have Been Worse

"You know, Stalin has turned out to be an enemy of the people," I said to Genka as we went out to play in the yard. I remember very well how unusually mild the weather was for late October in Tallinn. I had just heard—most probably overheard—my parents talking about it at home. We were both of us six, and the year was 1955. "What are you saying? Surely not!" Genka was incredulous.

"Honest! I swear it!" I said. "Cross my heart, hope to die, he's turned out to be an enemy of the people!"

Genka was hesitating whether to believe me or not. His face still reflected his doubt as he picked up a stick and a piece of dirty old rag from the grass, hung the rag on the stick like a flag, and went into the street. I followed him, without understanding what he wanted to do. Solemnly carrying his homemade banner before him, Genka began to march along our Graniidi Street, proclaiming at the top of his voice: "Lenin is an enemy of the people! Lenin is an enemy of the people!"

Folk coming in our direction gave us strange looks. Some of them, it seemed to me, slowed their pace, and once, turning round, I noticed that one man was following us with his eyes. Of course, I didn't understand a thing—I only saw that we were drawing attention. Moreover, perhaps from the way my parents had talked about it, I felt that these matters were not to be noised abroad. Years later, recalling this incident, I thought that my feelings might even have been hurt by the profanation of Lenin's name: for a six-year-old Soviet child, this name was already surrounded by an aura of sanctity.

But in the first place, I could not bear being misquoted and misrepresented. I grabbed Genka by the arm and whispered into his ear: "I didn't say Lenin, I said Stalin!"

Immediately, without demur, he changed his tune and, still marching along the paved sidewalk with his banner, announced: "Stalin is an enemy of the people! Stalin is an enemy of the people!"

Passersby still stared at us, and I felt intensely uneasy. But abandon Genka or even ask him to shut up, I could not: such a failure to stick by my own words would have been as good as going back on them! How long we went on marching like this, I don't remember. By pure good fortune, nothing untoward occurred.

And all sorts of things could have happened. Hearing such blasphemy about Lenin, somebody or other among the passersby might have taken an interest in the children's parents. And to call even Stalin an enemy of the people in 1955, just two years after his death, was still risky: his denunciation by Khrushchev had been taking place behind closed doors. It is possible that in a purely Russian city, such as Moscow or Leningrad, the fate of my family, including my own future, would have turned out differently as a result of Genka's demonstration. But the incident took place in Tallinn, the capital of Estonia, where the Soviet regime was universally hated. In our neighborhood, I think, about two thirds of the passersby would have been Estonians and not Russians.

At any rate, nobody did stop us. Nobody came up and said to Genka: "Boy, who taught you to say that?" And Genka did not reply, pointing at me: "It was him." And nobody then said to me: "Boy, where did you hear that?" or "Boy, where do you live?" And I did not take anybody to our block of flats, number 22 Graniidi Street. And my father was neither arrested nor even expelled from the Party.

Never did my parents learn about this imprudence of mine.

Much later, when I was an adolescent, and afterward, when I had enrolled at Moscow State University, my mother—and sometimes my father too—told me that I ought to show more discretion in what I said. I did not take these warnings seriously, for I considered my parents to be products of another era. "In Stalin's time you would have rotted in a labor camp long ago for a tenth part of what you've been discussing with your pals," my mother used to say to me with disdain—probably both for my garrulity and for the state system. "You're a fool, you understand nothing at all. You haven't been through what we went through."

"But what was it I said wrong?" I complained to a friend of the family who was younger than my parents. But he likewise shook his head: "It's under the liberal Khrushchev that saying such things is no more than dangerous. In Stalin's time you'd immediately have been picked off."

I was lucky: I grew up in the most liberal period Soviet Russia had seen for over half a century. It could have been much worse.

That surreal demonstration in the street of Tallinn at the age of six can, however, be seen as a kind of synecdoche not only for my childhood and youth in the Soviet context but also for something very personal, devoid of any context, a microcosm hinting perhaps at those "things under heaven and earth," which Hamlet ranged against science.

The pattern of my whole life has been to live dangerously close to the flames—sometimes so close as to get burnt—then right at the last moment to run away, catch my breath, live quietly for a time, and then face yet another fire.

My first sexual experience, at the age of eighteen, was with a lovely, romantic nun from the Moscow monastery where I was for a while employed as a teacher of English. It was painful for me to part from her when her monk brother intervened, but fortunately he wasn't of a murderous disposition.

Then one day I discovered that my closest friend in Russia, the man I had trusted wholeheartedly and confided in, had betrayed me. Still, in the end it didn't matter, though it left a scar.

A drunken captain came to my workplace in Riga brandishing his revolver and threatening to shoot me. As luck would have it, I was out buying booze to celebrate our boss's birthday and missed him by a whisker.

My brushes with the Soviet secret police, whose long arm tried to reach me even later outside the country, could have ended disastrously for me. Almost by a fluke—or miracle—they didn't.

At the height of my nervous breakdown in London, I became fascinated with Soho and its prostitutes. During my last and nearly lethal escapade, I was saved by a tough policewoman.

However, the nearest I got to total self-destruction was through supposedly beautiful things: romantic love and religious faith, along the banks of the Thames, in London, Reading, and Oxfordshire. Love and faith led me merrily along and down an alcoholic path, which, amazingly, opened into a teetotal high road leading to better things.

I shall describe all those events when I come to them, in a more or less chronological order, but the weird sensation occasionally gripping me for a split second that I may have some kind of a guardian angel dates back to that little declamatory walk along a Tallinn street. I did, after all, have an inexplicable sense of relief after it, when I was back home, and I still remember the happiness that enveloped me as if I'd just escaped some grave danger.

On the whole, my contemporaries and I accepted the political and social conditions imposed by the Soviet Union. We could not draw comparisons, since we knew very little about the freedoms and traditions of the western democracies. The BBC and Voice of America, which we tried to listen to in our search for information, were usually jammed. So we lived, quite contentedly, on two levels. On the one hand, within our own circle of friends, we criticized the obvious lack of freedom in our country, while on the other, being young and educated, we enjoyed life.

Walking through the corridors of Student House, the main building of the University of Moscow, we exchanged snide jokes about walking on the bones of Stalin's prisoners, who had been engaged in building it. I even penned this poem, imagining myself as one of them:

"With Vicious Force the Storm"

With vicious force the storm has slammed
The window shut, and suddenly
The lights turned off and all around
The air is dark as the somber sky.

Such darkness as if night has driven
Into its net the rising tide,
And everywhere in Moscow shares
The crushing blizzard at my side.

A Prisoner, I stand where there's
No record of my having been
And sense the darker destiny
That waits for me beyond this scene.

(Moscow, 1968, translated with Peter Porter)

But all this did not stop us from relishing the excellent food served in the "National Dishes" canteen. Nor did it prevent us from enjoying our privileged position as students in the greatest university in the country. In the university cinema we watched films that were not on general release—Tarkovsky's *Andrey Rublev*, for instance. Most students, including myself, who came from other cities, fell in love with Moscow and were proud that our faculty was at its very heart, facing the Kremlin and Red Square. We went to theaters and cinemas, art galleries and student balls, and in spring and summer we liked to walk in the large gardens of the Faculty of Biology. As future graduates of the State University of Moscow, we had good job prospects. And in our third year we moved from our hall of residence annex, where we lived four to a room, to the main building where conditions were simply regal: only two people per room, though the rooms were half the size. Amid such privileges, politics receded into the background. We exchanged quick glances when our lecturer in Party history urged us to talk about the achievements rather than the shortcomings of the Stalin era. We nudged each other when our lecturer in biology—in 1968, mark you—referred respectfully to the murderer of Soviet genetics (and, ultimately, geneticists) Lysenko, affectionately calling him by his first name and patronymic Trofim Denisovich. But on the whole, we were living it up.

"We" were only dozens out of thousands of students at the university. "One should swim with the stream, with the tide," so my sister's father-in-law urged me—an old man who had survived Stalin's occupation of Bessarabia. Indignant as I was with this whole approach, I nevertheless also swam with the tide. Even among those of us who held dissident views, there were differences of opinion. One young man who had no illusions about the Soviet system was ready to justify the invasion of Czechoslovakia by Soviet troops in 1968. "We can't give up Czechoslovakia, can we?" he challenged me. Another, though he disliked the invasion, nevertheless thought that the regime simply had no choice as during the Prague Spring, Czechoslovakia had been flooded by thousands of West German agents who had subsequently seeped into the USSR. He had got this "top secret" information from his father, a high-ranking university professor, who, in turn, had heard it at a closed session of the senior teaching staff. This sort of thing, surely spread about by the KGB, helped to explain the throttling of Czechoslovakia to the doubting intelligentsia. And explanation is almost acceptance, and the step from acceptance to justification is also a short one.

My fellow students reacted with some respect but even more with sarcasm when I appeared at a university poetry evening. On that occasion I read, among other poems, one which was really about the invasion of Czechoslovakia. This poetry evening took place only a few months after the events there, and my "Verses on Silence" spoke of "the silence of conscience in the cells of oppression and lies" and about troops inured to "obliterating frontiers with their jack-boots." (I wish I could have read the following, which I wrote at about the same time, but that would have been really suicidal:

> When rumbling tanks climbed up Hradčany's hill
> And blood for dew distilled upon the town—
> On ravished Prague—a woman of that city
> In throes of labor gave birth to her son.
>
> The child's first cry was spilled and drained away
> Beneath the soldiers' feet, their trampling noise,
> And once again the barrel of a gun
> Assumed protection of a Senate House.
>
> The father was not waiting for his offspring;
> The sun had clotted in Vltava's eyes;
> And in the square Jan Palach was ascending
> Jan Hus's fire and felt the flames arise.

As you invoke a blessing for your boy,
Raising your hands above the soldiery,
Mother, do you foresee what trials await him—
What fires, what martyrdom, what agony?

Moscow, 1969; translated with John Heath-Stubbs)

To forestall any questions, I had prepared a reply—to wit, that those verses were about American society and American troops in Vietnam. How many people understood—and how much they understood—I cannot tell: yes, the students clapped, the shrewd editors of literary magazines sitting as adjudicators and the representatives of the university authorities did not seem to react, no questions followed, but I was never invited to take part in a poetry evening again. My friends said afterward that I had taken an unnecessary risk, since Czechoslovakia was of no interest to anybody anywhere and was anyhow a dead loss. If one was to take risks, they all concluded, it had better be for something more worthwhile, like democratic freedoms within the USSR itself. In this way, without realizing it, they were reacting in exactly the way the state ideologists would have wanted. For there is only one way to take a moral stand against a totalitarian ideocratic system—and one must take a stand and not be tempted by its occasional charms. It is to have no truck with it at all, and that includes total rejection of the rules of its logic. If you argue that, in spite of his crimes, Hitler did give the German people full employment, or that you don't condone Stalin's misdeeds but have to admit his achievements in terms of the industrialization of the country, then you're already tainted with ideological leprosy.

Fighting the ideology, however, was almost futile: it penetrated everywhere, into the most secret recesses of the mind and into the unconscious. That's why, I think, it would be truer to describe our life in the Soviet Union as not even two-faced but simply as having a second dimension. It was as if our day-to-day existence as ordinary Soviet youth was accompanied everywhere by a shadow.

Underneath that ambivalence, though, was another, much more serious and complex and confusing one, clamoring irresistibly for attention. For there had been, and still were, aspects of the regime that were positive and humane, both before Stalin and after him, in my own lifetime, under Khrushchev and Brezhnev. I'm talking about the periods that were autocratic, authoritarian, or oligarchic rather than totalitarian—a phenomenon I'm tempted to term "socialism with a humanoid face."

My parents welcomed the "freedoms" brought about by the Revolution: my father, because they saved him from the poverty of his family, and my mother, because they allowed her to escape (temporarily, as it had turned out) the oppressive religious atmosphere of her parents' home.

Father, born in 1908, went to primary school under the Tsarist regime. As a snack he took with him old crusts of bread, because there was nothing else in the house. Other children were from more well-to-do families, and he felt ashamed of his poverty. So, at the age of seven, on his own, unassisted, he made up the lie that it was the doctor who'd ordered him to eat only the fossilized crusts, to strengthen his weak gums.

The whole town of Gomel was owned by Ivan Paskevich, prince, Field Marshal, and hero of the Crimean War, who died in 1856. In 1916, his daughter-in-law Irina gave a

Christmas party in their sumptuous palace to which she invited all children whose fathers were at the front during the First World War. Father's mother immediately rushed to look for decent clothes for him—shoes, trousers, jacket—and for herself too, because her own clothes were also too poor. So they all ran to and fro and finally succeeded in borrowing a jacket and a pair of shoes from their traveling merchant neighbor across the street. (A wealthy man, indeed!) His son had small feet, so the shoes were too tight for my father. As a result of all that fussing about, they were late for the lighting of the Christmas tree and got to the palace when all the Christmas presents had already been given out. Father was standing on the staircase crying. A woman coming down the stairs—a maid or governess—asked his mother why the boy was crying. She explained. The kindly woman straightaway went and brought a present. Then she took my father by the hand so that he could join other children holding hands dancing around the Christmas tree. She wanted to take his present away from him—only for a while, to make it easier for him to hold other children's hands—but he clutched it and wouldn't let go. And so he danced, grasping their hands and his present. His hands being wet, on account of the sweat and the wiped-off tears, the little package slipped out of them and fell on the floor. All the sweets were immediately trampled under the children's feet. He ran out of the round dance and burst into tears. They began to pick up the sweets and anything else that remained, to give it back to him, while he went on sobbing.

Post-revolutionary Russia opened all doors for these penniless Jewish children, and they entered the new bright reality with all the enthusiasm and idealism of youth. The moment the Young Pioneers League was created in 1922, my father rushed to join. (According to him, my mother became one of the very first Young Communist League members—something she vehemently denied.)

In the late 1920s, my mother's brother, a young hothead, nearly killed a neighbor who'd tried, illegally, through his connections with some higher-ups, to grab a piece of the family's house (that was the time when everybody had to live in cramped quarters—including, incidentally, the abovementioned Prince Paskevich's daughter-in-law, who had to move from their grand palace to a small, ordinary flat). The man was taken to hospital (he recovered, but never came back) and my uncle was sentenced to two years in a penal colony for adolescents. At that time, the country invested heavily in the future of her children, including the rehabilitation of young criminals, a period described most movingly by one of the world's greatest educators, Anton Makarenko, in his timeless work *Epic of Education*. According to my mother, the one and a half years his sentence had been commuted to had to be spent in a colony—just outside the town, surrounded by nature, like a resort home. The young people were treated and fed well and were allowed frequent visits from their relatives (if they had any, that is: many children were guttersnipes as a result of the Civil War and the following military Communism).

Looking from afar at the cruel and corrupt state of affairs in Russia today, the middle of the second decade of the twenty-first century, with the elderly begging in the streets (and dissenting investigative journalists dying mysterious deaths, but that's another and more frightening topic), I can't help wondering. In my time, no one went hungry. Everybody worked; there was no unemployment. The rich top brass never dared flaunt their riches in public, the way the oligarchy deliberately, ostentatiously does now in front of desperate poverty. And with all the bureaucracy and hierarchies there still seemed to be more caring about ordinary folks, what's called in America "the little guy," than there seems to be today. As a boy in Riga, I witnessed my mother's nighttime complaint to the Party man on duty regarding a long-distance call to Tashkent. The telephone exchange girl on the line was rude to her, saying she was too busy. It was essential for Mother to talk to her sister, whose little child was sick. Mother got the Party Headquarters number from Directory Inquiries and phoned them when it was past midnight. The man on duty on the other end of the line took the details. Ten minutes later, the telephone exchange lady called, apologized profusely, and without further ado connected Mother with Tashkent.

When struggling to get the exit visa, one of Mother's arguments was the fact that Father, a communist and therefore a supposedly ethical man, had left her with no alimony, no financial support of any kind. The Party Secretary almost begged her to submit a written complaint: "We'll make him pay dearly for that kind of immoral behavior!" "Just let me leave the country and go to my brother's," she insisted.

And finally they did.

Chapter 3: "The Thug Copped It"

In school, I was an active pioneer and, thanks to my sociability and my gift for speaking and declaiming poetry, took part in various ideological school jamborees. Once, when I was about fifteen, our school was named the "Pavlik Morozov" school. That young pioneer hero was an important martyr in the Soviet pantheon. During the collectivization years, he had informed on his own parents for attempting to hide their grain and prevent its requisition by the government. Such requisitioning would have meant starvation for a peasant family. To be informed upon meant either being shot out of hand or deportation to Siberia and a lingering death there. The boy—if he existed at all and if Soviet history is to be trusted—was knifed by his grandfather for being an informer, and so died.

A bust was solemnly unveiled in our school vestibule. All day pioneers stood on guard on both sides of it, relieved every hour. I, with my school pal Zhenia (short for Yevgeny) Konyaev, had the honor of being assigned the first watch. At the most solemn moment, when the entire school stood motionless before this bust and our pioneer leader ("scout leader" might be the western equivalent) had reached the dramatic climax of her speech, we were to break ranks, come up to the bust of the young hero, salute him with a pioneer salute, and, dividing in military fashion, take up our positions on either side of him.

And so, there we were, standing with our backs to the assembled crowd, looking straight ahead and saluting the fallen hero. Behind us, our leader in a trembling voice was saying: "And that's how the enemy butchered our Pavlik." And then my pal added in an all but inaudible whisper: "And a good job too!"

I began to choke with a quite uncontrollable fit of the giggles, and tears came to my eyes. In a couple of seconds I would have to turn round and face the entire school. I started coughing strenuously. Choked with my simulated cough and still with tears bursting in my eyes I took up my place of honor on the left side of the memorial. When I had turned right round, I was afraid to look at the faces in front of me. But everybody must have thought I had a bad cold or was even overcome by emotion and no one gave me a suspicious look.

Laughter did help to counteract the brainwashing, but it did not save, for the sheer repetition of slogans poisoned your mind, however much you may have derided them. To resist them, you needed a stronger foundation.

My attitude to the outside world I owed to my mother. Until my final exit from the country at the age of twenty-one, the influence she had exerted on me from childhood was completely at odds with the whole colossal state machine.

When I was about sixteen, I read or heard for the first time how there had been a mass shedding of hysterical tears at the death of Stalin. This phenomenon seemed odd to me for even those who suffered directly under him or who had known only too well the abject terror that had gripped the country—even they indulged in heartfelt weeping. I found out that some of those who had been preparing themselves to become his next victims had also wept for him. Among such, for instance, were many Jews who, after the notorious "Doctors' Trial," had expected any day to be loaded into cattle trucks. These transports had already been shunted at the larger terminus towns in European Russia, their destination being Siberia. The lamentation of the doomed for their executioner seemed like a mass psychosis, and I asked my mother: "It looks as if everybody was shedding tears when Stalin died. Did you cry too, Mother?"

Mother was indignant at my question and answered me scornfully: "The thug copped it—and I should cry?"

One story she told me a number of times in my early years, probably wishing to impress it on my memory, shook me profoundly. It referred to an event in Gomel, her birthplace, in the mid-twenties, toward the end of the period of the so-called New Economic Policy. One day her grandfather, a simple, semiliterate, pious old man was arrested by the security police. At that time, the psychopathy of the state took the form of suspecting everyone of hoarding gold. One glance at that impecunious family should surely have been enough to show how ridiculous such a suspicion was. But at that period, religious persecution was also being stepped up, and it is possible that the search for gold was only a pretext for the local Cheka to make the arrest. Perhaps the authorities wished to intimidate other believers by making an example of my great grandfather, loved and respected as he was by the townsfolk. The time, however, was still "vegetarian"—to use the word Anna Akhmatova applied to it, in contrast to what was to come, which might have been termed "cannibalistic." People in the town began to say: "Well, if folk like old Stambler, who wouldn't hurt a fly, get arrested …" And the authorities relented. When, three or four months after his arrest, the old man unexpectedly returned home, his own wife, who opened the door to him, did not recognize him. "Can I help you? Who are you looking for?" she asked.

Before releasing him, they had extracted from him a signed undertaking that he would never tell anyone about what had happened to him while in custody. And indeed, he must have been so frightened by the security police that he never told anybody just what they had done to him in their cellars.

My unconscious and conscious search for coherence in the identity that was woven into my life in the course of all those years, could to a large extent be explained by radical differences between my mother and my father.

My father, who used to tick me off for my "too negative" approach to the Soviet system, was an experienced journalist with many years of professional practice behind him. After beginning his career as a lieutenant in the navy during what the Soviets called the Great Patriotic War, he ended up as a front-line reporter with the rank of major. He was a member of the Communist Party, and the Party appreciated his journalistic talents.

"You silly boy," my father used to ask, "what do you know about the Revolution to poke fun at it so glibly?! It removed the Pale of Settlement; we Jews—especially the poor ones—were freed and could pursue any career we wanted. The idealized image your mother has of pre-revolutionary Jewish life is false through and through, and she knows it!

"I shall always remember one episode that deeply impressed my child's mind. I was around six or seven, so it must have been in the middle of the first decade of the century. My father—your grandfather Abraham—was, as you know, a cabinetmaker and a carpenter. We were a poor family. Once a very rich man in our town commissioned my father to make him some furniture—cupboards, sofas, tables or shelves, that sort of stuff—worth a lot of money. My father delivered the goods, but the man wouldn't pay. My father took me along when he went to his house, two or three times, to ask for the money owed to him. The wealthy man kept putting the payment off under various pretexts, blaming the creditors or the War—the First World War was in progress at the time—or simply saying he just happened to be out of money at that moment and asking him to come again later. Then one evening my mother went instead, again taking me along. There was a big dog in the yard of the rich man's house: usually it was on a chain, but on that occasion it happened to be untied. It jumped at us, and my mother was so terrified she screamed at the top of her voice. We ran for our lives. I've had an uncontrollable fear of dogs ever since. We never got paid, not a penny, by that man who was loaded with money. I welcomed the Revolution with all my heart. When the Young Pioneers Association was created in 1922, I became one of its very first members."

Of course, my mother's account of this same incident differed significantly. "Your father's made that all up. Being an atheist, he would have—lies come easily to these people. Can you really believe that a religious man, part of a religious community—all Jews, mind you, were religious then, before the communists came, eternal damnation upon them— can you imagine an Orthodox and surely bearded Jew refusing to pay what he owed for the furniture he ordered? Can you? For I surely can't!"

Once—to be more precise, in the early thirties—in a medium-sized town in Belorussia, there lived a girl. She worked as an assistant bookkeeper in one of the local enterprises that had been set up after the Revolution. One day, a girlfriend with whom she worked asked her: "Would you like to meet a nice boy?" All her friends had already got admirers, although she was prettier than any of them, and she longed to have one as well. But she kept her feelings to herself and answered with a proud show of indifference: "To meet a boy? I have no time for that sort of thing." Her friend, however, brought the boy along. He came to their workplace toward knocking-off time, and she could immediately tell by his excited manner that he liked her. He began to tell her about himself: he was a visitor to the town, his permanent home being in Moscow, where he was studying at a naval school and also taking some journalism courses. For a girl from a provincial town, the image of a student from the big city was full of glamor and romance. And he spoke beautifully, like a book. After her work was over, he insisted on seeing her home, even though she didn't want him to. Now all her acquaintances—and in a small town everybody knows each other—could see that she was going out with a boy. At her gate, he asked for her work phone number. Surely she would never have given it him! But she felt so embarrassed standing there with a strange young man—her parents might at any moment come out of the house and then she would definitely have died of shame. So, just to get rid of him, she gave him the number, hoping he wouldn't use it.

But he did use it—and the very next day too!

Just before he was supposed to call for her at work—again toward the end of the day—she asked her girlfriend: "Vera, listen, this boy is not from these parts—so how does he know old Abraham Dubnov? When he insisted on seeing me home yesterday we bumped into old Dubnov—and they greeted each other so warmly they might have known each other for years."

Vera burst out laughing. "You silly girl, he's old Dubnov's son. He just happened to leave here as a teenager to get his college education in a big city."

The young man started to come every day to see her home from work, and in a few months' time they got married. Her mother didn't attend the wedding: the groom was totally secular, and she had wanted a religious son-in-law, a scholar proficient in the Bible and the Talmud. He took his bride with him to Leningrad, where he was enrolled in the Naval Academy. She was glad to leave her native Gomel and the many pressures from her family.

My mother didn't like to talk about it, but the story goes in the family that she'd run away from home in her late teens, to ride horses and drive tractors on a collective farm. Mother considered Father a good-natured, well-meaning, trust-everyone wimp. She liked to tell a story about his having been offered the editorship of a major newspaper—a definite promotion since he'd been a deputy editor at a lesser publication. He shared the good news with an ambitious colleague who immediately rushed to the big newspaper's editorial offices and offered his own services. The paper's top brass weighed his candidacy against my father's and in the end preferred the colleague.

My father had been a naval officer and then a war correspondent. Mother regarded his military fortitude as indicative not of courage but of recklessness. She taunted him for being spineless and incapable of standing up for himself, for not fighting for promotion to the next military rank and not defending his honor before an ungrateful and abusive air force general.

The Soviet counterattack at Stalingrad began on November 19, 1942. Within four days, the 330,000-strong German forces had been encircled. The war correspondent for the country's military newspaper, *Krasnaya Zvezda* (*The Red Star*), Captain Leonid Dubnov (he would be promoted to major in the spring of 1945), alighted from a Polikarpov U-2 plane and went to look for the group commander, Colonel Sedov. The man had attracted his attention for having been much more successful than other air force commanders in dropping food and ammunition for the defenders of Stalingrad earlier in the month. While other air regiments' supplies mostly fell into the Volga or behind the German lines, due to conditions in the air and on the ground, Sedov's squadrons managed to get over half of their cargo through to where it was so badly needed.

The regiment was stationed in a village, the military lodging in houses, and regiment offices and airfield services being housed in huts.

The captain was a sturdy man of average height, five foot seven or thereabouts, with a strikingly handsome face. He walked resolutely past depots of arms, parachutes, mobile aircraft workshops, looking for the regiment HQ. The snow that had been falling throughout the day had changed to sleet and stopped by the time of the captain's arrival. The weather had turned bitterly cold. The village street was a dangerous glaze of ice, but the captain somehow managed to keep his balance and walked on and still on with disciplined, military self-assurance with the whistling wind whipping against his face. Gazing at the crisp snow blanketing the street and giving an involuntary shiver in the chill air, he wondered what kind of man Colonel Sedov would turn out to be. Just before the HQ a road full of potholes opened between two huts, leading to a bright, boundless field. Behind the fence that marked the end of the village and the beginning of paddocks or grazing ground, the airfield could be seen with some dozen Yakovlev Yak-7b fighter planes, as well as aircraft that flew the group commander. Patches of snow sloughed away in several places, revealing the bald ground underneath.

Showing his documents to the sentry, the captain entered the warm HQ room and brought into it the chill whiff of wind, snow and ice.

Colonel Sedov looked as different from the captain as humanly possible: tall and strapping, with a prominent roughly-hewn nose and slightly dilated nostrils (the captain's nose was delicately sculpted, like a figurine), furrowed cheeks and overlarge ears, he was not attractive but his strong cleft jaw, his black hair streaked with grey and his seemingly peasant manner immediately endeared him to the captain.

A month later, Sedov saw his portrait, with a no-nonsense frowning face, in *The Red Star*. Next to the portrait was a full-page article. The article was also brought to the attention of Lieutenant General Alexander Novikov, who only a few months before had taken command of the Red Army Air Force. Colonel Sedov was summoned to Moscow, appointed wing commander and promoted to the rank of brigadier general.

It was a hot summer night. The vast heaven of stars stretched from one end of the airfield to the other. The velvet canopy was alive with the coldly burning light of pale blue stars. It was clear as he had never seen it before. The captain had all the required permissions to fly on a night bombing raid, in his capacity of war correspondent.

The German attack in the Kursk-Belgorod region began on July 5, 1943, and was stopped, along the whole front, on July 23. On August 3, the Soviet counterattack was launched along the Orel-Kursk-Belgorod line. Medium Ilyushin Il-4 bombers played an important role in that action. As the captain approached the one assigned to him, he came across a small group of military men. A few were wearing pilots' helmets and suits, but the two officers among them were dressed in a general military uniform. The captain immediately recognized one of them, the former colonel and now brigadier general.

"Comrade Sedov, Brigadier General Sedov, I mean," he said excitedly, giving a military salute to the man who owed him his promotion. "I knew you were a wing commander on the Kursk front now, but I never expected—never hoped to see you just like that—to come across you by chance on an airfield!"

"Who are you?" asked the man impatiently.

"Why, war correspondent Captain Leonid Dubnov. I interviewed you at Stalingrad in November."

"Did you?" Sedov showed no sign of recognition. "And what are you doing here, may one ask?"

"I've got permission to fly on a night bombing raid, for an article for *Krasnaya Zvezda*."

"Not here. Petrushenko," he turned to the lieutenant accompanying him, "escort him out of bounds."

"But … but … I have all the necessary papers and—"

"Lieutenant, take the captain away, and I don't want to set my eyes on him ever again. If he starts arguing, put him under arrest. We're too busy to entertain visitors here."

To cut a long story short, the bomber my father was supposed to fly on was shot down by the Germans and all its crew perished.

I strongly suspect that Sedov knew just how dangerous those night flights were and kicked my father out—quickly and resolutely, avoiding arguing—to save his life. But my mother saw this as yet another feather in my father's well-deserved and honestly earned cap of humiliations.

I must stress that my memories of my mother's negative attitude toward my father date to a particular period, which began with a terrible calamity that befell our family in 1960. Before that, I do not remember any real quarrels or falling-outs. We seemed to be ordinary representatives of the Soviet intelligentsia. I don't remember ever lacking food, but it's quite telling that we didn't have a washing machine and my mother had to do the laundry—for the whole six-strong family—by hand.

I'm sure that as a communist employed in the ideological work of journalism, my father could have managed to secure a private flat for his family, but this would have required the ability to stand up and fight for his rights with a kind of nonmilitary courage he apparently lacked. At least in Tallinn we had to share the flat with only one other family: later, in Riga, the communal flat had four families besides us.

I remember our bigger room in Tallinn full of guests seated at the extended table at dinner. These were my father's friends and colleagues: journalists, doctors, writers. He was very proud of his beautiful and witty wife; she, bright and gifted but lacking education, basked in the attention of all these members of the intellectual elite. Occasionally she'd pinch me painfully under the table when she thought I was misbehaving. As she did so, she went on pleasantly talking with and smiling at the guests. I must have been about eight or nine. On a couple of occasions I couldn't take this kind of hypocrisy any more and said out loud, for all to hear: "Mother, why are you pinching me under the table?"

Mother gave a gentle and indulgent smile and addressed the whole honorable gathering: "The sweet naughty boy is at his jokes again!" And, a few seconds later, to me, in an ominous hiss out of the corner of her mouth: "I'll show you, you scoundrel!"

It must be said, though, in her defense, that these threats were never carried out. One of her saving graces was her sense of humor, and when, after the guests had left, my sisters mimicked her hypocrisy, speaking almost simultaneously out of both corners of her mouth—one corner for the guests, the other for me—she laughed heartily with the rest of the family.

Everybody also laughed when they once caught me after dinner drinking dregs of wine that I'd just poured from all the wine glasses on the table into one (it had turned out quite a sizable portion!). They admonished me never to do this again—but with indulgent smiles and giggles.

I look at the old family photographs in my album: in every single one there are gaping holes where my father had been. After he'd left, my mother took the scissors and just cut him out.

Years later, when studying English literature, I came across Robert Frost's poem "Home Burial" and was taken aback. I had thought that what had happened in my family was unique—and yet it was exactly what Frost was describing, step by step, with painful precision.

The disintegration of my family began in 1960, when my elder brother died tragically. My mother blamed my father for his death. She became much more religious, going back to her Orthodox family roots from which apparently she'd tried to escape, first by running away to a farm and then by marrying my father and moving to another, distant city.

My brother, who died when he was twenty-two—and I was eleven—had written verses in, more or less, the accepted Soviet style. Nevertheless, it seems to me that he was already on a collision course with the Soviet system. His surviving teenage poems, despite their conformism, showed a genuine talent. (He must have written poetry in his early twenties too, but there's no record of it, and it's tantalizing for me to guess just what degree of dissent that work might have had.) Having been forced, like all male students in those years, to take part in the development of virgin lands in the Asian part of the country, he spoke out sharply against the coercion and the conditions they had to work under. Such courageous openness was rare at the time. It is beyond any doubt that he was informed on and it is more than likely that the KGB took notice of his file and went after him, contributing to the tragedy of his later expulsion from the Polytechnic Institute. Perhaps his untimely death prevented the full flowering of a personality, the consequences of which could have been dire.

Vova—short for Vladimir—was too intelligent and had a sense of individual dignity too well developed for him to be able to go along with the regime. In his school class there was a tradition whereby each pupil was given a little present of some kind on his or her birthday. My brother, since he wrote poetry, was given an album containing verses written by his classmates. A few of those verses, instead of the panegyrics and good wishes expected on such an occasion, were devoted to criticism of his inordinate pride.

We shared our Tallinn flat with one other family. They were Ukrainians. The husband was an ordinary factory worker, and the wife, who originally came from a *kolkhoz* (collective farm), was employed as a cleaner in a works canteen. As representatives of workers' and peasants' power, they disliked our family. For we, after all, were part of the intelligentsia. They once had a skirmish with my brother in our communal kitchen. The husband insulted and even hit him. Exactly how he reacted, I don't know, but after that they took him to the local court for insulting behavior. They accused him, the son of an intellectual and himself a student, of treating them with disdain as representatives of the urban and rural proletariat.

Despite all the "liberalism" of the Khrushchev period, such an accusation carried serious consequences. The local court found my brother guilty, although it also delivered a mild reprimand to our neighbors for their lack of restraint. The court's decision was passed on to Tallinn Polytechnic, where my brother was studying. The council of the Polytechnic planned to consider his case in one of its routine sessions. Expulsion threatened my brother. However farcical this sounds, the only hope for a positive outcome lay not in my father the journalist—for all his years of experience in influencing the populace through the printed word—but rather in my mother the housewife, who had scarcely read anything in her life. But she was brainier and a stronger character than my father, and even her use of language—vivid and passionate—left my father's journalistic clichés far behind. She was, indeed, a born orator who drew ever more fire from her burning convictions. My father had never had such convictions, much less the courage of them.

My mother, I think, would have succeeded in defending my brother before the council of the Polytechnic, but she had to leave the town. Her sister, who lived in Tashkent, sent a telegram begging her to come. This sister had married in her forties, and now she needed help from her older and more experienced sister to nurture her first baby.

My mother hesitated at first, knowing that she couldn't safely leave her son's fate to his father. She went to see the principal of the Polytechnic. After she had talked it over with him, he agreed that there were insufficient grounds for taking measures more drastic than a reprimand or something of the kind. On the basis of this assurance, she took a plane to Tashkent.

In the meantime, the principal also had to leave for somewhere and was absent from the Polytechnic council session. (One may even suspect he made himself absent deliberately, to be safe rather than sorry—that is safe rather than finding himself at loggerheads with proletarian honor.) My father, judging by the result, did not give an outstanding performance. Later on, my brother told my mother with indignation that, while the council was temporarily adjourned, my father had smoked and chatted with his own son's chief accusers. The council decided to expel the student Dubnov for disrespect of the working classes. When my mother came back, it was too late to do anything about it.

"Your Party!" she shouted bitterly to my father. "You've spent your whole life serving it, and now your own son has been thrown out, and you couldn't help him!"

"It's his own fault," my father attempted to justify himself, "he really is far too conceited."

I think Mother was partly right: because of his fear of conflict, my father failed to use the trump card of his Party membership, the ideological nature of his work as a journalist, and his war record. Nor had he tried to make use of his personal contacts with the Party hierarchy. But, after all, he did not belong to the state elite, being only an ordinary Party member and an ordinary, albeit well thought of, journalist. When it came to a clash between an ordinary communist belonging to the intelligentsia and the ostentatiously working classes, the Party might not have come down on his side. And I must also add in my father's defense that when, six years later, the university entrance commission turned me down in spite of all my A's in the entrance exams, he showed a measure of resilience. He secured an interview with Latvia's Deputy Minister of Education, after which the commission reconsidered my case and reversed its decision. Perhaps by that time he had acquired more weight and leverage—and even courage; perhaps my case was different; perhaps the time was somewhat different too.

But, to return to my brother's case, those neighbors of ours remained unsatisfied with the ruling of the local court and got in an appeal even before we did. They were encouraged by the fact that, although innocent, my brother had been convicted by the court and expelled from his polytechnic. What's more, they had already found out how to play upon their belonging to the masses. Their appetite was whetted. In the event of a successful appeal, they could hope for financial compensation from us and even our eviction from the flat. In the latter case there was a chance that, if they played their cards right, capitalizing on their being injured members of the proletariat, they might even get the whole flat to themselves.

As soon as the case was referred to a higher court—the city court, in fact—my parents approached an advocate by the name of Pipko, one of the best lawyers in Tallinn. The city court, having reviewed the findings of the local court, found its decision groundless and overruled it. The judge even imposed a small token fine on our neighbors. Apologists for what is called socialist justice would doubtless say that right triumphed in the end, but I wouldn't. Now the fight for the reinstatement of my brother in the polytechnic might have started. But by this time he was already in Tashkent, where my mother's sister—whose baby, incidentally, had not survived—managed to square the local polytechnic. This was achieved through bribery, so that the authorities of Tashkent Polytechnic were not too scrupulous in asking my brother to show them all the usual papers from Tallinn, which would have revealed that he had been expelled.

My aunt's brother, my uncle, also lived in Tashkent. Together, each in their own way, they looked after my brother as much as possible, but they could not prevent the tragedy that was to occur.

One day my brother went with his lame friend Mishka for a dip in Komsomol Lake, the only swimming hole in Tashkent. Having gone into the water once and then sunbathed for a bit, they left, but after only a little while Mishka suddenly decided he would like to go into the water again. With only one leg, he probably felt embarrassed to go in all by himself. He began to talk my brother into going in with him. My brother didn't want to, as if he had a premonition. He said: "We've had enough, let's go home." Mishka, however, went on urging him: "Come on, just once more." So they went back to the lake and back into the water. It was just as they were about to come out that my brother took one more dive. The water was too shallow, and he broke the vertebra of his neck.

Once more my mother urgently took a plane to Tashkent, this time not for her sister's but for her own child's sake. My brother lingered on in agony in the hospital for a few days after she arrived, and she was with him shortly before he died, when he fully regained consciousness and spoke to her.

After she came back to Tallinn, the personal situation in our family got worse and worse. Mother was continually hysterical, screaming the night through "My son, my son, where are you?" She called my father "murderer," for, according to her logic, it was because of my father's failure to defend him that my brother had been expelled—and had he not been expelled, he would never have gone to Tashkent.

I personally wonder if it wasn't my brother's death that ultimately saved me from submitting to the Soviet system. On its own, my mother's influence might have proved powerless in the face of the terrible pressure the state brought to bear on my youth and education. But death, erupting into my life when I was only eleven, threw everything else into the background. I was an impressionable child, and at times I fancied that somebody I happened to see in the street was my brother. I would quicken my pace, pass him, and then look back to see his face—only to realize it was a stranger's. In the light of the haunting mystery of death, all the Young Pioneer jamborees and, later, the whole of Marxism-Leninism seemed to be poor substitutes for existence.

Another factor that helped me to preserve myself relatively intact from the state was its persistent generalized racism (against practically anybody who wasn't Russian) and specifically, as it touched me, anti-Semitism.

Chapter 4: "This foul regime—a curse upon it!"

Any man is able to stand aloof from an unjust society. But it helps if he feels different to begin with.

Admittedly, there wasn't much out of the ordinary about my childhood apart from my being Jewish.

Set into the wall that divided the big and the middle-sized rooms and heating both there was a white-tiled stove. It was nice to lean your back against it or to warm your hands on it. The opening of the stove was in the middle-sized room (I don't know why it wasn't just called "the small room": there were only two rooms in our flat). I liked to watch the fire behind the heavy wrought-iron grating. Every now and then Father or Mother would poke it up, add a piece of wood or coal, and rake the embers to the front. I was not allowed to do this. When I was five or six, I started my first serious revolt. I don't recall what it was all about, but my parents evidently decided to teach me a lesson.

"We don't need a son like you," they said, put an old tattered coat on me, thrust a stale piece of bread into my hand and told me to be off and seek my fortune. I can still see my father turning aside and smiling. This came to pass on a cold winter's night. There was black frost outside. What really shook me was that the coat they had given me was not the new, smart one that had recently been bought for me, but a nasty threadbare good-for-nothing one. I fought back my tears for quite a while, but when the front door was flung open, I could do so no longer and burst into a violent fit of sobbing. I was allowed to stay.

At the age of seven I wrote my first poem, describing the strife of the elements on the Northern Sea. It was a typical piece of juvenilia, but I'm still glad my very first lines were not about the Young Pioneers or something of the sort but about the ocean itself—and in turmoil!

Sometimes I had to help my father carry logs from the cellar up the stairs to our flat. I did not like this job: the cellar frightened me, even when the electric light was on. I suspected that there were rats lurking in the darkness behind all the latticed doors.

Even in the daytime, the cellar was a bit creepy. But with Sashka, the neighbors' boy, for company, I would muster just about enough courage to make a quick dash through it, running out onto the stone steps that led up into the yard. After the half-darkness of the cellar, the sun in the yard seemed to shine magically. All the divisions in the cellar were neighbors' bunkers, but just before the exit, on the left, there was a strange room with a big tub and a bench.

In the comer of the yard, by the fence, there stood a tall horse chestnut tree. I would often climb it and sit comfortably near the top and read my books, occasionally spitting on the heads of passersby who must have thought it was raining unexpectedly, with the sky blue and the sun out.

The fence meant a lot to me. If I stood on its lower bar and jumped up, I could sometimes see the smoky-blue streak of the sea. Occasionally, in a high wind, I could even smell the faint tang of the salt water.

Once I was showing Natasha, a neighbor's little girl, how to strike sparks from the stone pillars on either side of the yard gate, and a spark flew into her eye. She ran home, screaming, covering her eye with her hand. A minute later her mother ran out and chased me all round the yard. I scurried round the house with all my might and main. She shouted: "Wait a minute!" I dropped my homemade flint-lock in order to run faster. She picked it up and began to shout: "Stop—here's your thingummy!" But I didn't fall for that trick. I simply shouted back: "Throw it to me then!" and kept on running. Try though she might, she couldn't catch me. And Natasha's eye healed in a matter of days, and she and I stayed good friends.

On another occasion, Sveta, an older girl, the boss of our whole yard, bashed me for refusing to kowtow to her. Blood dribbled out of my nose, and my mother carried me in her arms to Sveta's flat in order to show her parents what their daughter had done. But Sveta and I likewise stayed good friends.

Later I made friends with Vaino, an Estonian boy from the neighboring yard, whom the Russian boys cold-shouldered. Together we climbed over fences in the evenings. We would take with us some crusts of bread smeared with garlic and climbed over one fence after another. Each new yard was a discovery, different from all the others. And you can imagine our excitement when, after three or four fences, we would suddenly find ourselves in a totally different street, far from home!

Sometimes there were dogs in the yards, and then we would hurriedly climb back over the fence. It was Vaino who taught me when it was safest to pick apples from a tree growing in the yard belonging to his block of flats. I clambered over the fence onto the roof of their shed and, lying flat on my stomach, drew the apple boughs toward myself.

I was bought new felt boots, and one evening, in the company of Vitya, the Ukrainian boy who lived in the next yard but one, I ran in these boots along the drowsy, snow-covered streets. We rang doorbells and scampered off to avoid being caught.

Our family had a Finnish sleigh, the slats of its seat broken, and I would push off along the icy street, the wind whistling in my ears. The best time to do this was in the evenings, when it was dark and the streets were deserted. But my parents insisted on my being back by a stated hour, and if I was late, I was punished by not being allowed to ride the sleigh for two weeks.

My play in the yard was often interrupted by the rattle of the top-floor window as it opened and my mother summoned me. This summons would either be a call to lunch, or else my mother wanted me back in the house because of the ruckus I was raising. When it seemed more likely to be the latter, I would quickly hide and the other children would tell her I wasn't around. "All children scream when they play," she fulminated, "but you just sound like nothing on earth!"

When I was about five I went off in search of the sea. One summer evening, without saying a word to anyone, I walked to the end of our street and turned left. It seemed to me that it was in that direction I had seen the blue streak from the top of our fence. As I walked onward I was helped by the smell, which grew stronger and stronger. At length I stopped, upon seeing patches of blue through the gaps in a gate. I walked through the gate. I'm not quite sure what happened next, but I remember sailors giving me things to eat and taking me to sit in a cinema that was open to the sky. I sat with my new friend, Grisha the sailor, in the third row. The sea behind the screen was beginning to turn black. The film, as I now realize, was a love story. Grisha became upset when I started crying—at a crucial moment in the plot, I think. Other members of the audience—sailors and their girlfriends—shushed us, and Grisha led me quietly out of the cinema and back through the gate. There he pointed me in the right direction to get home and returned to watch the rest of the film.

So homeward I went. It must have been already about eleven at night. I got lost along the way but was befriended by a husband and wife who were taking a late-night stroll, arm in arm. I told them my address, and they walked with me to the corner of our street. There, an extraordinary sight met my eyes: my parents, my sisters and my brother, and even a few of our neighbors were scurrying to and fro all along the street. They all looked very funny. As soon as they spotted me far off, the whole lot hurled themselves in our direction. They thanked the husband and wife over and over again, while the latter insisted over and over again that it was nothing. My father, as always, had evidently failed to exercise the necessary vigilance; I remember how my mother scolded him: "The child vanishes from six o'clock on—and what does he do about it? Nothing!" My brother gave me a sharp slap, but the whole family was so relieved I had returned safe and sound that I wasn't even punished.

Our caretaker, an elderly Estonian woman, had an unmarried daughter called Aasta who was in her forties. Aasta always looked swollen, which must have been due to some disease. This would not have been helped by the fact that she also drank. But her mother drank even more, and would often not be seen fulfilling her functions as a caretaker for days on end. The local authorities tried to break her of her drinking: they even compelled her to undergo treatment and finally threatened her with the sack. Aasta, having been classified as an invalid, was not obliged to work, so they were both dependent on the mother's tiny income. Because of this, the more threatening the authorities became, the more Aasta would beat her mother when the old woman got drunk. The mother shrieked so terribly that her cries could be heard all round the yard. Once I overheard my parents talking about the ingenious methods Aasta used to inflict the maximum amount of pain on her mother without any bruises showing. For nights afterward I couldn't sleep, thinking about it. All the neighbors kept saying that something ought to be done, but apparently nothing was or even could be done. The shrieks continued.

When I was nine, my parents bought me a subscription to the *Pioneers' Pravda*, and every Tuesday evening that snowy winter I went home from school full of happy anticipation. The paper was serializing a science fiction story about the adventures of a group of pioneers in outer space.

I retained an affection for this paper, and when I was fifteen sent it my first "mature" poem, written in dutiful adolescent imitation of Mayakovsky. The paper replied with an effusive letter, saying that these verses—and any others I might have written—should be submitted to an adult journal. I was greatly encouraged by this.

Once I had mastered my letters, I resolved to keep a diary. My parents bought me a nice, thick notebook with hard covers. One March morning before school (I was in the second shift, which started at two), I came out of the house and began breaking the thin ice on the puddles with the toe of my boot. A passing Estonian boy I didn't know wanted to do likewise. This led to a clash and we got into a fight. He was the stronger, and won. When I got back to the house, I opened my diary and made the first entry: "Today I have drawn blood from a passing Estonian." This was the end of my attempts to keep a diary, at least in this form. (When I reached seventeen, I did start writing things down, but for a different purpose—not to describe my life but to preserve interesting episodes, thoughts, and anecdotes for possible future literary use.)

It wasn't difficult to get the better of me, for I was rather weak ("Every morning he got out of breath with his dumbbells," my mother would say later on about my father, "why then didn't he make you do physical jerks along with him?" In that case she was actually right; it wasn't until a few years later, when I started jogging and fell in love with physical activities, that I became able to defend myself successfully against school bullies (some three decades after, jogging and my now strong physique would save me from death by alcohol.)

Once at school a Ukrainian boy called Prikhodko chivalrously called me out to a duel for my having allegedly impugned a girl's honor. When we played at tag in the course of our PE class, I had, in order to turn more quickly, grabbed at her elbow. My fingernails had not been cut, and I scratched her skin. The duel of fisticuffs took place during break in the basement changing rooms, with a second apiece. We exchanged a few blows, and his second hastily awarded the victory to him. My second turned out to be spineless and failed to defend my interest. When we came back to the classroom, the girl asked: "Who won?" "Me!" Prikhodko answered proudly. She was disappointed. "I'd rather it had been you," she told me, and never spoke to Prikhodko again.

One day on my way to school I happened to see a very plain girl who was perhaps in her late teens and said loudly, for anyone to hear: "Gosh, what a gorgon!" A few people turned round and looked at her. I was very pleased at this opportunity to use a learned word and that people had reacted to it positively, noticing my erudition.

At the age of about nine I was admitted to the Young Pioneers and began to sport a badge and a red tie. Disorganized as I was, I was always putting the tie away in the wrong place, and the next morning I would be unable to find it. Our form teacher threatened me with expulsion from the Young Pioneers if I ever showed up again without the tie. More than once my sister Lena came to the rescue by pinning a piece of red rag to the collar of my shirt, tucking its ends underneath my sweater.

We went to Leningrad once to visit some relations there, and I was allowed to go to the Hermitage Museum on my own. What I liked most of all there were the lead seals on the showcases, hanging down below them. Taking advantage of moments when the attendant was in the next room, I would unwind the wire and tear off the seal. In this way, in the course of only one visit I succeeded in collecting about a dozen of them.

Another thing I remembered in Leningrad was the flat where our relations lived—my father's sister and her husband. It was huge, and there were about a dozen families living in it. Our relations occupied two rooms at opposite ends of the flat. In order to get from one to the other you had to pass through many corridors and remember which turnings to take. I gradually learned to get my bearings from the toilet and the bathroom, which were halfway along the journey: there would either be queues outside them or they would be occupied and the light on inside. Once I had passed them, I only had to take two turnings to the right and one to the left. I remember hearing my relations telling my parents that before the Revolution not only this apartment but the whole building had belonged to one family. I found this hard to believe. Later, when I got back to Tallinn, our schoolteacher told us that before the Revolution only a very few people lived in affluence while the rest of the population were deprived, and suffered. Not observing any affluence around me, I felt like asking her whether the present situation was more just, when everybody suffered, as in that Leningrad apartment with all its families. But I was too shy—and that was just as well, for the question was a silly one. A few years later, having made friends with the son of a big Party official in Riga, I discovered that alongside the general overcrowding and misery, there were people who were very affluent indeed.

There was in our class a boy called Tolya. His Estonian surname contained a number of *aa* sounds. His Estonian father had abandoned his family and, his mother being Russian, Tolya went to a Russian school, although he was as fluent in Estonian as in Russian. His mother worked as a cleaner in our school, and they were a poor family.

He and I became friends and went to a skating rink together. Later on I gave him a book to read, which I had borrowed from the local library. It was a children's story called *Matthew the Young King*, by Janusz Korczak, the Jewish writer and educationalist who was murdered by the Nazis together with the children he was in charge of and refused to abandon. It was a beautiful book, with fine, colored illustrations. I advised Tolya to join that library and said that he could then return the book for me. A month later, I got a reminder from the library that the book was overdue. I reminded Tolya, but he swore that he had returned it already. I went back to the library. The librarian, a young girl, listened to my story very sympathetically and even spent a long time checking her records. Finding nothing there, she said with an embarrassed smile that my friend must have forgotten to return the book and if it could not be found I would have to pay the fine. Once more I went back to Tolya, and once more he swore that he had returned it. My parents paid the fine, but I felt confused. Tolya was a friend, and he had taken his oath so passionately, hand on heart, that I was simply unable to doubt him. On the other hand, the book had certainly not been returned, and he changed his mind twice about approximately when he had returned it, and he did come from a very poor family, one which had never possessed such a thing as an expensive book with pictures. In this way, I learned something about life.

My next important lesson had to do with Chopa (a nickname based on his longish surname). He was the class idiot, bullied by everyone. Beatings-up in our class usually started like this: somebody would be scrapping with somebody else and would knock him down. Then the crowd standing round would start kicking the loser in the ribs. I myself had to go through this a couple of times. And when one day, during break, I saw Chopa on the floor and Trunov sitting on his chest, I stopped in my tracks. Everybody around was kicking Chopa, and I too gleefully raised my boot—and then suddenly drew back. It seemed to me that there was something wrong about doing this. But everybody else was kicking him—I myself had been kicked the same way, lying on the floor—so again I raised my boot. And then the bell rang.

Estonian was a compulsory subject in our Russian school. This first alien tongue I learned made a strong impression on me. Yiddish I don't count since I had picked it up unconsciously: whenever my parents wanted to discuss something they did not wish me to know about, they would use Yiddish, and in this way, by degrees, I came to understand it. But the Estonian language was something completely new. I learned to pronounce its strange vowels, and their sounds still haunt me. I remember how I tried to say the word *väike* (small) and how the bilingual Genka Logunov corrected me: "It's not *vyaike* but *väike*."

Gradually I became more and more obsessed with Estonian (later I read a book on the relative euphony of languages: Estonian was placed second, after Italian). I would stop passersby who looked Estonian and would try out my knowledge of their tongue on them. I asked them the time, the weather forecast, the way to the cinema, and so on. They gave me strange looks, but would still reply, quite adequately and to the point, and it pleased me immensely that I could understand them. Vaino, the Estonian boy from the next yard, would smile when I tried to talk Estonian to him, but he never corrected me, out of tactfulness.

Gradually, though, into this more or less ordinary Soviet boy's existence, a strange and disturbing new thread began to be woven.

In my own yard we were all friends, boys and girls, and the boys all fought among themselves, and still remained friends. So it was a painful shock to me when an older Russian girl from Vitka's yard gave me one look and said: "A little Jew!" Just like that, with no particular animosity, simply stating the fact that I belonged to a caste below hers, like in India. And I think I actually fancied her (I must have been about eight and she probably in her late teens)! I was terribly hurt.

I think now that my being in between the Russians and the natives, first Estonians and then Latvians—and knowing how the former despised the latter and the latter hated the former—helped to put my own ethnic humiliations in perspective.

Serezhka Trunov shared a desk with me and was my pal. His parents were Party officials of some kind. Once we had a row, and he ostentatiously moved himself to another desk, announcing that he did not want to sit with me anymore because I was a Jew. "In our country all are equal," said our form teacher. She did not allow him to change his place.

That was in Tallinn, when we all were children. In Riga, as we got older, the references to my Jewishness got more varied, and I also received some dubious compliments from a couple of my classmates of the kind "you're also Jewish, but you're all right."

As we were going through the painful time of sexual awakening and maturation, in our mid- to late teens, for at least one boy in my class an attractive and sexually aware Jewish girl was a mythical, archetypal Biblical harlot—Delilah, Salome, Lilith—exotic, dangerous yet irresistible. "That Jewess there—see how she's spread her legs!" he (let's call him Borodulin) exclaimed almost involuntarily when our entire high school was at a cross-country event in Mežaparks ("forest park" in Latvian, in the north of Riga). His tone expressed extreme disapproval. Then he saw that it was in fact I who was standing the closest and hastily explained: "It's not that she's a Jewess, it's that she looks so lewd—lecherous—horny!" (Funny how Borodulin reminds me now of Dostoyevsky: some of the latter's Jewish figures are equally ambivalent, their archetypal dimensions and his own metaphysical terror of them showing willy-nilly through his tabloid-style anti-Semitism).

Eckensdorff, a pupil who claimed to be an ethnic German, once said in class that the name Ivan had come from the Hebrew. The class mistress, Antonina Ivanovna, was shocked. She mocked his claim to German ancestry and said that a Jew was either a genius or a cretin, he belonging to the latter category. Then another pupil, Vladimir Shkodin, a typical Russian boy, said he'd read a book by the famous Leo Ouspensky called *You and*

Your Name, which had traced the origin of Ivan to the Hebrew Yohanan via the Greek Ioannis. The teacher was horrified: "If even such a purely Russian name as Ivan becomes suspect, there's no knowing where that could lead!" Bravely, Shkodin went on defending his version, even promising to bring the book by the distinguished onomastician to school the very next day. The bell rang, the teacher fled the class, a few fellow pupils, me included, surrounded Shkodin, and he explained to us just how the Jew Yohanan had become the Russian Ivan.

All this may sound pretty innocent, but I also witnessed a much uglier face of Russian Jew-baiting when a Jewish girl from a class in the same year had been hounded to such an extent that the school authorities finally had to take action and organize a special theatrical performance, with pupils reciting all sorts of anti-racist material culled from Soviet literature.

Meticulously, vexatiously examining all evidence now, I have to acquit myself of any belated self-accusations: there was absolutely nothing I could have done to help that girl. The school was big, and parallel classes hardly communicated; I immediately agreed to take part in the recital when my form teacher asked me and declaimed a Mayakovsky poem against anti-Semitism, but that was the end of my involvement. When later I encountered the girl alone in the school corridor, I asked her about the situation. The girl wore the thick-lensed glasses I've always associated with high achievers, and looked bright; appearing grateful for somebody's interest in her situation, she said she was transferring to another school.

When I was ten or eleven, I had my first encounter with Hebrew, under rather strange circumstances. It was when my older sister Milla took me for the first time to the oculist.

I had two sisters. Lena, the younger of them and nine years older than I, was the one who helped me out with my pioneer's tie; she liked to make a general fuss of me and dress me up like a doll. She had perfect taste, and was considered the beauty of the family. She got married in Tashkent, as a result of having been bitten by a dog. This mishap delayed her departure from that city, and in the meantime she fell in love.

My other sister, Lyudmilla—Milla for short—was fifteen years older than I. She was attractive too, but with a less striking beauty, and was thought of as the intellectual of the family.

Somehow my parents hadn't had the time to notice that I had a lazy eye that could hardly see and, as a result, a slight squint: my father had been too engrossed in his journalistic work, while my mother regarded medicine in general with some suspicion. The old distinguished-looking oculist heard my sister out, tested my eyes with various instruments, and then shook his head, regretting that I had not been brought to him sooner. "Where were your parents all this time?" he asked. My sister sheepishly said nothing. After that he told me to read rows of letters on a slowly revolving illuminated screen.

I asked: "How—from left to right or from right to left?"

"It's in Hebrew that you read from right to left," he replied. "Do you know Hebrew?"

I blushed and said that I didn't.

"A pity," he commented. "It's a very fine language indeed, and one should make every effort to learn it." He glanced at my sister, who likewise became a little embarrassed, but said nothing.

I realize now that it would have needed considerable courage to say such a thing to strangers. For it was some ten years before the great upsurge of Jewish national conscious-ness within the Soviet Union, which followed the Six Days' War.

I remembered this episode shortly after the Six Days' War when the KGB began bad-gering my sister. Up till then I had not even thought of her having any un-Soviet ideas. Like all her contemporaries, she was a member of the Young Communist League and she worked on a young people's newspaper. Her troubles started like this. When she was al-ready twenty-seven—a desperate age for a girl in the perennially pre-feminist Russia—she met a young man and fell in love with him. That was in Riga, and when he returned to his home in Leningrad she went there to see him. Mother warned her not to go: "If he's really fond of you, let him come back to you." But my sister found a good excuse for going anyway: the young man was interested in Zionist literature, and she had just got hold of a Zionist pamphlet from a friend of our family. And so, in spite of what my mother had said, she went to Leningrad, saw the young man, and passed the pamphlet on to him. He was arrested and immediately informed on her.

Her case was handled in Riga by a certain Lieutenant-Colonel Ivanov, of the KGB. One day, as I was walking with my mother along Rūpniecības Street, where we lived, she suddenly whispered: "Look—there goes Ivanov, over the road!" This man had a heavy, stony face with a scar. He was walking slowly, as if carrying a burden. I could never have imagined him smiling. This, then, was the man who had interrogated my sister—several times in the course of two months. She never told him who'd given her that Zionist pamphlet. She maintained that she'd simply found it, dropped by someone, she didn't know who. The KGB, I'm sure, were not taken in by this. But in the end they did not press the matter further. Maybe somebody or other in their ranks—perhaps even the glum-looking Lieutenant-Colonel Ivanov himself—still retained some shred of humanity and saw before him a girl in love and therefore merely irresponsible. Perhaps he or one of his superiors had a grown-up daughter who'd fallen for someone. But the most likely explanation is that the KGB half forgave my sister because they did not regard her as re-ally dangerous. In the post-Stalin period, some degree of reasonableness began to show itself—not, of course, in terms of common human values and justice, but relative to the nature of the regime itself. The state was learning to distinguish between its true enemies and those who were simply silly enough to find themselves out of line. My sister was seen as belonging to the second category and that, I think, was why they dealt with her rather leniently—considering their savage standards, that is. She was, of course, expelled from the Young Communist League, but in any case she would have had to leave it in a few months' time on account of her age, so it didn't make much difference. Naturally, as such things went, she was also dismissed from her paper and then couldn't get any job at all, not even as a bookkeeper or housekeeper.

And then she married another young man—a very honorable student of medicine working on his doctorate who was incapable of betraying anybody—and they went to live in Tselinograd. There he began to practice as a doctor and she began again to do journalistic work with the local television and radio stations. By comparison with Riga, this city in Kazakhstan was a dump, and its media outlets a joke compared with her previ-ous newspaper, an important publication in a large city, but at least she could continue working in her own field. Needless to say, it would have presented no great difficulty for the KGB to ensure that she would never again be engaged in journalistic work of any kind—journalism was, after all, one of the most ideologically sensitive occupations in the country. A few telephone calls would have sufficed for them to check her new address and employment. But she was left in peace. Or they simply didn't bother. Likewise, her new provincial employers must have failed to look closely into her occupational past for reasons easy to guess. She was, after all, an experienced reporter coming from a place they could only dream of: the capital of Latvia, a formerly foreign country, the westernmost corner of the USSR's European territory. (For her part, she didn't let them down and played a significant role in building up the local TV, which, at the time of her departure, could rival that of almost any city in the state.)

When I was nine, my brother came back from the virgin lands. He looked scruffy and could hardly stand. With the kopecks he had earned he bought me a mouth organ as a present. He badly needed a wash, and this took hours, for it involved heating bucket after bucket of water on the stove. His clothes stank. My mother shouted out a few times: "This foul regime—a curse upon it!" She always spoke of the Soviet system as if to compare it with some alternative one, of which, of course, she could have had no inkling.

Twelve years later she used the very same words on the occasion of my brush with the state system. This took place in 1971, in Brest-Litovsk, on the Soviet-Polish border, when we were leaving the country for good, with visas for Israel in our pockets

The official who was checking our luggage went through my correspondence with two or three men of letters whose names were known to educated people. After that, he asked my mother to go with him: he wanted to talk to her.

I was nervous: maybe they had been informed of my file having just been passed to the Latvian KGB? It turned out the man had tried to persuade her to leave for Israel without me, on the grounds that my future should, in his opinion, be brighter in Russia. In that crucial moment my mother did not lose her presence of mind. As far as I could gather, she had answered the official politely and reasonably, but her reply was a categorical no.

In the circumstances it was essential to keep a cool head. Although we had secured an exit visa, we were still in Soviet territory, and theoretically we could have been turned back at any moment. Returning from her interview with the customs official, to my question about it my mother muttered under her breath: "This foul regime—a curse upon it!"

Thus it was that this phrase for me associated our departure from the country with the fate of my brother, who had effectively been destroyed by the system.

Chapter 5: Travels from Language to Language

I still have the mouth organ my brother gave me as a present when he came back from the virgin lands, and I remember word for word the few poems he'd had the time to write, including one about me as a first-grader at school.

And, of course, there was that tragic city of Tashkent, where he died.

I was taken to Tashkent twice, at the ages of eight and nine. I remember a journey on the train, which lasted a long time, when I was greatly puzzled as fields and forests gave way to sand and camels. I went to school there for the last two months of the school year and made friends with an Uzbek boy called Mamadzhan. He used to take me to one of the splendid bazaars of Tashkent, with all its luxurious fruits and vegetables. Mamadzhan's father had a stall there, where he sold melons. Initially, the Uzbek language did not appeal to me at all. In the first place, its alphabet was the familiar Cyrillic and therefore it didn't really seem like a foreign tongue—unlike Estonian, which was written in Latin characters. And second, its sounds could not compare for beauty with those of Estonian. But gradually I warmed to it and when, at the end of my stay in Tashkent, Mamadzhan's mother—who was a primary school teacher—recited verses of Alī Shīr Navā'ī in the Middle-Turkic proto-Uzbek Chagatai language, I was completely taken in and even learned a few lines by heart. I still remember them, from *Layli va Majnun*, one of the epic poems comprising his quintuple *Khamsa*. The sounds and the melody of the verses are very lyrical and breathtakingly beautiful.

I probably got this feeling for sound from my father, who was a great lover of music. My mother, on the other hand, was tone deaf. Once, when she was a schoolgirl, my mother attended an audition for her school choir. Afterward, every candidate was handed a piece of paper on which their degree of musical aptitude was noted in abbreviated form. The first choir rehearsal took place in the great hall immediately after the auditions. My mother turned up along with everybody else. Their pieces of paper were checked at the door. "What have you got?" she was asked. "I've got an SN!" my mother replied proudly. "'SN'? *Slukha nyet!*" ("Tone deaf!") was the reply, and she was told to go away.

I suspect that my own sense of pitch was ruined at a very early age by her lullabies. But if you think I'd give up so easily, you're dead wrong!

There was a Russian family living in our flat in Tallinn before our Ukrainian neighbors.

From five o'clock onward I would take up a position at the door, which opened from our private corridor into the main one. When the entrance door of the flat slammed, I knew my hour had come, for that was the head of the family himself coming back from work. Accosting him at the threshold and all but barring his way, I'd ask him to listen to my singing. He'd agree graciously, give a slight sigh, and lean on the kitchen table by the window. I struck a pose opposite him and began to sing "Katyusha," "Evenings near Moscow," and many other songs. Every now and then he would glance aside and smile. Sooner or later some member of my own family—my mother or one of my sisters—would burst in, in order to drag me out of the kitchen. "Aren't you ashamed of yourself?" they scolded me at the top of their voices, as if I at the age of seven or eight could comprehend such niceties. "A man's no sooner got back from work than you pounce on him." After that they would apologize to our neighbor: "How many times have we told him he's not to pester you! Don't stand any nonsense from him—just tell him you're busy—and that's the end of the matter."

"Not at all, not at all," he would protest sheepishly. "He isn't at all in my way."

He had a daughter a few years older than myself with the odd name of Veta (short for Yvette, as I now know). Everybody called her by the diminutive form "Vetka" (Twiggie). She would often invite me to her room, sit me on the windowsill from where I could see trees outside, and then tell me lots and lots of fairy tales.

Another older girl in our block of flats, Nadya, would take me for walks and recount to me the plots of films she had seen. One of these I can still remember: it was *Roman Holiday*, featuring Audrey Hepburn. To me, the story sounded pretty boring, but Nadya, who must have been getting on for fifteen, went on about the star and her role with much enthusiasm. When, as an adult, I saw the film myself, I remembered Nadya and her romantic delight in the story.

I'm grateful to these Russian girls in the Estonian capital for their youthful warmth and kindness. I wasn't very good at fighting other boys: I could just about do it when I had to, but I hated it. In Tashkent, though, nobody took me for walks or showed much interest in me, and I felt pretty neglected. Besides, it was too hot there and too many women wore black veils, which frightened me. Once, on a hot afternoon I was walking along Darkhan Street, where we lived. The sun was blazing down. There was not a soul about—obviously everybody had taken refuge from the heat. Suddenly, a woman wearing a black veil appeared from round the corner and headed in my direction. Under the black material, her nose and cheekbones stood out with terrifying sharpness. She was coming straight at me and there was nobody at all who could have come to my rescue in case of need. When there were only a few yards between us, I couldn't take it anymore and, with a wild scream, I broke into a run.

In this alien city, Mother treated me with particular—not to say *cruel*—strictness. Whenever we had to cross a road together, she would grab hold of my hand, giving it a painful squeeze. I tried to wrench it free, saying that I would walk side by side with her, but without holding her hand. She was not prepared to accept this compromise and retain her grip on my hand, squeezing it even more painfully. After this I was prepared to agree to hold her hand, on condition that she didn't squeeze it. But even this she would not concede. Once I tried to wrench my hand free, and then she twisted my arm and slapped my face. I burst into tears and refused to move. People gathered round and became indignant: "What sort or a mother is this who torments her own child in such a way!" they were saying. I felt doubly humiliated by their pity.

I despised myself for not running away (the way my wild Tashkent cousins would certainly have done in such a situation—not that they would have ever found themselves in it, to begin with!), going to the police and saying I didn't want to return home.

It was characteristic of my mother that she never could understand a growing boy's need for independence. "You had it in you, right from the start, a devil of contrariness," she would still hold it against me many years later. "A mother tells her eight-year-old child to hold her hand, and he, deliberately, just to spite her, insists on walking on his own."

If my father was rather weak-willed and a trifle shallow (Mother, though tone deaf herself, was right to ridicule the silliest possible popular records that he liked to play, and which somehow peacefully coexisted with his love for classical music), her own principal shortcoming was her autocratic character. I often discussed their fundamental incompatibility with my sisters, and later on, after our parents got divorced, we all came to the same conclusion—that what our mother really needed was a husband much stronger than herself. What she ought to have had, we all decided, was a husband rather like her own older brother, Uncle Meir.

I recall Uncle Meir somewhat vaguely, from our Tashkent days. He died not long after he had left the Soviet Union for Israel, of a heart attack. His death rendered our own exit from the country more complicated: we no longer had any close relatives abroad.

I have warm memories of him. He was, admittedly, something of a despot. "So what?" my mother tried to justify him, "he beats his wife—but what else could he do? He alone supports her and their six children. He lugs heavy carcasses of meat about on his back in the heat of the summer, just to save a kopeck or so with which he could have paid someone else to do it for him. Any other wife would have been ready to wash his feet. But when *he* gets home, late at night, hardly able to stand upright, what does he find? No supper on the table: she, you see, hasn't had the time to get it ready. All that good food has gone to waste and been thrown into the *aryk* (irrigation ditch). His children are never at home—they're roaming the streets somewhere, armed with knives, along with those gangs of Uzbek boys. And he screams at her: 'Where are the children tonight?' And she answers: 'I've no idea.' And, then, quite naturally, he beats her up." ("They all took after our grandmother," said my sister Milla, showing me a photograph of an old woman with a shrewd, strong-willed face and pursed lips.) But Uncle Meir also possessed sensitivity and goodness of heart; me he always treated kindly.

Uncle Meir's first wife and all his children by her perished at the hands of the Germans. How he himself escaped, I don't know, but I know that he loved his first wife very dearly. When, a few years after the War, the matchmaker offered him a match simply telling him that the bride came from an Orthodox family, he made no inquiries about her character or, indeed, whether she could cook.

It was largely through learning the story of his family that I began to realize that life and people were more complicated than they seemed. When I listened to my mother, Uncle Meir emerged as a hapless martyr to his second wife and their children. But when I listened to my sisters or my father accusing him of total lack of self-control and of being a tyrant, or when I myself witnessed his treatment of his wife, I was just as shocked as they were and ready to point an accusing finger.

Together with an assistant he ran a butcher's stall in the local bazaar. Officially, the stall was like any other meat trader's stall, but in point of fact it dealt in kosher meat. From beginning to end, everything about this was illegal, obviously requiring a multiplicity of bribes. There was the ritual slaughter of the beasts, the processing of the meat in a special way, its delivery to the bazaar, to a state-owned stall, and its sale to Orthodox families. Uncle Meir did almost everything himself: with his large family every penny counted.

"And what's his reward after a hard day's work?" my mother would demand of me dramatically. "Careering all over the town to save his children from being murdered!"

Once Uncle Meir's eldest son Yashka (short for Jacob) was told to go and take the family nanny goat into a ravine to graze. He took me along with him and asked me to hold the goat by her tether while he went away for a bit. I consented, to my own near-undoing. The moment he'd gone, the goat pulled strongly down the slope toward the *aryk*.

I had not the strength to hold her back and was dragged after her down the steep ravine, slipping and sliding and slithering, and nearly falling into the rushing waters of the *aryk*, whose bed was full of sharp stones. In this manner she dragged me about, up hill and down dale, for the space of some two hours. To let go was out of the question, for then she would have run away, and I knew that a goat cost an enormous sum of money.

There was nobody about, and it was already growing dark. I fell down several times and only by a miracle did not tumble into the *aryk*. At last Yashka reappeared and took the goat from me. I complained bitterly, accusing the goat of treachery and gross insubordination. She—perverse creature that she was—immediately became tractable in his hands and put on an air of innocence. Her face had an almost human expression, as much as to say: "I simply can't understand what all this fuss is about."

Yashka had come back in a good mood: it turned out that he had been with his gang, and the gang leader had agreed that he could drop out, at least for a time. Yashka had explained his request to drop out by claiming that he had been threatened by his father. His father had indeed said that he wouldn't put up with his son going out at night heaven knows where and that if it went on he himself would turn him in to the police.

I cannot help thinking that if Uncle Meir had not carried his family off to Israel in the nick of time, one or other of his children would have ended up either in prison or knifed.

One night I couldn't get to sleep and felt a craving for roasted sunflower seeds. I got up quietly, so as not to wake anybody, went out into the yard, unlatched the gate, and, looking stealthily around, slipped into the street. An enormous moon was shining, and the sidewalks and alleyways were in black shadow. I knew where the Uzbek woman who sold sunflower seeds lived—in the last house but one at the end of the street. I knocked on the door. There was no reply. I knocked louder and louder. At length, lights began to go on, first in one window, then in another, and then in a third. I heard excited and even, it seemed to me, anxious voices. Someone's head stuck out of a window and scrutinized me for a long time. "What do you want?" a man's voice asked.

"I would like a jar of sunflower seeds for five kopecks, please," I said, clutching the five kopeck coin in my fist.

"And do you know what time it is?" asked the head.

"Yes," I said, surprised at the fact that nobody in such a big house seemed to have a watch, "it's half past one."

The head lingered for a while, studying me, and finally withdrew. A couple of minutes later, the front door of the house creaked open and the old Uzbek woman produced a jar of sunflower seeds. I gave her the five kopeck piece, emptied the seeds into my trousers' pocket, gave the jar back to her and said, as I had always been taught at home, "thank you very much indeed." For some reason she kept on smiling and shaking her head. After having taken a few steps in the direction of our house, I looked back. The woman was following me with her eyes, and she was still smiling.

The best thing about Tashkent, however, was not even its sunflower seeds, but its *aryk*s. Their babbling could be heard in the streets of the innermost parts of the city as well as the dirty deserted lanes on the outskirts. Often you couldn't see them at all for the grass and weeds that overgrew them or because their course lay in deep gullies. Then their presence would be made known by the faint noise and the scarcely perceptible coolness of the air round about them. The play of light and shadow upon these thin streams fascinated me.

Both my visits to Tashkent lasted for just a couple of months, during April and May. I had to finish the school year in a local school. Since it was a matter of only a few weeks, the teachers left me alone for the most part and made no demands upon me. Besides, the academic level of these Tashkent schools was simply laughable by comparison with my Tallinn one. On a few occasions I fell asleep during class, on account of the heat. The teacher would sometimes say tactfully: "The last desk, do you mind if we trouble you?"

On my second visit to Tashkent I was obliged to move out of a bright spacious room we were renting from an Uzbek family—unofficially, of course—to a shed at the end of the yard. The reason for this move was that there was no separate entrance and in order to come and go we had to pass through the landlord's living room. He said he didn't mind, but my mother felt it would be an intrusion. Then the landlord built three steps under the window of our room, which was on the ground floor, and suggested that we should use the window as a door. Both I and my father who'd come with us on this occasion applauded the solution, but my mother, after consulting Uncle Meir, rejected it. It turned out that Jewish law forbids the use of a window as a door. Because of all this my mother and father had to rent another and smaller room, whereas I was given separate accommodation in this shed, which seemed to be at world's end.

Once, late in the evening, during a terrible downpour, I ran to the house of a school friend who had promised, earlier, during lesson time, to lend me his book of Japanese fairy tales. He was greatly astonished, not expecting me in such a deluge. Hiding the book with its marvelous pictures inside my jacket, I ran back home through the drenching rain. Once in my room, I lay down on my bed and began to devour the stories. There was paper covering the ceiling, and over it rats or mice were scuttering. Sometimes I could even see a little foot thrust through. Outside the window the storm still kept on.

There was an occasion when another schoolmate of mine invited me to his home. In front of the entrance of his typical mud-built Uzbek house he told to me about various races and their characteristics. First he spoke of the Russians, whom he disliked. Then he said: "And Jews are also bad, aren't they?" To tell the truth, I don't know what kind of retort I would have made at the age of ten, but at that point his parents came out and interrupted our conversation. They glanced at me in an unfriendly way, said something to him in their own language, and went back into the house. He became slightly nervous.

I asked him: "And you—what nationality do you belong to?"

"I'm a Tartar," he replied with considerable pride.

This pride—after his relegation of the Jews to such a low rank—surprised me somewhat. By that time I knew that in the Soviet hierarchy the Asiatics were on the lowest level. Among these, the Tartars were at the very bottom. By comparison with them, even the Jews themselves could be seen as a privileged race. Even anti-Semitic Russians regarded Jews with a certain grudging respect—a race they hated but had to take into account (this attitude became especially predominant after the Six-Day War). But as for the Tartars, quite a lot of Russians scarcely regarded them as human at all.

I heard my aunt say that anti-Semitism in Uzbekistan was entirely due to Russian influence. And the fact that a Tartar boy should have been indoctrinated, from his earliest years, with the racial prejudices of what was in effect a colonial power, still seems odd to me.

One blazing afternoon in early summer I was lucky enough to discover something to occupy myself with. I found that if a piece of wire was hammered with a stone it could be beaten thin to make a passable model sword. From this point onward I began to search all the streets for pieces of wire lying about. I would work diligently at hammering these through a whole afternoon, sitting on the sidewalk, while every now and again passersby stepped over me. I even managed to sell a couple of my artifacts for five kopecks apiece to members of my own family, and this acknowledgment of my youthful craftsmanship and its market value made me feel extremely proud.

Upon returning to Tallinn after my second and last visit to Tashkent, I went to a pioneers' summer camp where my eldest sister was a camp leader. There I made friends with Kostya, a boy with a humorous turn of mind who intrigued us with his abbreviations game. In the evenings, when we were all lying in our bunks, he would start asking: "What is PDGPLF?" Nobody knew. "Why, it means 'Police Department Granted Permission for Loud Farting,'" he explained. Then he would set another puzzle: "What is HLAPH?" Again no one could guess. "You idiots," Kostya would say, going on to explain as if it were obvious: "The Higher Leadership Allows to Piss Heartily." At other times he would tell us frightening ghost stories: "And then he suddenly remembered how the bogeyman had told him that at a certain crossroads on a certain highway on a dark and stormy night he would come after him for his pound of flesh—and here he comes now!" At this point, Kostya would stamp his feet on the floor, emitting hollow groans, and we would all be scared out of our wits and start shrieking. I liked Kostya very much, and we often walked together among the reeds by the river.

My sister organized a poetry recital competition. I chose Krylov's fable "The Ass and the Nightingale" as my piece. This fable is still one of my favorites: even now I occasionally recite it to myself, and cannot resist quoting it here, in a translation John Heath-Stubbs and I did together:

> Seeing the nightingale, the ass, said he:
> "Look here, as I have heard tell,
> You are the chap that sings so mighty well.
> I'd like to have the opportunity
> Of judging for myself that skill they praise,
> To know if it is all that it's cracked up to be."
> With that the nightingale his art displays:
> He chirps and trills
> A thousand melodies drawn out and linking:
> Now to a tender languor sinking,
> Now from afar a plaintive reed-pipe shrills,
> Scattering his grace-notes through the groves.
> Then everywhere all things were listening
> To the small chorister Aurora loves:
> Zephyrs were hushed and birds forbore to sing;
> Flocks took their ease, the shepherd swain,

Admiring, gazed upon him and meanwhile,
Listening to the nightingale, now and again
Granted his shepherdess a smile.
The singer ended. And with puckered brow
Cast down, the ass opines: "Upon my word,
A fellow listens to you without getting bored!
But still it is a pity you don't know
Our old rooster: if you had found out
A tip or two from him and heard him crow,
You'd be a real champion, I don't doubt."
Hearing the judgment made, my nightingale, poor thing,
Is off, and on the wing;
Over the fields he flies and far away.

God shield us from such judges, I will say.

After I had delivered this poem, a girl, considerably senior to me, followed with a poem in praise of our Soviet land. Then about a dozen more children recited various poems.

I was awarded the first prize—a bow with a set of arrows tipped with rubber suckers (it was subsequently broken by one of my cousins: the few toys I did have were always reduced to fragments by one or other of my relations). The girl who read after me and who I thought was much better got the second prize, a book.

I felt I hadn't deserved the first prize, and I asked my sister, who was one of the judges, whether she hadn't allowed her position as camp leader to weigh in my favor. I can still remember how offended she became when I asked her this. She told me that the decision did not rest with her but with the whole panel of judges, who had unanimously decided that my performance was the best.

My carefree days in the summer camp were suddenly brought to an end by my brother's death. One telephone call to Tashkent changed everything. From the pioneers' camp we went back home to Tallinn to await my mother's return. My father was, I think, away on a journalistic assignment. "Could I go to the cinema?" I asked my sister about a week afterward. "It's not a comedy and indeed not a jolly film at all—it's about the War."

"Well, you can go if you like," she said. (My mother held it very much against my father that as soon as one year had gone by after his son's death, he would ask her to if they could go to the cinema again. She herself would never see another film for the rest of her life.)

A few months later we exchanged our flat in Tallinn for one in Riga. My mother could no longer bear to stay in a town where everything reminded her of her son. My father hired a big van, making an arrangement with the driver, who was not supposed to use it for any other purpose except those assigned to him by his factory. So on we rolled along the road through the spring forests. I remember many books being in the van, and among them the collected works of Lenin in a vast number of volumes. My mother cruelly mocked my father for dragging such junk along with us. He attempted to justify himself by saying that he had tried to give these volumes away free to several friends and neighbors, but nobody would take them. It would have been a pity to throw them away, he said, and anyhow they might come in handy in his journalistic work.

After a whole day traveling, with occasional stops for snacks by the roadside, we drove into a city. At first we were passing through the outskirts, but as we approached the center it became clear to me that this city was much bigger than Tallinn. As our van turned yet another corner and began to slow down, I noticed the name of the street—Rūpniecības— and read it to myself in the Estonian way as if there had been two dots over the vowels instead of horizontal strokes. On the way I had already noticed other unfamiliar words on shop signs with long strokes written over some of the vowels.

Later I discovered that a horizontal stroke—macron—in Latvian did not signify at all the same thing as the umlaut in Estonian: it indicated the length of the vowel rather than its quality. In point of fact, the two languages are totally unconnected, Estonian being a Finnic language and Latvian an Indo-European one. I was not just passing from one province of the Soviet Union to another but into a completely different linguistic world.

Chapter 6: The Tongues

I was perhaps oversensitive to the auditory aspects of different languages (it was no accident that later on I became interested in such related subjects as phonetics, phonology, and likewise in voice production). But an awareness of language in general was something I shared with all my close friends. When making a new acquaintance I could usually find out whether we had common ground from the very first words he spoke. To paraphrase Shaw, in modern Russia the moment a man opens his mouth it becomes clear precisely what measure of scorn he deserves from another speaker. But even so, the richness and variety of pre-Revolutionary Russian speech has never wholly disappeared.

Soviet totalitarianism failed to take into account the subversive potential of the Russian language. To be logically consistent, those in power should have instituted some kind of Orwellian newspeak while abolishing the living language and making its use an indictable offense. But the Soviet leaders permitted—and in many cases even encouraged—the reading of the Russian classics. This was done mainly in order to legitimize the transition from the old regime to the new and thus to gain the support of the intelligentsia. But, having allowed the continuing circulation of the classics, the authorities opened the door to a comparison between the depth, beauty, and integrity of these writings and the shoddy barbarism of what was taking their place. When I was seventeen I wrote down in my notebook two quotations I wished to remember. One from Tolstoy: "Try to do your duty, and you will at once discover your own worth." The other was from Chekhov: "You cannot be deprived of your honor—it can only be lost." The Soviet authorities should have forbidden such phrases: they teach a man to think for himself. This encouragement to think does even more harm to the system than any quotations from the classics on the subject of liberty, such as these lines from Pushkin:

> The heavy shackles shall fall off,
> Prisons shall crumble; by the door
> Freedom, in joy, shall welcome you,
> And brothers shall the sword restore.

(translated with John Heath-Stubbs)

It was drummed into the Soviet people from the cradle that pre-Revolutionary Russia was one vast dungeon. Facts were constantly distorted; the propaganda machine, perfected over decades, worked without a hitch, and very few Soviet citizens would have thought of applying the words of the classic authors decrying the lack of freedom in Tsarist Russia to the contemporary situation. Hence the apparent paradox that broad humanistic statements from the Russian authors of the past could be more subversive than their overt championing of liberty. Set against the intellectual strength of the giants of Russian literature and their mastery of language, the poverty of the officially approved way of writing could be sensed, even if only subconsciously.

As for the actual leaders of the state, their lack of even elementary knowledge of how to use language was beyond belief. Their speeches were not broadcast live, so there was nothing to stop their clangers being corrected on the soundtrack before the actual broadcast. But this was never done. The standard of the leaders' grammar was obviously not considered important. From top to bottom, the blatant illiteracy of the country's "thinkers" was a part of everyday life. Our philosophy lecturer at the University of Moscow would lard his discourse with such gems as, "It's easy, throughout my opinion, to tell friend from foe" and "In art, man presents the vast capabilities of his organism." If he felt more disposed to use figurative language he would say something of this sort: "With its sharpshooting muzzles, Soviet ideology uninterruptedly sets the dogs on the helpless malice of our enemies."

Language is like litmus. It shows anybody who knows how to use and interpret it the nature of what he or she is dealing with. It is no surprise that it should betray the intellectual quality of the speaker—and indeed of the whole system—and one finally got used to what amounted almost to an officially sanctioned disdain for words. The barbarism of language was so ubiquitous that all of us grew tired of parodying it. Instead we developed an ever-greater sensitivity to sincerity or its camouflaged absence. In those days we quite liked the poetry of Andrey Voznesensky (I was, as an émigré poet, to have a wonderfully comic encounter with him and his KGB chaperones in London in the mid-1980s, but more on this later), even though some of his rhythmic and stylistic experiments seemed to us excessively preoccupied with form for its own sake. But on one occasion in a close circle of friends somebody was reading aloud his recent poem "Lenin in Longjumeau," for which he had received some state award or other. This poem's insincerity was so obvious that pretty soon we dismissed it and began to argue about the connection between the artist's personal integrity and his gift. I still hold to the conclusion we eventually reached—that the artist's compromises gradually lead to the withering away of talent.

Sincerity or its lack, though, expressed itself in words. So, once again, in our attitude to the authoritarian state, we couldn't get away from language. We divided people into "us" and "them" by the way they used it. We could suss "them" out pretty fast, often after only hearing a single phrase. "We" spoke a living, supple, human tongue, whereas "they" sought to express themselves through official clichés. Even in the course of my first student affairs of the heart I could not overlook a girl's linguistic habits, however much she attracted me in other ways. With a degree of shame I now recall how I would quote to my pals some of my first dates' phrases and how much we laughed at them. I say "with shame" for it was, after all, rather caddish. But each of these youthful infatuations soon came to an end, because one cannot go on loving a person whose speech one does not respect. On the other hand, when one girl said a simple sentence with a simple intonation, something like "It's raining—there's a storm coming on," I immediately warmed toward her and before long fell in love.

So we would pick our friends by the phrases they used, and careful attention to words often allowed us to take risks—at times quite dangerous, considering the number of informers around. I recall an incident that took place at an exhibition of paintings in Moscow. I was standing in front of a picture by a contemporary Soviet artist titled *The Kremlin in Morning Mist* or some such. This mist, however, looked excessively roseate, and a stranger standing by made a joke about it that could have got him into serious trouble. Giving me a close look, he said that the Kremlin in mist was a rather interesting idea. His tone was almost imperceptibly ironic. I replied in the same vein—that, indeed, the Kremlin in mist was a decidedly intriguing concept. Then he said: "And doesn't it seem to you that the Kremlin in red mist is a particularly fascinating thought?" Again, I followed his lead—we engaged in further chat and turned out to be kindred souls.

The need to conform to the regime while simultaneously psychologically resisting it led to our employing figurative language: carefully veiled political references, elaborate metaphors, subtle irony, plays on words and, above all, parody. The more adeptly a man could make use of language, the more outlets he had for his thought and for therapeutic laughter.

All these things did help, but unless you were prepared to potentially pay for disobedience with your very life, you had no choice but to be infected with the bacillus of obedience. And if you became free by emigrating while still relatively young, you'd be lucky if you were completely cured.

Among the most important manifestations of human dignity is, I think, a person's reaction to a demand and the way this demand is put. Some fifteen years after I left Russia, a telling little incident happened. I was to meet a Russian friend of mine by the ticket office in London's Finchley Road tube station. He stole up behind me—just for fun—and, suddenly grabbing me by the elbow, said: "Come along with me, comrade." It needed only a fraction of a second for me to turn round and recognize him, but in that fraction of a second I felt my whole being cringing and about to submit to the order. And then, while I was telling him off for making such a stupid joke, I recalled a scene I had witnessed when still a boy in Riga. A family friend once took me to see an old gentleman who lived alone on the outskirts of town. This man came from a distinguished Russian aristocratic family. One of the very first things this octogenarian told me, a fifteen-year-old, was that he had not one drop of Tartar blood in his veins but was a direct descendant of Ryurik (the Norse founder of the first Russian dynasty). Then, as chance would have it, there was a knock on the door and a police officer had to be admitted. I don't remember exactly what it was all about, but the police officer demanded that the old man accompany him to the station, where he was wanted for questioning about some offense that had been committed. The phrase the police officer used was the standard one: "Come along with me, comrade." To this the old gentleman replied, rather haughtily: "I am not at leisure to come with you; I find you distasteful and your choice of words offensive." He carried his point—he had, of course, grown up before the Revolution—and the officer left.

Riga in general gave me a further powerful linguistic push. Our moving there from Tallinn was significant not only for my encounter with a far greater variety of Russian, but also for my getting to know two completely new sets of sounds. These were the Latvian, which I heard spoken all around me, and the English, which I then began to study at school. The curious diphthongs and lengthened vowels of Latvian were quite different from the corresponding phonemes in both Russian and Estonian, but I was always open to any new phonetic challenges.

Study of the local language in Russian schools took up four hours each week (it is noteworthy that in Latvian schools twice as much time was devoted to the study of Russian). Both these languages, being national languages within the Soviet Union, began to be learned in the second form (at age eight). But the study of Western European languages (English, French, and German) began in the first year of secondary school (for eleven-year-olds). As I commenced my secondary schooling in Riga, I had missed out on three years of Latvian. At first, quite fairly, I was told to join with a few other new pupils who were from the Russian Soviet Republic and whose situation was similar. We were excused from attending the general classes in Latvian, but had to stay behind two days a week for special tuition. We did not take these lessons very seriously, and in general the attitude in Russian schools to languages other than Russian was rather offhand (later I noticed that English elicited just a little bit more respect than Latvian—and that was largely because some boys were crazy about pop music with lyrics in English). The Latvians reciprocated this contempt and disliked learning Russian intensely. The telling difference—which was also reflected in the amount of time assigned to the study of Russian and Latvian respectively—was that whereas a Russian speaker could get by in Latvia without knowing any Latvian, a Latvian had to know Russian to succeed, even in his own republic. The realization of this made the indigenous population even more resentful of the Russian language and its speakers. I remember an incident in our neighborhood bakery. A Russian who was just in front of me in the queue asked for a particular kind of bread and was told there wasn't any left. Then a woman behind him asked for the same kind of bread in Latvian and was immediately served with it. The man, who was already paying for a different kind of bread at the cash desk, happened to notice this and became annoyed. "Why did you tell me you hadn't got any?" he asked the assistant. She pretended not to understand Russian and poured out a stream of Latvian words. The man went to complain to the manager, who also was Latvian. She must have realized what was going on and became nervous. She summoned the assistant, and the two of them had a hurried consultation, in which I could just catch "Ivan" being repeated several times by the assistant (the Russians, by the same token, called all Latvian men Jānis). Finally, the manager, speaking in what was obviously deliberately broken Russian, apologized to the customer and explained that there had been only one loaf of that particular kind of bread left and that the assistant had overlooked it.

Asking Latvians the way in Russian could also lead to complications. Once a distant relation of ours, called Dmitry, came to stay with us from the depths of Siberia. He looked like a typical Russian, and his accent was *echt* Russian, not often heard in the streets of Riga. The first days of his stay were mainly occupied in going from one end of town to another, having been continually misdirected. By degrees he learned to rely only on those who spoke Russian with a pure Russian rather than Latvian accent, but at first he had been totally foxed. I couldn't help laughing at all this. I think that my own attitude to the confrontation of Latvian nationalism with Russian imperialism was ambivalent. Not having been born in Latvia, but just happening to have been brought there, I found little common ground with the locals. Moreover, by virtue of my mother tongue being Russian and my attending a Russian school, I felt myself to be much closer to the dominant Russians. Even so, I did sense there was something wrong in indiscriminately calling all Latvians Jānis. That was when my closest friend, himself a Russian, applied this name to the husband of our Latvian teacher, who had brought him with her to one of our school's social evenings: "Look—there's Astrida with her Jānis." I liked Astrida, who had taken seriously my translation of a poem from Latvian into Russian and encouraged me, and I felt that she and her husband didn't deserve this kind of thing. Generally speaking, I never felt wholly at ease with the chauvinistic attitude many Great Russians took toward inhabitants of the national republics within the Soviet Union, and the Russians' patronizing attitude toward Latvian nationality and culture, which I could observe all around me, occasionally embarrassed me. Besides, another close friend of mine in Riga was half-Jewish, half-Latvian, and he kept on trying to convince me of the superiority of everything Latvian.

So when I saw our cousin Dmitry, with his Pollyanna Komsomol optimism, innocently thrusting his pristine Russian sounds on all and sundry, totally oblivious of the fact that most of them hated it, I could not but feel that he deserved whatever he got.

In the group of newcomers with whom I had at first been placed at school—who mostly came from such great Russian centers as Moscow and Leningrad—the attitude to local language and culture amounted to total indifference at best and open ridicule at worst. I turned out to be an exception—not because I was particularly diligent or very keen on Latvian, but simply because I was interested in languages and learned them readily. By the next year our teacher had transferred me from this special group to the general class. I thought it unfair that I should be expected to keep up with those who had been studying Latvian for four years. All the same, my grumblings were of no avail: the teacher refused to send me back to the special class. The year after that, I came top of the class in Latvian, along with two other pupils who were bilingual.

Although I liked this first teacher well enough, it is her successor, the aforementioned Astrida Janovna, whom I really remember warmly. This is partly because, as she taught me in the upper school, I remember her much better. More importantly, I owe her a debt of gratitude for encouraging my budding poetic aspirations when I was about fifteen. I particularly liked one poem of Jānis Rainis (1865–1929), the best-known Latvian poet of the Romantic school, who occupied a central place in the curricula of both Russian and Latvian schools. This place was given him not only because of the merits of his work, but, even more so, because much of it was imbued with revolutionary enthusiasm. The poem I liked was called "The Prodigal Son"; I quote it here in English translation:

> Evening delays, rain falls, the north wind blows.
> The prodigal's in rags, with feet unshod.
> To fill his belly, then, do you suppose,
> The path back to his father's house he trod?
>
> But don't you mark how his demeanor shows,
> Though weak and ill, he's proudly unsubdued;
> The rags about his body crimson-hued.
>
> Not to be harnessed he comes here again
> But as a judge to drive you from the fayne.
>
> (translated with John Heath-Stubbs)

Moved by the rhetoric and the romantic imagery of this poem, I translated it into Russian verse and, having plucked up enough courage, showed my translation to Astrida Janovna. She liked it very much, and I also think that she was touched that somebody in a Russian school should show such enthusiasm for Latvian literature. She advised me not only to continue translating, but to try my hand at writing original verse. Her encouragement—together with that of the *Pioneers' Gazette*, which I have already mentioned—played a crucial role in my life.

The following year, I won the first prize for reciting a Latvian poem in a competition organized for the Russian schools. The poem I recited was another one by Rainis, about the coming of a new generation who would change the world. The message of this poem was virtually indistinguishable from dozens of cheery offerings in Russian, on which we were brought up and which proclaimed the death of the old order and the advent of universal happiness. Still, there was one difference that I must have felt when I chose this poem. Its feeling for nature was genuine and deep, and I was stirred by the musical quality of those lines that spoke of the natural world. After I had been awarded the first prize in the competition among Russian schools, for some reason I was entered for the Latvian schools competition.

I still remember how nervous I felt. It was one thing to recite the work of a major Latvian poet—in fact, the symbol of Latvian culture—as one among other Russian speakers. But it was quite another to do so in competition with the Latvians themselves. And the audience also was totally different, being composed entirely of Latvians. Moreover, the auditorium was vast and full to capacity. I began to recite the first lines of the poem, in an intentionally quiet voice, trying to linger on the long vowels and to pronounce the diphthongs the way Astrida Janovna had taught me—in a Latvian, not a Russian manner. The audience listened in complete silence. It must have been obvious to everyone, the moment I opened my mouth, that my mother tongue was not Latvian but Russian. I got a lot of sympathetic applause, but, needless to say, did not win any prize.

It was not because I failed to win the prize, however, that I felt piqued (in any case, the prizes were announced later). It seemed to me that the amount of genuine goodwill on the part of the organizers was negligible and that the purpose of dragging me into somebody else's competition was to use me as yet another example of love and fraternity among the Soviet nationalities. I also felt angry because my turn to recite came near the beginning and I was obliged to sit there for over an hour listening to only half-understood selections from the Latvian classics, all the time conscious of curious glances in my direction. But gradually I became interested and paid more attention. What I was experiencing must have been the first awakening of an interest in the auditory aspects of poetry, which later became a preoccupation. There was something else about the situation that I enjoyed—as the only outsider here, I felt in quite a privileged position. And toward the very end a thin, pale, plain girl (who was to carry off the first prize) recited an excerpt from one of Rainis's dramas with so much conviction that I forgot my grudge completely.

When, in my final school year, I had got rather tired of the ubiquity of Rainis on our syllabus, I was lucky enough to discover Alexandrs Čaks (1901–1950). At that stage, I found him more congenial: he wrote about big-city loneliness, poverty, and squalor, and his meters were less bound by convention. In contrast with the "revolutionary" Rainis, Čaks had been no more than tolerated officially. Most of his poems either dealt with purely personal feelings or were sketches of urban life. Although the latter did often picture the plight of ordinary folk, this was presumably not enough for the ideologues of Soviet culture. After Latvia had been incorporated into the Soviet Union, Čaks tried, under increasing pressure, to write the required panegyrics of the regime, but not very successfully.

I found the official attitude to Čaks puzzling. Later on, when I came across some writings by the Ukrainian poet Vasil Simonenko, I discovered that he had been treated in the same way: not totally suppressed but virtually ignored. The work of such poets might appear in periodicals, but if it was ever published in book form it was provided with an introduction that contained so many reservations and criticisms of the author's shortcomings that it seemed calculated to put the reader off rather than encourage him. In fact, I believe that these introductions were designed not so much for the reader as to placate the authorities. There must have been some people in the state publishing houses with genuine taste, but this was the only way they could get work they admired into print.

To the same period as my discovery of Latvian poetry belong my first readings of English poetry. I tried to puzzle out in the original Shakespeare's sonnets, the poems of Byron and Langston Hughes, Shelley and Carl Sandburg, Keats and Whitman, Wordsworth, Ogden Nash and Hardy, between the ages of fifteen and twenty. A girl I knew toward the end of this period, who was finishing her diploma in English Literature at the University of Riga, supplied me with some of the poems from her textbooks—among them I recall Yeats's "No Second Troy" and "The Sorrow of Love," both wistful and plaintive, although the former also struck me as somewhat aggressive under the surface.

I liked the English language and its poetry so much that when I was fifteen I thought that I might transfer to a special school in which the time devoted to English was not the two periods a week that we had but eight or ten. I had also heard that some general subjects, such as history, were taught in that school through the medium of English. Specialization in Soviet schools began from the end of the eighth year (the fourth secondary school year), after which full-time education ceased to be compulsory. At this point, those who wished to continue their studies could transfer to a specialized stream in either their own or another school. This streaming was invariably the case for those who wished to take the sciences or mathematics; a special English school, however, was a great rarity. When this school turned out to be for Latvian rather than Russian speakers, I made no further inquiries, and remained in my old school. Afterward, I found out that there was also an English school in Riga for Russian speakers, but it was already too late to transfer. Professional advice to senior pupils on careers and scholastic opportunities was almost nonexistent in Soviet schools: the parents had to ferret out information for themselves. Furthermore, those schools in which a foreign language featured prominently in the curriculum must have been in a special category: they were obviously designed to train future diplomats, trade representatives, translators at international meetings and conferences, and other members of the elite. This elite is largely self-perpetuating, and my chances of getting accepted would have been slim. It was my father who found out that such a school existed in Riga—for Latvian speakers—undoubtedly through his connections as a journalist. However, even he could not be expected to know that there were two such schools in the city.

The possibility of taking a course in English language and literature continued to haunt me for several more years. The Moscow Institute of Foreign Languages was the first place I approached after leaving the department of psychology at Moscow University. I left the university on account of my decision to apply for an exit visa; I wanted to explore the possibilities of continuing with higher education in case this exit visa should be refused. I finally succeeded in transferring to the department of English literature at the University of Riga. But before long it was discovered that I had applied to leave the country, and I was expelled from the university before I had had a chance to start my course. At length, in Israel, while continuing my studies in psychology, I chanced to stroll into the English department—and this had unexpected consequences.

When I had first encountered the English language at the age of eleven, among those of its sounds that were new to me I was particularly intrigued by the "w." I also felt warmly about the "th," which required dexterity of the tongue.

"Put your tongue between your teeth," I would instruct my friend and fellow pupil. He did as I said—and his tongue hung out like a dog panting in the heat. "Don't stick the whole of it out, but just the tip! Now say 'thin' and quickly pull it back again." My friend would first draw his tongue in and then pronounce "tsin," "ts" being the sound that Russian speakers ordinarily substitute for the unvoiced "th," whereas the voiced "th," as in "then," was pronounced "dz."

Our teacher would sometimes correct my pronunciation of other sounds. What her own pronunciation was like I cannot now recall, but it would be fascinating if I could. Of course, hardly any Russian teachers of English in schools had ever been to an English-speaking country. Some university teachers must have done a little bit of training abroad, but even where this was the case it could not have been for more than a year. Pronunciation was learned by hard slog in a language laboratory. As for the standard of grammar and vocabulary, it was, I think, quite high, although here too lack of experience abroad must have put these teachers at a disadvantage. They could hardly learn current spoken language by studying H. G. Wells, Shaw, or even the columns of the *Daily Worker*.

When I commenced my first secondary school year, my sister Lena was already studying at the university faculty of philology. She told me about various features of English that do not occur in Russian and gave me the correct terms for them. The next day I would repeat what she had taught me in the classroom. Scarcely did our teacher have the time to write the name "Pete" on the blackboard and to say that the final letter is not pronounced than I eagerly put up my hand. She gave me permission to speak, and I would say in a loud voice: "That letter is called 'the mute e'!" At first she welcomed my knowledge and enthusiasm, but after a bit began to show signs of embarrassment. And then it so happened that one of my classmates came up to me at the end of the lesson. She was a quiet, intelligent girl called Natasha Petrova, and we were to remain classmates for the rest of our time in school. I remember exactly where she came up to me—it was in the corridor just outside the classroom door—and the fact that this has fixed itself in my memory shows, I think, what a strong impression her words made on me.

"Boy," she said to me (the school year had only recently started, and I was still new), "it's not done to show off like that in front of your classmates." I felt terribly ashamed, and after this I would raise my hand only when a question had been put to the class.

Our first English teacher, Bella Davidovna, was a young Jewish woman who had probably just taken her university diploma. She must have had a sense of humor because she often smiled (and there would be sparks of laughter in her big dark eyes) at my thin figure, my high-pitched, girlish voice and my earnest enthusiasm for an alien tongue's linguistics and phonetics. She was succeeded by another lady, Octavia Karlovna, who had a more sarcastic sense of humor and who saw us into our final school year. I think she might have been of German or perhaps even English origin: her first name and patronymic sounded most unusual; her Russian had an odd flavor, and her excessive courtesy in using the polite second person plural *vy* (corresponding to the French *vous*) when addressing a member of the class, children though we were, was also a sign of her foreignness. I liked her very much, not least because of her eccentricities. She treated me with a mixture of encouragement and irony. Once, when she was introducing us to the use of the conditional in English, I must have particularly impressed her by being the only member of the class to get the hang of it. After this, whenever I made a mistake she would say: "You think you know everything—but you don't. Much, yes, but not everything." I would feel slightly uneasy at this remark, for I had never claimed to know everything.

Sure enough, in due course, she put me in for the annual English competition between the local schools. Having won the first prize, I was entered for the city competition. This was held at the opposite end of town; I remember going there on a tram and telling the very nice woman conductor, when she asked me, all about where and why I was going. She wished me luck.

The choice of topics on which we were asked to write in the main part of the competition upset me: they were something like the October Revolution, Komsomol Heroes, or Soviet Cosmonauts. After much deliberation, I chose the last as possibly the least dreary. The winning entries were to be announced some weeks later, and we all had to assemble again at the same place. Two or three prizes were announced for various achievements— such as composition, vocabulary, perhaps also proficiency in grammar—and I hoped that I would get one in something or other. But I got nothing at all.

It so happened that coming back on the tram I encountered the same conductor. She immediately recognized me and eagerly inquired how I had done. Imagine how red my face was when I had to tell her that I was coming back empty-handed. But she consoled me in a motherly way. Back at school, Octavia Karlovna said in her usual manner: "There, there; much, but not everything."

My father, trying to encourage my interest in languages, once took me to the seamen's club in Riga. One needed a pass for this, but my father was admitted as he carried a journalist's card. There I ran into my first real live Englishman. He appeared to me to be phlegmatic in a typically English way (probably he was drunk). My father beamed with pride as he watched us talking together from the next table. Having ascertained that the man was indeed from England, I asked him what city he came from. I couldn't understand his answer, so I had to ask him the same question more than once. He kept on saying something that sounded like "Ool." Finally, unable to identify it, I said that I supposed it must be quite a small place. At this, for some incomprehensible reason, he became indignant and replied that on the contrary, it was a very large city. I thought that I knew all the large cities in England, so I asked him to repeat the name again. Upon hearing the same sound once more, I said with final conviction that it must be nothing but a very, very small place indeed. He got quite hot under the collar and said emphatically that it was one of the biggest cities in England.

Years later, I remembered this incident and, poring over a map of England, realized that the Englishman, in his Yorkshire accent, must have been saying "Hull."

After all these years, while always conscious of my organs of speech, always adjusting and deploying them, I've come to be convinced that perceiving life and people through another tongue—even another accent—means a different perception of reality.

Chapter 7: "All Potatoes Look Alike"

Riga was a major port—but a river port, not a sea port. Whereas Tallinn had been actually in sight of the sea, to travel to the beach from Riga took about an hour overall, including a twenty- to thirty-minute train journey. But very close to where we lived was the Daugava River embankment (in Russian this river is called the Western Dvina). Its estuary being not far off, it ran wide and was an important feature of the city. My friends and I often went for walks on its embankment, and one of the most cherished memories of my youth is of a whole night's walk there with my classmates after our graduation ball.

I feel that I was fortunate in that each time I moved it was from a smaller to a larger city, and each time I found myself either living or working closer to the city center. In Tallinn, our flat was on the outskirts; in Riga, we were within quarter of an hour's walk of the central Lenin monument. But there were disadvantages inherent in this change.

There are three factors that influence urban children's development everywhere—their family, their school, and street life—but there is, in the Soviet Union, an additional one. That is the communal apartment.

Once, when my parents argued about ideology and the Soviet reality, my father taunted my mother: "You're nothing but a housewife—what do you know apart from pots and pans?"

My mother asked him in return: "And you, what about you?"

"I'm a mouthpiece of the Party!" answered my father proudly.

After that, every now and again, she would mock him (quite deservedly, in my opinion): "You, 'mouthpiece of the Party.' Why does your family have to be huddled in two tiny rooms and share the apartment with four other families? Can't your Party do something for its mouthpiece?"

My father had no answer. He'd make a desperate gesture with his hand and leave the room.

Our living conditions were not only very uncomfortable but bureaucratically complicated in a way typical of Soviet double-think. Officially, such overcrowding was not allowed. We had to conceal the fact that all five of us occupied two rather small rooms, and one of my sisters was not registered as living with us. My mother constantly worried that one or other member of the families we shared the place with might inform on us, and she had to take this into account in the course of the continual feuds and alliances that went on in the apartment. However, when some officials did check how many people were living in our rooms (I'm almost certain that somebody must have informed on us), nothing very drastic was done about it. Soviet law in fact laid down the minimum space per person in living accommodation—and our space was half that. But the authorities obviously had no solution, and my father's newspaper must have put in a word for him.

So, when we swapped our Tallinn flat for a more centrally situated one in a much larger city, we had to put up with living conditions that were far worse. In Tallinn, our rooms with their own little passage had been away from the kitchen and the communal corridor; in Riga, the corresponding rooms were divided from one another and situated at opposite ends of the communal flat. They were less than half the size of our Tallinn rooms. The smaller one, entered from the kitchen, was really tiny—only eight square meters. Before the Soviet Union exported its "democracy" and its living conditions to the Baltic states, this room would have been occupied by a single servant girl. The area of the other, bigger room was twelve square meters. In these cramped quarters we five lived, managing, like the majority of Soviet people under the same or even worse conditions, to cope with studying and working. My father's capacity for work was simply staggering: after a whole day at his newspaper office, he would often stay in the kitchen till long past midnight finishing an article. My elder sister Milla also worked hard and sometimes—especially after she had been transferred to the section of her youth newspaper which dealt with rural matters—went on trips to various towns and villages in Latvia. Father and sister would occasionally sit together at the table, and he, being the older and more experienced journalist, would instruct her on how to write.

For my part, I wasn't interested in the least in their day-to-day work or indeed their profession. In general, the falsehood and truth of the adult world left me indifferent in those years: having discovered the world of books, I plunged into it headlong. I read everywhere: at the dinner table, in the lavatory, in bed at night, with a flashlight under the blankets. At that time, in our first years in Riga, I read omnivorously: Thomas Maine Reid, Dickens, Jack London, Ernest Thompson-Seton (called in Russian Seton-Thompson), *The Kalevala* (one of my favorite books, treasured from Tallinn), Walter Scott (whose verse I was to discover and admire later in the free translation by Eduard Bagritsky), fairy tales of various nations, Tolstoy, Victor Hugo, and so on. As for poetry, I attempted to read an anthology of Soviet verse that had belonged to my brother. It had been published in the 1940s, the Stalin era. No matter how hard I tried, I found it difficult to get anything out of it. On the other hand, in school we were being introduced to Pushkin, and I enjoyed the ringing quality of poems like "Song of Oleg the Seer."

My mother would cry out that the child was going nuts; she forbade me to read at the table (I would still snatch moments between courses), and once she even caught me with my flashlight under the blankets (this, of course, didn't stop me: I simply became more wary and began to prick up my ears for footfalls in the kitchen coming up to the door). Sure enough, she blamed my father for this passion—and even saw it as part of the bad genes stemming from his own father, who sometimes came to visit us and read children's books day in and day out.

Grandfather Abraham had been a simple illiterate cabinetmaker and carpenter who learned to read very late in life. My memories of him mainly belong to those years—the early 1960s—when he was still hale enough to come and visit us, although he was already in his eighties. (He died at the age of 99, and I was moved when I heard that the congregation to which he belonged in Leningrad gave him a veritable slap-up funeral, "fit for a real saint," as those who had witnessed it wrote to us, long after our exit from the country.) I loved him for his simple, unassuming nature, his childlike sense of fun, and his being a cabinetmaker. It was probably through him that I soon became fascinated by fretwork and would spend hours on end sawing figures of deer and other animals out of plywood. Some of my relations on my mother's side—as I realized later—couldn't forgive her for marrying into such a common family, whose head, Grandfather Abraham, spoke Russian incorrectly to the end of his days. This marriage of hers was particularly objectionable, as I gathered, to her maternal branch, the Maneviches. They consisted almost entirely of members of the intelligentsia—doctors, engineers, and so on—in a word, the intellectual elite. My being constantly bludgeoned with their names might well have turned me against them, but I could see that they were really bright, from their photographs in the family album. My mother often said things like: "Comb your hair back, so that we can see your high forehead: it's the only thing you've got that takes after the Maneviches—otherwise you're the spitting image of your father and your Grandfather Abraham."

That really got my goat, and I would shout back angrily: "What if I do want to be exactly like Grandfather Abraham?"

"You mean you'd like to be besotted with children's stories in your old age?" Mother would ask sarcastically.

I would reply "Yes," but with less conviction.

When he was not engaged in making furniture for us, Grandfather would lie on the sofa reading books intended for children of primary school age. He was completely enthralled by his reading, and his features reflected everything that went on in the story. If he chortled happily, you could be sure that the jolly chums had succeeded in escaping from Daisy the rampaging moo-cow. If a shadow of anxiety fell upon his face, one could guess that our heroes had got a nip from Gussie the neighborhood gander. Sometimes Grandfather forgot himself so far as to read aloud syllable by syllable: "And-Pe-tya-shout-ed-to-Van-ya-pax!" whereupon he laughed, overjoyed that everything had come right in the end.

He had the reputation of being a first-rate cabinetmaker who had dedicated his whole life to his craft. But when he used to come to see us in Riga, his eyesight had deteriorated quite a lot. Nevertheless, he insisted, after our move, on personally making at least some of our furniture: the bookcase, the wardrobe, and the kitchen dresser. We couldn't refuse, firstly for fear of offending him and secondly simply because we hadn't got the money for new furniture. Some items—I think a couple of old divans and a table or two—we had brought with us from Tallinn. Grandfather's furniture was skillfully enough made, but was distinctly on the old-fashioned side. Moreover, the cheap plywood, which was all my father managed to obtain at a discount, using his journalistic connections, was clearly not good enough. Grandfather's failing powers must have accounted for the fact that there were nails sticking out inside the shelves and drawers. Because of these nails, all of us from time to time got scratches on our hands. In theory, we knew the position of those nails (for instance, in the wardrobe at the very top of the second shelf from the bottom, on the left-hand side, there was a particularly nasty one), but time and again we would forget about them, especially when in a hurry. On a number of occasions we tried to hammer them in or to bend them so that they were closer to the partitions and more out of the way. But once this led to the collapse of a whole shelf, after which all we dared do was give the end of the nail a slight tap so that it would stick out rather less.

The smallest number of nails was in the bookcase particularly beloved by me. On its upper, glass-fronted shelves stood editions of the classics, as well as other volumes of verse and prose in fine bindings. On the two lower shelves, behind plywood doors, were kept all the slim books, those with soiled covers, and textbooks. As fresh books were bought and the old ones read, the need arose for somewhere to house third-class volumes. When, some half-dozen years later, we came to Riga, and a telephone was at last installed in our flat, a place was found for these books in a small cupboard we fixed up under the phone.

To have a telephone was, at least in those days, something of a rarity. In Tallinn, we had not had one at all. For me personally its appearance was an important event. Now I could chat to my friends, find out what had been set for homework if I had forgotten, and arrange to meet after school. The phone proved to be a milestone on my way from books to the actuality of human contacts. Between the ages of nine and sixteen I was a real bookworm, but gradually the emotional stresses of adolescence and my initiation into the urgent complexities of adult life rendered books less important. What took their place was one's own concerns and discussing them with one's peers. During my Moscow years, my friends and I hardly read at all, but talked continually among ourselves, sometimes all night long.

The other members of our communal flat were frequently irritated by my endless telephone conversations with my schoolmates. Occasionally, when they needed the phone themselves, they asked me to cut it short. I gave in, but felt aggrieved. I was particularly humiliated and annoyed on those—admittedly rare—occasions when someone who happened to be near the phone answered it and said I was not at home. In fact, I was always in our smaller room behind the kitchen, but they were either too lazy to summon me or expecting a phone call themselves. Sometimes I would hear the telephone ringing, but I had scarcely opened the door into the kitchen before I caught the voice of one of the two particularly tiresome old women quietly saying: "He's out." Immediately after, I rang up my schoolmate Zhenya Konyaev and, sure enough, it was he who had just phoned. If I took up the matter with these two women it was useless: they simply said they had called for me at the top of their voices, but there had been no reply.

This attitude of theirs to my telephoning rights seemed to me particularly unfair. After all, had it not been for our family there was little chance they would have had a telephone in the flat. Initially it was installed only for us; it stood in our larger room and was registered in our name. We got it relatively quickly (after only two years' wait) thanks to my father being a journalist. Ordinary mortals had to wait much longer—and, indeed, to consider themselves lucky if they ever got a telephone at all. But, as was to be expected, no sooner had we had the telephone installed than our co-tenants began to beg us to let them either use it or allow somebody else to call them—in which case, we would have to go and fetch them. In the end, my parents decided to place the phone in the communal corridor, so that we would not be disturbed unnecessarily. Further, paying the rental for the phone could now be shared by all (local calls in Russia were free). But since it remained officially in our name, we could always take it back if we wanted to. Finally, my mother got fed up with our having the sole responsibility of collecting and paying the rental when everybody was using the phone. For this reason—and also as a gesture of goodwill—we agreed to cancel its registration as our private phone and make it a communal one. Later on, my mother regretted this and thought it an unforgivable stupidity. Losing control over the phone meant that she had given up a valuable bargaining point. The day our phone was out of our hands, we were on a par with everybody else in the flat.

I think I learned a lot from this episode. I had a direct experience of just how short-lived human gratitude can be. On the other hand, surely this was natural enough in its own way. We had indeed done a good turn for the four families living cheek by jowl with us—and a very valuable one too in the context of Soviet domestic conditions. For this, one might have expected their appreciation to have endured a little longer. But we had done what we had done of our own free will and had no right to expect anything special in return. Moreover, I sensed how the passing of time changes the significance of any action. With my own eyes I saw the black object exchange our room for its place in the corridor opposite the front door of the flat, and with my own ears I heard expressions of enormous gratitude. But the fulsomeness of this gratitude soon began to dwindle and after a while vanished altogether.

Now imagine the following situation. In the communal larder you have inherited from previous tenants there is a very convenient shelf. It is close to the window and at eye level. Another woman in the flat has an inconvenient shelf, in a damp corner and lower down, so that she has to stoop all the time. She starts by saying how lucky you are to have that shelf and then goes on to commiserate with you on your cramped living conditions, which, surely, even the notoriously niggardly regulations don't permit. So you either swap shelves with her or, if you're too attached to your own shelf, make a concession to her in some other field. You can even ignore her implied blackmail if you're prepared to take the risk. But whatever your reaction may be, it will do you no good reminding her that it's thanks to you she can use the phone whenever she likes and how difficult her life was before. All this is no longer relevant. Then some of the original tenants leave, new families move in, and no one cares when and how a communal phone appeared in the apartment. So you live in the present and face the facts as they are.

On the whole, we were fortunate enough in the people we had to share with in Riga. In spite of all their shortcomings—one a thief, two of them half insane, another an alcoholic, and so on—they were not without human warmth and decency; they appreciated my mother's intelligence and understanding of people and from time to time asked her for advice or simply confided their troubles to her. Nevertheless, it was my easygoing father they really warmed to. "We all respect Ida [a form of Adele, my mother's name] Solomonovna, but Leonid Abramovich—there's a really big-hearted man for you." (My mother liked to quote these words as further evidence of my father's spinelessness, usually adding one of her stock of Jewish, Russian, Belorussian, and Ukrainian proverbs, such as: "It's the bent tree all the goats go at." Later I discovered that she also knew another saying, which had passed into common currency from *The Wisdom of the Fathers,* a collection of Talmudic lore: "God loves whom men love." But it never would have occurred to her to consider applying these words to her own husband.)

In the course of our eleven-year stay in apartment eleven at eleven Rūpniecības Street, some rooms in it changed tenants. Lyolya and Valdis's family moved to another part of town, while Sofya Samuilovna had to move even further—she died.

I still remember her with some uneasiness, for she really did look like an old witch—albeit twentieth-century style. She was a chain smoker and coughed continually. My mother referred to her as "the lumpen proletariat." I did not know what that meant, but I gathered it alluded to the old woman's one-time participation in the Revolution and in post-revolutionary terror. My mother insisted that Sofya Samuilovna's total loneliness in her old age served her right—especially as she was Jewish and, according to my mother, it was none of her business to get mixed up in that sort of thing. "That's just the way those trollops who interrogated innocent old men and women looked and behaved," my mother would say when Sofya Samuilovna made one of her appearances in the communal kitchen. She always wore some kind of leather jacket over her rags; her lips would be painted bright scarlet, with a cigarette casually dangling from them. She lived just behind the partition wall, and at night I was sometimes awakened by her rasping graveyard cough. Then one day a gloomy hush fell on the whole flat and some men appeared with an oblong wooden box, which they trundled into the old woman's room. My mother burst out crying along with one or two neighbors: "Sofya Samuilovna has passed on."

Lyolya was the mother of Valdis, a boy some three years my junior. They were a Latvian family, and since Latvians don't use patronymics I had no way of addressing her at all. To call a woman old enough to be my mother by her first name would have sounded overly familiar, while Auntie Lyolya would have been too childish. As for her hypothetical patronymic, nobody knew what her father's first name had been, and she herself, when asked how one should address her, would say: "Just call me Lyolya." On official documents and at their place of work, everybody in the Soviet Union without exception had a patronymic. At school we naturally addressed our Latvian teachers by their name and patronymic, and later on, when I was working at the State Latvian Institute of Urban Construction Planning, I could not conceive of using anything but the same form of address with my Latvian colleagues. But among themselves they called each other by their first names or surnames only. Having an alien custom imposed on them must have been for many yet another unwelcome reminder that they were not masters in their own republic. Understandably, such people never conformed to the custom unless obliged to, and certainly not when away from work.

Valdis had a father too, but I hardly ever saw him and didn't even know his first name. He was some kind of state, or Party, official and seemed to me to be a highly important person. He gave this impression by his embonpoint, his deliberate way of walking, taciturnity, and the fact that he was often late returning from work. I realize now that he could not have been all that important. Had he been, this family would hardly have been living three to a room. But at that time the deference that Valdis clearly had for his father spilled over onto me. Valdis really did hold him in awe and the following scene remains clear in my memory. That year I had had a chess set for my thirteenth birthday and quickly learned the moves from a book (at that time I learned everything from books). Valdis already knew how to play, and we had games together, which he mostly won. His father took an evident pride in his ten-year-old son's victories. Sometimes, coming home in the evening, he would look in at the kitchen where we played, in order to appraise the situation on the chess board. On such occasions he would usually stand there for a minute or two without uttering a word and then go back to his room. Once, when Valdis was losing, his mother told him that it was time to go to bed. He must have been very eager to get the better of me and told her that he would come in a minute. A little later, she called him again, and once more he answered her in the same way. Then his father appeared. Without raising his voice, he reminded Valdis that his mother had told him to go to bed. Suddenly turning pale, Valdis jumped up and began to mutter something about how desperate he had been to finish the game. Without even arranging our next meeting, he trotted along the corridor, continually justifying himself and saying he was sorry. His father followed him unhurriedly.

My mother would often point to this kind of discipline as a good example for both me and my father. I was in no such awe of my father; instead I was afraid of his sudden outbursts of passion—his "kicking over the traces," as my mother called it. These tantrums usually happened as a result of her nagging. One typical small scene from our Tallinn days has stuck in my mind.

"Ivanov's little girl trembles at her father's every word, even though he's just an ordinary fellow, not a journalist, let alone a Party member. But in our family the children don't take any notice at all of their father," I heard my mother's voice in the corridor.

"Where, who takes no notice?" my father raised his voice in assumed sternness.

"That child is taking a whole hour to put one sock on," she continued as if she had not heard him. "He's been told that he's going to be late for school and that Father will be here in a moment. Why, he couldn't care less, he just goes on taking his own sweet time with his sock and singing."

"I'll show him, just let me get my hands on him!" my father "kicked over the traces" and rushed into the room. I was standing on a chair, pulling my trousers on and singing a song we had recently learned at school at the top of my voice:

> It's fun on skates, it's fun on a sleigh,
> It's fun on the mountain to tear away—
> But much more fun, with laughter and glee,
> To dance around the New Year Tree!

(translated with John Heath-Stubbs)

"Here's fun on skates for you!" My father gave me a painful slap on my behind. "And here's fun on a sleigh!" He gave me another. "And that's for tearing away on the mountain." The last one was almost unbearably painful. I burst into tears—and soon enough, toning down my sobs in order to listen, I could hear my mother berating my father for always working himself into tantrums instead of taking a firm hand with his children. According to her, by beating me up so cruelly and unexpectedly he was sending me into veritable hysterics ("Can't you hear the child is having a fit?" and I would immediately turn up the volume to prove her right) and in general ruining my mental health. ("No wonder the child is growing up different from everybody else!") I was glad to hear my father so scolded, because it served him right for punishing me, but I also wished my mother had not egged him on to begin with: she must have known only too well what his reaction would be.

But the older I grew and the less time my father had to spend with us, the more infrequent those outbursts became. On the whole, I enjoyed a large degree of freedom in the family, and in spite of all my mother's efforts to impress me with the father-son relationship in Valdis's case, that remained totally alien for me.

Mother and I both genuinely regretted their family's moving out. But no one could fairly say that the Orlovs, who took their place, were less interesting.

For one thing, there was somebody of my own age group, and a girl to boot. She was called Klava and was only a year younger than I. Although she went to a different school, we still had enough common ground to discuss homework, lessons, and teachers together. Sometimes we played japes—as, for instance, once when the doorbell was out of order and we were asked to write a note to be placed on the door, informing callers of the fact. We spent a whole hour drafting it, and it ran something like this: "The buzzer has konked out, having done so much service to mankind. Would-be wayfarers are kindly requested to plant their weary bums on the floor. In case of emergency please knock with your head." Once on the door, this note's lifespan proved to be short. No sooner had the first caller arrived than we were each summoned by our respective mothers and given a dressing down. (I can only guess what her mother said to her, but mine, as usual, attributed the affair to my weakness of intellect.)

Alik, Klava's half-brother—they were meant to have two fathers, neither of whom was around—must have been in his late twenties. He had been married, but was now divorced. Alla, his ex-wife, occasionally came with their little daughter to see him. I thought Alla very pretty and couldn't understand why he would have divorced her. I heard Lyuba (Lyubov Ivanovna, that is), Alik and Klava's mother, saying something to my mother about Alla having been unfaithful, but I was rather hazy as to what that meant. Some attempts were made to bring them together again, but although she remained fond of him, she had too many boyfriends, and it all came to nothing. He himself was hardly a model of virtue. Once, sitting in the lavatory, I overheard a conversation in the kitchen between him and Tonya. She was the daughter-in-law of Zinaida Alexandrovna (a very stout but energetic woman who made the floor shake whenever she walked down the corridor). Tonya was married to Zinaida Alexandrovna's son Sergey, a young officer who was away most of the year doing some kind of paper work in Egypt. Tonya was attractive in a typical Russian way: she was quite tall, opulently proportioned, and often wore her hair plaited in one rich dark braid. Sergey was decidedly on the short side and seemed rather puny, especially when standing next to his wife. (Zinaida Alexandrovna said that he took after his father, her own late husband—and I couldn't help laughing trying to imagine what that couple must have looked like when they went out together, as Sergey was only about a quarter of his mother's dimensions.) Alik, on the other hand, was built like a guardsman and as handsome. At the time this overheard conversation took place, Sergey was in Egypt, but I think he was expected back any day. "Whatever are we to do, then?" asked Tonya (she sounded almost in tears). "Why, nothing," Alik replied with a laugh. "We were just ships that pass in the night." "But it just can't be like that!" Tonya said pleadingly. "Why not? That's the way the cookie crumbles." When I emerged from the toilet into the kitchen, they stopped abruptly, for reasons I did not understand.

Lyuba was a veritable battle-axe. On two separate occasions she nearly killed first the older and then the younger Kvele. These two Latvian women, mother and daughter, moved into the room that had been Sofya Samuilovna's. The daughter was an old maid of about forty to forty-five, called Skaidra. Her mother must have been in her sixties. Both always seemed to be suffering from various ailments. Skaidra's face was usually puffy, while her mother had swollen legs and walked with difficulty. Before they were allotted Sofya Samuilovna's room they had been living in some kind of basement, which was regularly flooded when it rained. For them, moving from a place like that to such a posh house—with a spiral staircase covered by a glass dome—must have been a real step up in the world. That being so, the fact that the mother had to climb four flights of stairs with her swollen legs paled into insignificance. She worked in a cigarette kiosk on Suvorov Avenue. Occasionally I would encounter her moving at a snail's pace along our street or up the stairs, stopping every few steps. Once, having bought a glass of beer from a beer tanker parked near her kiosk, I went up to her to get some matches. She was genuinely pleased to see me, and her face became wreathed in smiles. This moment remained one of my most vivid and moving memories, since in all those quarrels and shifting alliances that went on at home, our families happened at the time to be on different sides and I had more than once been intentionally rude to her, just to keep our end up.

I think it was largely because of Lyuba that we were at odds with the Kveles at all—and indeed, later on, when she moved out, we became quite friendly with them. We could hardly refuse Lyuba our support, for our family and hers were on very good terms. She took our side in every apartment dispute, and she was a useful ally as all were afraid of her tempestuous disposition. The fact that she had a young and muscular son made her position even more formidable: although Alik usually did not get involved in these feuds, he was still a force to be reckoned with. On the few occasions when he did involve himself it was for some major cause, and then his entry on stage would be really impressive.

Maria Tikhonovna also had a son—Victor—who was likewise young and broad-shouldered, but he turned out to be no match for Alik. Moreover, he was often away at sea, and anyhow lived elsewhere and only visited his mother occasionally. Maria Tikhonovna must have been getting on for seventy. She was a quiet old woman, but she had a mind of her own. My mother said that when it came to intelligence she could knock spots off everybody in the place. Victor must have inherited his mother's laconic manner: except for "Hello," I hardly ever heard him utter a word, either to me or to the others. Indeed, I had the impression that even to his own mother he said nothing but "Hello mother" and "Good-bye mother." Like Alik, he was quite handsome, and in addition to his wife he had a mistress. Sometimes he would come to visit Maria Tikhonovna not on his own, but with one or other of them. Each of them tried to get into Maria Tikhonovna's good books by bringing her various gifts.

"Ida Solomonovna," the old woman would say, "look what an expensive Orenburg kerchief my daughter-in-law has given me—how much could a thing like that cost? And these fur boots, Victor's girlfriend bought them for me. Which do you think are nicer?"

"Why, both presents are equally nice," my mother would answer diplomatically.

Maria Tikhonovna was in the habit of stealing things now and again. Once, when I was in our smaller room, deeply immersed in a book, she tiptoed in, evidently believing there was no one there. Imagine her surprise when she saw me! Muttering something like, "I keep on calling: 'Ida Solomonovna, Ida Solomonovna,' but I get no answer," she beat a hasty retreat. On another occasion, when she had invited my mother and myself to admire the new mirror bought for her by Victor's mistress, we noticed something familiar on her table. It was a table runner that we had brought with us all the way from Tallinn, which had then disappeared.

"It's a lovely mirror," my mother said, "and I like this table runner too. I wonder where such a nice one could be got?"

"Oh I really don't know," answered Maria Tikhonovna without batting an eyelid. "It was Victor who brought it for me from abroad, years ago."

Mother did not inquire further in exactly what foreign parts one might find a table runner with an Estonian national design. Instead, she told me off for neglecting to lock the door when going from one of our rooms to the other or to the telephone. But it wasn't just me—all of us, including herself, frequently forgot to do this. It was hardly practicable to lock the door—and take the key with you—every time you had to pop into the other room to fetch something (I also felt slightly embarrassed doing this in front of our co-tenants, showing they were considered not to be trusted). And when the phone was ringing and you had to rush to answer it before it stopped, there was simply no time. But if that same phone call turned out to be for you, then the room could remain unwatched for some considerable time. Although we had hardly anything worth stealing, articles—pieces of cutlery, small plates, doilies, and little vases—would regularly vanish. To be fair, I have to say that some of these might have been stolen not by Maria Tikhonovna but by Zinaida Alexandrovna, Tonya's mother-in-law. Maria Tikhonovna I called a professional thief; Zinaida Alexandrovna was in my eyes no more than an amateur. It is true that she likewise was not above filching other people's property. She too strolled into our room once and, according to my mother, on more than one occasion she helped herself to our meat from the pot cooking on the stove. But she lacked Maria Tikhonovna's persistence and finesse—not to mention her audacity. Indeed, would she ever have had Maria Tikhonovna's nerve in sequestrating potatoes from the communal larder?

These potatoes—five kilos—had been bought by Lyuba at the local shop in Janki Kupala Street, in the morning, and by early afternoon half of them had vanished. But Maria Tikhonovna had not reckoned on Lyuba's fighting spirit. For, having a pretty good idea who the thief was, Lyuba quickly organized a posse to go through all the rooms in search of the missing potatoes. Sure enough, they were found under Maria Tikhonovna's bed, and a hilarious exchange took place between Maria Tikhonovna and Lyuba.

"Here they are!" shouted Lyuba triumphantly. "These are my potatoes!"

"Nothing of the sort," answered Maria Tikhonovna in a sweetly reasonable voice, "I've just bought them at the greengrocer's by the post office."

"You're a liar! This is just the amount that went missing! And they're the same color!" She rushed back to her room and returned with a specimen potato—so that everybody could observe the similarity.

"All potatoes look alike," answered Maria Tikhonovna, not at all put out.

"And why do you keep potatoes under your bed then?"

"Why, it just happens to be a habit of mine."

"Okay, just you wait," said Lyuba. "When Alik comes home, he will sort it out."

Alik got back from work a couple of hours later. The whole apartment could hear Lyuba briefing him on the situation; the word "potatoes" continually reverberated in their room. "I'll kill her if she doesn't give them back," said Alik, coming out of the room and heading for Maria Tikhonovna's door. Lyuba ran after him, begging him at the top of her voice to try not to use force—unless he really had to.

But it was not for nothing that my mother had such a high opinion of Maria Tikhonovna's resourcefulness—it turned out that the old woman had already found time to summon her son Victor. No sooner had Alik started banging on her door shouting,

"What's all this business about the potatoes?" than the doorbell rang twice. (Each family had its own number of rings, and each new set of tenants inherited the code of its predecessors. For us, one had to ring no fewer than five times.)

"That'll be Victor!" cried Maria Tikhonovna gleefully as she went to open the door.

"What's this potato business?" asked Victor of those gathered in the corridor. "Why can't you leave my mother alone?"

"We'll have to find out whose mother it is that can't be left alone," Alik rejoined, and went on to suggest: "Let's take a little walk together—we'll leave the women out of it."

They returned after half an hour, and that marked the end of the matter. Lyuba later told my mother in confidence that she had got her potatoes back. This had to be done discreetly because part of the agreement between Alik and Victor had been that the affair should be settled in a quiet way, so that Maria Tikhonovna should not lose face. Victor must surely have known about his mother's little ways, and I think it was not just Alik's superior physique that made him concede the point.

Alik did not intervene in Lyuba's skirmishes with the Kveles, but this did not stop her from holding the possibility of his intervention over them. They, for their part, threatened to complain to the police that they were continually intimidated by the prospect of physical violence.

I could never understand what the whole thing was all about. I now think that it was mainly a matter of the disparity of their temperaments—Russian and Latvian. This national difference was aggravated by Lyuba being naturally headstrong while the Kveles were not a little dotty. The older of the two would occasionally break out into a weird loud laugh in the middle of an argument with another tenant. Sometimes she would do this for apparently no reason at all, except that she found herself alone in the kitchen with someone from the enemy camp. This laugh was meant to express her contempt for them. The behavior of Skaidra, the daughter, was even more interesting. Once, when I was about seventeen, at the height of our feud, she failed to call me to the phone, but slammed the receiver down before my very eyes (nobody ever phoned the Kveles, so she could afford this tactic without fear of retaliation). Having done this, she retreated to her room, which was just behind the telephone. After a few seconds, the phone started to ring again, and I lifted the receiver. It was a friend of mine who said that he had just rung and asked for me, but somebody had cut him off. The Kveles' door opened slightly—Skaidra clearly wanted to hear what was being said.

"I know very well who it was," I replied in a deliberately raised voice, "and I'll make sure, right now, they'll never do it again."

So saying, with a heavy tread I approached the Kveles' door—which immediately shut—and banged on it loud enough to waken the dead. Skaidra and I were the only people in the flat at the time.

"I'll send for the police!" she shouted in response to my banging.

"Why the hell didn't you call me to the phone?"

"And I won't call you next time either!"

"So that's the way it is? Just you wait!" and I opened the door of her room. All I wanted was to scare her a bit, but she began to squeal so loudly that I was terrified myself and left her to it.

After that she would regularly appear clad in nothing but a very short nightie at her doorway whenever I—or, for that matter, anybody else from our camp—happened to pass. No one knew exactly why she did this, but we conjectured that it was simply to annoy. If so, surely this was not very effective, since the light bulb in the corridor was so dim that all one could make out was a vague pink and white blur.

"Aren't you ashamed of yourself?" my mother would say to her. "Fancy doing that kind of thing—at your age too! Just what are you trying to get out of it—to tempt someone with your flabby body?"

"Why, your own son enjoys looking at me!" Skaidra would answer.

"My son?" my mother laughed. "My son can look at young girls with young bodies—he doesn't have to gawk at someone like you."

(I considered this sadly ironic, for already my mother's jealous attitude to my most innocent and tentative relationships with girls was quite intolerable.) Then, after a few days of Skaidra's exhibitionism, Lyuba decided that the joke was over and complained to Alik. "Where, where did you say she stands naked?" he thundered coming out into the corridor. (There was dead silence in Skaidra's room.) "Just let her try it on again!" She never did.

Sometimes the seeds of a political drama could be discerned in this farce. "Why don't you go back to Moscow where you came from and leave our Latvia to us Latvians?" Old Kvele would occasionally mutter in the kitchen, to which Lyuba invariably replied: "When was Latvia ever yours? It's always been Russian!"

One evening the whole flat was aroused by wild shrieks coming from the kitchen. We all ran there—and saw Old Kvele lying in the middle of the floor with her feet waving in the air. Skaidra, who was in the bathroom, immediately began joining in her mother's screams. Together they made such a hullabaloo that even people from adjoining flats came rushing in to see what was the matter. Lyuba, who continued to occupy herself with her cooking, as if nothing had happened, eventually told us what it was all about.

"I was making some soup, and never touched her—when all at once she began to say under her breath: 'Go back to Moscow, what are you lot doing here, go home!' Well, finally I got fed up. So I shoved her nose in her own frying pan. I did it quite gently, just to teach her a lesson, but straightaway she started screaming blue murder. The bloody shammer!"

For a long time after this the Kveles kept threatening to take Lyuba to court, but never did so. They must have realized that Lyuba had a trump card in her hand—namely, Old Kvele's anti-Russian outbursts.

They likewise failed to take legal action on another occasion when Lyuba might really have killed the younger Kvele. But that was Skaidra's own fault. The thing was that she sometimes listened at Lyuba's keyhole. Precisely why she did it is still a bit of mystery to me. Nothing anti-Soviet could possibly have been said in that family—and anyhow I doubt whether Skaidra would have gone as far as to inform on them. My guess is that she listened in order to try and find out what moves her chief enemy was planning. She had nothing to do, and in her empty life any triviality could grow out of all proportion and lead to paranoia. "I hear every word you're saying in there," she would sometimes remark in passing to Lyuba—and on one occasion she even spelled it out: "We know very well in what connection you mentioned our names yesterday." At first Lyuba paid no attention to these insinuations, putting them down to Skaidra's muddled mind. But once, coming out into the corridor, she saw her jump back and run to her own room. "It looks as if the bitch really is listening at the keyhole!" she said with surprise. "Never mind, I'll teach her."

A few days later, Lyuba managed to catch her enemy in the act—she must have heard Skaidra, or perhaps saw her standing there through the keyhole. She suddenly flung open the door. The door-handle was quite large, and Skaidra was really very lucky not to get her skull cracked. As for Lyuba, nobody could blame her: hadn't she got the right to come out of her own room whenever she felt like it? How was she to know someone might be skulking there?

Apart from matters of life and death, the struggle between the warring factions was also conducted in a multitude of minor ways. Thus, Lyuba once refused to pay her share of the electricity bill after the Kveles had bought two new bulbs to replace the burnt-out ones in the communal corridors. These new bulbs were a hundred watts, whereas the old ones had been only sixty watts. I was delighted at this brightening up of the dark gloomy corridors along which all of us were obliged to run backward and forward over and over again every day. And surely the difference in the electricity bill, after it had been divided between five families, would have been negligible. But for Lyuba the thing was a matter of principle. "They'll bedizen themselves with light bulbs, and I shall have to pay!" she fulminated. "Isn't it enough that the younger hag sits at home all day, when everybody else is out working, and burns up electricity in the loo! And the older hag keeps forgetting to turn it off after her! And we all have to pay for those madams!"

I believe that if it had been put to the vote, the majority of the tenants would have been in favor of the hundred-watt bulbs. But as Lyuba refused to pay for the extra power, to work out her share of the bill according to the old system would have been well-nigh impossible. So the flat relapsed into its former state of dimness.

The Kveles tried to annoy all of us in matters pertaining to the bathroom. This needs explaining in some detail.

One of the happiest events of my teenage years was the inauguration of a new water tower in Riga. This now meant that the water was on tap about as many hours per day as it was off. (On average, that is: it did not at all mean that it would be on, say, for two hours at a time, and then off for two hours. Such a timetable we could only dream of. In practice, the water behaved with total unpredictability, appearing whenever it felt like it and treacherously vanishing at crucial moments.) For me personally the improvement in the water supply meant that I was much less often obliged to carry buckets of water up the back stairs from a lower floor. Everybody in our flat still found it advisable to lay in stocks of water (drawing it when the pressure was highest), but now there was less need for this, and it was only in very rare emergencies that one had to make calls on neighbors on the lower floors. (We were lucky, because our floor was the highest, and so the building of the new water tower affected us for the better.) Another reason I welcomed this advance in Soviet technology was that the atmosphere in our flat became rather less tense; my mother almost completely stopped shouting out, "The water's running! Quickly—fetch a bucket!" and then scolding me for being too slow. But in the matter of taking a bath these bonuses altered nothing. It was still impossible to have one at normal times, because the water could not be relied on. It might be off, or it might stop just when you most needed it.

I am talking, of course, about cold water—there was no running hot water in the flat at all. If you wanted to have a bath, the water had to be heated up beforehand on the stove in a number of saucepans, kettles, and cans. And if after all this trouble there turned out not to be enough cold water to add to it for a decent bath with a rinse afterward, then the whole operation would have been a waste of time. So it made more sense to have a bath as late at night as possible, when the water would be available.

Skaidra must have expended an enormous amount of time and energy on spying out the enemy camp's intentions in this matter. But it must have been worth her while—and indeed, on one or two occasions she succeeded in frustrating us. She did this by occupying the bathroom—having made a dash there from the kitchen with a kettleful of hot water— just before we were about to use it. This kettleful would have only sufficed to wash her hair, for which purpose she would hardly have had to wait till two in the morning. What's more, she remained in the bathroom for over an hour with this single kettleful—obviously just to keep us waiting as long as she could.

When my mother told Lyuba about this, the latter was triumphant. Skaidra would never have had the nerve to play such a trick on her, and she had repeatedly reproached my mother for taking too soft a line with the Kveles. But Lyuba was elated not only at being in a position to say "I told you so!" She saw the incident as clear confirmation of her views on Skaidra's fitness for work. Everybody in the flat knew that Skaidra had a heart condition, but opinion was divided between those who thought that she was too ill to work and those who put it down to sheer laziness. "So when it comes to helping out her elderly mother by sitting half a day in the kiosk she's too ill—but as for being on her feet all night in order to play a dirty trick on people—all of a sudden she's spry enough!"

Human nature being what it is, one should not so much wonder at the fact that such overcrowded conditions brought out the worst in people as appreciate that with all this they still retained some measure of common decency. Thus, it now seems to me that Lyuba felt a degree of compassion for the older Kvele. How to explain otherwise her condemnation of Skaidra's failure to contribute more than just a couple of hours a week to help her mother out in the kiosk? My own mother, at the height of all this intolerable squabbling, would sometimes say that the Kveles were more to be pitied than blamed. "The things they get up to are both despicable and silly," she remarked, "but what can one say? They're sick, the two of them, the old woman can hardly drag herself along. To have lived for years where they were before, in that damp cellar, would be enough to drive anyone mad."

The Kveles themselves, after we became reconciled with them, showed many likeable traits. The old woman would treat me to sweets from her kiosk every now and again, while Skaidra went out of her way to be particularly polite and helpful when a phone call was for us. We, for our part, often asked if we could get anything for them when going out shopping.

My mother was basically on good terms with all the tenants, and both Lyuba and her predecessor Lyolya, after her family had moved out, would sometimes come to visit her. Neither of them, on these occasions, showed any desire to see any of the others.

The Petrovs—husband and wife—moved in to take the place of the Orlovs. It was difficult to judge their ages: the wife always seemed worn out by work and her husband's excessive drinking, and as for him, I hardly ever saw him standing upright and so didn't really get a good look at his face. He couldn't have been more than about fifty, but everybody called him "Old Petrov." He worked in Riga's famous radio and gramophone factory VEF—the same one where Alik Orlov had worked and where I was to spend one of the ghastliest periods of my life (a term of industrial or agricultural labor was obligatory in Soviet schools). Old Petrov drank all the time, but especially at the end of the week. Then one could hear his wife's shrieks coming from their room. Occasionally I distinguished something about the miserable life she led and threats to do away with herself. She would emerge in tears, trying to sneak along the corridors as quickly as possible to avoid being observed. On paydays and for a couple of days afterward, Old Petrov moved exclusively on all fours, and instead of uttering articulate speech he mooed or giggled. His wife kept running after him in the corridors to retrieve him. Once she managed to catch him in the nick of time as he was muttering "Sonny" and offering me vodka.

"Haven't you got enough pals to drink with? Leave the boy out of it!" she scolded, dragging him back by the scruff of the neck (they had a long way to go, because while she had been complaining to my mother about her lot, he had succeeded in crawling almost as far as the kitchen). "He'll drink with you, to be sure—that'll be the day! He'd rather read a good book," she added, obviously in an attempt to please me and thus make up for what she saw as her husband's assault on my refined sensibility. Little did she know that I had already started my training as a drinker—part of the initiation of almost every Soviet youth—and that "a good book" was now much less of an attraction than going to a bar with my friends. Only a month or so later I came home totally drunk for the first time and collapsed in the doorway of our room.

"Go to Old Petrov—that is, if you can get that far—and kiss him on both cheeks," said my mother, shaking her head. "You're two of a kind now."

Chapter 8: Religion

I did many politically risky things and Mother was right to say that if she had not applied pressure on me to leave the country with her, with my blabbering mouth I'd most likely have ended up in a labor camp in Siberia. Thank God she never found out that I'd complained about her religious pressure on me to my teacher. The Soviet Union being a militantly atheist country, such a complaint could have had unpleasant consequences for her. I might even have been forcibly taken away from her and passed on to my father and his second wife. (In my defense, I can only say that I complained to the same teacher that Mother had hoped would bring her husband back, that is, this was a teacher I knew to be decent and sympathetic. Even so, it was stupid and dangerous.) The young woman was very understanding; she nodded and said: "It's her undereducated generation with its superstitions; make allowances for your mother and don't pay attention to her religious poppycock."

As I approached thirteen, Mother became determined that my Bar Mitzva should be celebrated in the Riga synagogue. I had been against this, and so had Father, but, typically, our objections had been overruled, even though it was he who had to pay for my teacher.

Religious instruction was only semi-legal, if not forbidden outright, and was still sometimes persecuted. The teacher was a funny little middle-aged fellow, with a Lenin-style cloth cap covering half of his face. He always scuttled very quickly along the corridor and into our room, so as not to draw the attention of the neighbors. I remember him warmly, mainly because of the tactful way he tried to calm things down between me and my mother on those occasions when, in protest at one of her never-ending attempts to push me too far and boss me around, I'd refuse to study with him.

Within a few weeks I could read Hebrew, albeit very haltingly, which didn't stop me from trying to assail in the original the first sentences of *The Book of Ecclesiastes,* whose beautiful translation into Old Russian I already knew and admired.

For the ceremony I was meant to appear in the synagogue and recite the customary Biblical sentences in the traditional singsong way. My teacher sang a few words and asked me to repeat. After I had done so, he said that one could also declaim—the singing wasn't really obligatory. He also gave me a little speech in Russian to address the congregation with—a standard one, obviously, handed out to all boys in my position. I was nervous rehearsing the speech, short though it was: it was meant to be delivered by memory, and I was afraid of missing something out. I had to thank both God and my parents and also promise everybody to duly fulfill my obligations before God, parents, and humanity at large.

My recitation was a great success. The elders of the congregation—looking old and funny to me—all shook my hand, saying things like, "Well done, you're a real innovator, congratulations on your declaimed delivery, that's the way the young want to do it now, what a deeply felt recitation, a sign of the times," and so on. If only they knew that all that "super-modernism" was because I couldn't sing!

Father, who'd been against the whole thing, and had still paid for it, came to see the ceremony, very surreptitiously, from behind the glass of the hall door. That was a remarkable act of bravery, for a communist journalist. In an attempt to avoid recognition he was wearing dark glasses. Even on a slow day, any place of religious worship in the country had spies; they'd have definitely been out in force for a ceremony involving Soviet youth. In fact, one or two of those kindly and funny-looking elders could themselves have been part-time KGB informers. A well-tried and time-hallowed combination of threats and inducements would have recruited most elderly people, who would not have quickly forgotten the recent horrors of Stalinism. My father was lucky to get away with nobody on his tail. It wouldn't have required a great analytical mind to put two and two together—the boy whose father was absent from the ceremony and the strange man wearing dark glasses in the dark hall, peering through the glass. Actually, he had already got off the hook once by the skin of his teeth over my circumcision. That apparently had been done with his full consent, but after somebody informed on him, Mother had stepped forward to take all the blame. She said she had done everything on her own, in secret from her husband, knowing he'd be against any religious rite. She must have played her role so well that instead of losing his job as a journalist and being expelled from the Party, Father got away with only a reprimand—part of which severely upbraided him for letting his wife take over and run the family affairs. Long after Mother's visit to the editorial offices of the paper where he worked as a reporter his colleagues would still, every now and then, recall her appearance and sadly shake their heads: "Poor Dubnov—with that sort of wife …" (Informing on each other being *de rigueur* in the country, another colleague of his told him about everyone's sympathy for him.) I can't help wondering now whether their pity was just a result of Mother's theatrical performance or her real personality, which had come through even in its exaggerated version.

Anyway, to come back to my confirmation rite, as the formal part was over and people crowded around to shake my hand, I stole a few glances toward the door leading to the hall. The silhouette of the man with dark glasses was no longer there.

Then all of us—Mother, my sisters Milla and Lena, and the latter's boyfriend Slava—invited the small congregation to have a few drinks and cakes with us, to celebrate the event—and presently it was over. I was glad to be out in the autumnal sun nipping fresh air and to walk through one of those beautiful parks in Riga where the leaves were still turning, even though it was November.

"What God where you talking about?" Slava asked me.

"How do you mean?" I asked.

"Remember, you talked about your responsibility to parents, humanity, and God? I'd like to know, what did you mean by God?"

I was only thirteen and became embarrassed by this intellectual probing of an older man and an atheist. "Stop it, leave the boy alone!" Lena came to my rescue.

Religion felt to me like somebody else's domain. The synagogue that represented it was in every sense—linguistic, cultural, and aesthetic—an alien world. (As for ethics, I knew and respected only general morality; religion seemed only vaguely related to it.) Going off the straight, orderly, main thoroughfares of the city to delve into a confusingly, arbitrarily woven tapestry of miniscule alleys of the old town the synagogue was located in, where I'd often forget which way to turn, was a depressing experience. Unfortunately, following my father's departure, Mother began to appeal more and more to my sense of filial responsibility:

"You're not going to let your mother, abandoned by her husband, appear alone in the synagogue for the High Holidays, are you?"

"What difference does it make?" I'd try to wriggle out. "The seating's separate for men and women anyway, isn't it?"

"Mother and son must come together and leave together," she insisted. "And as for the separate seating, your presence or absence will be noticed in any case, and then people will gossip, and it's one thing if they say I was with my son and another if they start pitying me as having been abandoned by both my husband and my son!"

So I had to join her, fortunately only a few times a year.

On one of those occasions a noteworthy event took place. There was a foreign tourist in the synagogue, a young American girl. In the mid-1960s this was a most rare thing, and immediately the parishioners began to suspect that she was a KGB informer. Although I must have been only fifteen or sixteen, I happened to be the only one around who spoke some kind of English, and so I was delegated to investigate. After the solemn Rosh Hashana or Yom Kippur prayers—I can't remember which—I went up to her and asked where she was from and if she spoke Hebrew. The girl—in her early twenties or so—was from Brooklyn, New York, and she said that although she prayed in English and not in Hebrew, "Guard" would know her heart.

Greatly puzzled by that, I asked her again about just who would know that intimate place of hers—only to get the same answer: "Guard." To me this made little sense, as I had never heard of guards, sentinels, sentries, and wards being the best readers of pious hearts, but as the girl kept lifting her eyes all the while, I finally realized she meant "God." So I gave her a pass, even though, I must admit, her being heavily made up and constantly looking up to heaven looked very theatrical to me. (Since then I've had more than enough opportunities to see a lot of theater in houses of prayer, with loud sighing, ostentatious eye rolling and arm lifting and so on. The one powerful image I can recommend for that sort of spectacle comes from Sergei Paradjanov's classic film *Shadows of Our Forgotten Ancestors*, in which a rich man looks proudly and at length around the church for everybody to see the gold coin he's about to drop on the charity plate.)

After Father left, Mother began to take over my life more and more in every way. Partly attempting to turn me against him and partly, I suspect, out of sheer loneliness, she would corner my close friends when they came over and complain to them about "the kind of man who'd leave his own son." I felt terribly uneasy and rather ashamed of her for those intimacies shared with adolescents in their mid-teens. Fortunately, I had very intelligent and tactful friends, from good families, well brought up and, most importantly, with dissident views. Zhenia Konyaev was an ethnic Russian. He was extremely reserved with everybody, including his parents, and opened up only with me and, to an extent, one mutual friend of ours, Vladimir Kosov.

Not even Zhenia's parents knew that what he really wanted was to enroll at Moscow Patriarchal Academy to become a priest; I was the only one in the world he shared this ambition with. I was sympathetic—I would have been so to anything that challenged the regime—but, given my own unease about religion, also quite puzzled. But still, most of all I felt moved and privileged: I was, after all, Jewish, and for him to have shared his Christian yearnings with me rather than anybody else was a sign of very special and intimate trust. It was probably just as well, though, that he had to admit that this vocation was unattainable: his parents would have never given him the go-ahead, and he wasn't strong enough to embark on his own on a career that the all-powerful state totally opposed, even if it did not formally forbid it. So he'd chosen for himself the beaten track of an engineer and planned to enroll at the local polytechnic after graduating from school.

His father, a war veteran missing an arm, would every now and then come to our flat to spy on him and get information from me. He was a very nice and polite man, obviously worried about his reticent son whose school record was rather mediocre and whose future plans were unknown to him. My mother respected and sympathized with him. She'd make him a cup of tea, and they'd exchange meaningless pleasantries, and then she'd leave and go about her business in the kitchen, while I'd sit uneasily, waiting for the silence to break and for him to ask his usual: "But—what's *he* going to do? What are his plans? Is he going to graduate from school? Will he go to university?"

I'd paint a rosy picture of a purposeful, even single-minded young man, every step of his future meticulously planned out in his mind—the opposite of my friend, his son. He'd leave, greatly relieved—and would always remember to ask me to keep his visit secret from his son. I was in a quandary: betray my friend or betray his dad? Finally I couldn't take it anymore and told Zhenia, having made him swear he'd not say anything to his father. From then on he'd coach me, every now and then, on what to tell his parent about his future plans on the next visit. (They sounded pretty positive; it was only odd that with such ambitious plans his grades had been so low—definitely not good enough for a polytechnic.) Once his dad came to us rather upset; it turned out that his son had confronted him over those visits. "What's he doing snooping around behind my back? Doesn't he realize it humiliates me?" my friend defended himself when I, in turn, demanded an explanation. Finally we agreed to consider this as a one-off *faux pas*; he promised solemnly he'd never spill the beans again, and things went on as before: he'd tell me what to say, and I'd calm his father down.

My second closest friend, Yuri Afremovich, was half-Latvian, half-Jewish. He was absolutely bilingual—Russian and Latvian—and attended a Latvian school. His sympathies were generally with the Latvians; he admired his reserved and composed Latvian mother, a chemistry teacher at university, who hardly said a word, and disliked his journalist father because of his volubility, lack of dignity and self-respect, and what he called "a typically Jewish zany humor and ridiculous clowning." It therefore surprised me and made me respect his principles and his audacity when at the age of sixteen he chose to register as a Jew rather than Latvian. That was the age when Soviet youngsters received their passports, and the nationality entered in them could not be changed afterward. So that was a fateful lifelong choice. Life would have been easier for him if he'd registered himself as Latvian, but he said he didn't want it to look like he was trying to run away from his Jewish half. Perhaps, considering he looked quite Jewish, it was his pride, more than anything else, that made him choose thus: had he not, many people would have despised him as yet another cowardly Jew trying to pass himself off as something else. Still, I met many young men and women who had preferred that option, especially at Moscow University, where, in our psychology department, half the student body looked unmistakably Semitic (most even confessed to being half—or more—Jewish), yet their passports said they were Russian or Ukrainian. In their defense—and, again, to my friend's honor—it should be said that Soviet institutes of higher education still had the so-called Jew quota, according to which the number of Jews shouldn't exceed a certain low percentage. This policy had been inherited from the Tsarist regime, but had become covert rather than open.

Yura (familiar version for Yuri) was unemotional, reasoned, and composed, obviously taking after his mother. My mother preferred him, partly because he was half-Jewish, but mostly because he was so calm and sensible—not to mention a patient listener. It angered me that she habitually hijacked my friends to pour her heart out to them, complaining about me and about my father who'd so heartlessly dumped his little lamb and was ultimately responsible for the latter's transformation into a stubborn and rebellious donkey. My friends defended me, but Yuri did it more cleverly, acknowledging her grievances to an extent, only to subvert the main accusations, so in the end she must have felt at least partly justified. Zhenia had neither the patience nor the strategy for that kind of interaction.

Chapter 9: "Dinky Little Cunt" and the Young Communist League Secretary

On the eve of my matriculation exams, two events took place. One showed Mother and her family at their best, the side I most cherished; the other, while not bringing misfortune, showed me as naïve and reckless, prone to falling over myself, which had led to my first brush with the KGB.

A pair of newlyweds in their mid-twenties, on their honeymoon, came to spend a week with us, all the way from Siberia. The girl was a very distant relative of Father's. They didn't know he wasn't living with us anymore. "Why don't you give them his phone number?" I asked. "Let *him* play host to his own relations." "No," Mother said. "They came to me and it's my responsibility to be hospitable."

They stayed for a week, and Mother fed them. I thought it was crazy. We had no money: Father didn't give her any of the maintenance required by law, and she was too proud to ask. She was a typical—and in many ways exemplary—homemaker (I hate the word "housewife"), cooking and laundering and washing up for the whole family, in difficult conditions, with no running hot water; often with no running water at all. Having dedicated her whole life to her family, she had no profession. And suddenly she was left with no income and had to earn a living, working initially as a saleswoman in a kiosk and then as a bookkeeper at a factory that made washing machines. But she was adamant about not turning out guests who came to her house. She'd inherited this attitude from her parents and grandparents, who—both the educated branch and the simple folks—had been warm-hearted and kind people. Curiously, my father's ancestors—both the learned, including the historian Simon Dubnov, and the illiterate—likewise shared this trait of hospitality and generosity. I'd like to talk more about those grandparents and great-grandparents of mine at some later stage. But it's to them that I owe my own preoccupation with making sure every visitor crossing my threshold does not leave thirsty or hungry.

So we put at their disposal my little room next to the kitchen while I moved into the bigger room where Mother slept. It was very crowded there.

One day I had to pick something up in my room, in the middle of the day. The guests were supposed to be out. Still, I knocked, just in case, and entered. The young husband was taking pictures of his newlywed wife. The latter was half lying on my bed, her skirt pulled up. She had no underwear on. Upon my entrance she got a bit flustered and pulled her skirt down, but the man didn't show any sign of embarrassment. In fact, in a couple of days he proudly showed me the negatives of the film, pointing at his wife's bare breasts and crotch. When, some three decades later, I saw that distant relative of ours again—now a middle-aged woman, long divorced, with a grownup son, and a neighbor of my sister's—I couldn't help feeling slightly amused at the secret glimpse I'd had of her intimate places. Little did she know!

The young man seemed generally sexed-up. When Mother persuaded me to take him round Riga's parks (I didn't particularly want to), he started photographing local girls sitting on benches showing their stockingless legs (it was summer). One had particularly long and shapely legs, and she showed them rather generously. She didn't bat an eyelid when he positioned himself right in front of her and used up half a film on her and her legs.

After that he asked me, giving me a conspiratorial nudge, "Would you have liked to shag her?"

"Her nose is too long," I answered sheepishly.

"It's not her nose you'll fuck, is it? It's her dinky little cunt!" he said, singing out the last three words with the utmost tenderness.

I tried to reconcile this new knowledge—the negatives and the dinky little thing as opposed to the nose—with what I'd read in the *Complete Medical Encyclopedia*, but the only results were confusion and an embarrassing arousal.

My introduction to KGB types was, in retrospect, quite comic.

Always having been attracted to water, I often went to the embankment for a walk, with friends or alone. The Daugava was wide here, nearing its estuary, and ships dropped anchor nearby. I befriended a young Polish seaman and showed him around. When seeing him off as his ship was about to sail back, I was apprehended by a couple of vigilantes, only a few years older than myself and waging war against foreign currency transactions (the best apprenticeship for a KGB career). They must have thought I was active on the black market, buying dollars off foreigners and selling them on the side. One look at my infantile face and behavior—that of a well-brought-up adolescent from a good family—would have dissuaded anybody with a bit more intelligence from pursuing the matter, but these curs were obviously too bent on furthering their secret police careers to be more careful about who they picked on.

In a couple of days I got a letter summoning me to the Young Communist League Headquarters in the city for an interview with the League's secretary. At school I was told a request had come for my character profile, which they had immediately complied with, giving me a most flattering write-up. My sister Milla talked to her friend (let's call him Alexander), who was older than her and had much more life experience. A distant relative of his—second or third cousin—had some tentative connection with the KGB. (Alexander himself was an outspoken critic of the regime—within a close circle of likeminded friends, of course, like our family). It was Alexander who first suggested the black-market explanation—that the lowest-ranking secret police trainees had mistaken me for an illegal foreign currency dealer. He was certain that after receiving my school report and talking to me, the higher-ranking authorities in the organization would realize their error and let me go. He was equally sure that it would not be a young communist secretary interviewing me—that was just a ruse—but a KGB official. He wanted to coach me before that encounter.

In the early 1980s I described the whole event, more or less autobiographically, in a short story titled "The Polish Ship," which first appeared on BBC Radio 3 and then was published in *Literary Olympians: Crosscurrents' Anthology* (Westlake Village, California, 1987). Originally written in Russian, it was translated into English by my close friend Chris Newman and myself. Here's the passage where the young hero is being prepared for the KGB interview by Alexander the family friend, followed by the real encounter:

"A secretary, is it? Hm … hmm … We have seen such secretaries," Alexander was chuckling to himself. "My young demented friend, could you perchance inform us as to the true identity of this so-called secretary?" He was relishing every moment of his role playing.

"It is … it is …" Vladimir desperately searched for an answer, "not a secretary. It is somebody else."

"Well done," the older man said patronizingly. "That was clear from my question, I should have thought."

"Will it be, perhaps, some security man?"

"Much better. We're getting there. I'd place my money on some reasonably high-ranking KGB official. Well, now it's about time to act out the scene. Leave the room and come in when I call you."

Vladimir hurried excitedly into the corridor, closing the door behind him. Half a minute later a strange, dry voice, bearing only a vague resemblance to that of Alexander's, called him from within the room.

"You can come in now!"

Alexander was sitting behind a table examining a thick file of documents. "Sit down," he said, motioning the boy to a chair close to the table. "You know, I am sure, why we asked you to come. We have here a testimony from the two young members of the Social Order Brigade who apprehended you and a report from your school. I have also now read your statement; you seem to be an intelligent young man. We'll have a little discussion in a minute. But first let me tell you who I really am. I am not the Secretary of the Young Communist League."

At this point, Alexander broke off and looked at the boy questioningly. Vladimir didn't know what to say; there was an awkward silence, which was finally broken by Alexander's loud groans.

"Have you fallen asleep or something?" he asked Vladimir in a sarcastic tone.

"Why—what was I supposed to do?"

"'What was I supposed to do?' Just listen to him! O *sancta simplicitas*! You were supposed to express surprise! Are you capable of doing that or is it too much to ask?"

"But why should I be surprised? Wait … wait … I see … I'm not meant to know who he really is—I'm meant to think he's the secretary. And I have to play along with him."

Alexander's face relaxed into a satisfied smile. "Good. These people don't like it when their masks are removed. If they choose to reveal their identity, they must do it themselves. But let us go on …"

"Where were you on the night of March the twelfth when the Swedish ship docked here? Didn't you go out with your friend Sergei?"

"The Swedish ship … er … Yes, I remember! We did go out that night—we went to the quay. As I explained in my letter, my friend and I have this rather silly custom of greeting ships. Both our fathers were sailors, you know—must be in the blood."

"All this sounds fine, but why, why, I wonder, this interest in things foreign? Egyptian queens, Swedish ships?"

"It's not just Swedish—there was also that Polish ship, and last year one from East Germany. They are not really foreign, they are like ours, they are brotherly countries. And anyway, all those ships are good for us, they bring us a lot of trade. As Pushkin said: 'All the flags will be our guests.' Trade is also good for world peace—you know, our country is the most peace-loving in the world."

The eyes of the man behind the table became distant. "Peaceful coexistence with capitalist countries is only temporary," he said. "Our ultimate aim is to destroy them. Didn't you learn this at school?"

"We did, we did!" Vladimir quickly retorted. "But Lenin also says that the capitalists will themselves sell us the rope that we'll hang them with—so we must trade with them."

"This is true ... You seem to be a good Soviet boy ... But I still cannot understand why you shouted all those things you did on the quayside. That was very bad—to abuse those fine young men bravely serving their motherland and to shame your country before our Polish guests. Why did you do this?"

"I don't know." Vladimir seemed to be at a loss as to how to reply. "I really don't know. I was so angry—the way they dragged me off like that—like a criminal when I didn't do anything wrong. I was only seeing off my Polish friend—and he invited me to come to Warsaw and see all the new factories and housing estates there. And they searched me and confiscated his farewell present. I just lost my head, I was so angry. And they wouldn't believe a single word I said. I really didn't know what I was doing. I get like this sometimes—you can ask my parents."

His questioner looked briefly at the open file before him and nodded, almost imperceptibly.

"Yes, yes ... I see ... It's clear to me now that you are not what we thought you might be. We thought you might be ... but it's no longer important ... Nor am I, for that matter, what you thought I was. You thought I was the Secretary of the Young Communist League. But this is who I am."

He slowly drew from his breast pocket a small identity card with the letters "KGB" on it and brought it close to Vladimir's eyes, while not removing his burrowing stare from the boy's face.

Vladimir gasped in astonishment. "I thought ... I thought you were ..." he began to stutter. The hard steely eyes finally relented.

As Chris and I were translating the story, he commented: "It would be quite effective if, after the break, when the real thing started, this Alexander turned out to be the interviewing KGB man himself."

"Can't do that," I said. "That would go against the truth."

Recently I telephoned Chris, who is now living in Berlin, reminded him of the story and his comment, and told him about the news I'd just had from my sister. We both had a good laugh.

"Why," my sister had said the day before that phone call, "didn't you know? Our mutual acquaintance found out, after the Soviet Union had fallen apart and many archives had opened up, that Alexander had been in the KGB's employment."

CHAPTER 10: MADONNAS

In April 1917 everybody saw a Red Cavalry horseman riding across the moon: a portent of the October Revolution to come. One evening some townsfolk were walking through the forest near Gomel when all at once a huge wild man, his face distorted in a mad grimace, ran toward them. Taken aback—perhaps even frightened—they shouted to him to stop, but he paid no attention to them, as if they weren't even there, and went on running past them and into the thicket. Sure enough, hard on his heels came the Revolution with all its crazy and savage bloodshed.

Such were the stories my mother told me. She was bright and gifted, but uneducated, having finished only four years of primary school. Her superstitions had also touched me directly—and most painfully.

After my brother's death, Mother guarded me vigilantly. She wouldn't let me go on school outings, and I felt an outcast at school. Everyone else went: I was the only one left out. Mother's reasoning was particularly cruel. After I begged and begged and she still refused, on the very eve of one particular outing, she was gracious enough to explain to me her thinking on the subject.

"Had you simply asked, calmly and quietly, with no passion, 'Mom, can I go?' I might have agreed. But as you were all agog, so unhealthily bent on this outing, alarm bells began to ring in my head."

Then, to illustrate her point, she told me a story.

It had happened in a little town or village in White Russia before the Revolution. Late one evening a young unmarried man living with his family became restless. He was dying to go out for a walk. His parents noticed that there was something overblown, worryingly exaggerated about that craving of his. It's late, said the young man's parents, why don't you go for a walk tomorrow morning? No, he said, I've got to do it tonight—and he rushed to the door. Fortunately, it was locked. Seriously alarmed now, suspecting perhaps some unclean otherworldly influence, they locked the windows too. The young man's behavior became quite frightening: he beat his fists against the door, the windows, the walls, wailing all the while. At last he broke down and fell to the floor, half-conscious. Next morning, he was his own normal self. Some townsfolk passing by told them about a young and sad woman's voice they'd heard last night coming from the lake on the outskirts of the town. The voice was complaining: "My lover hasn't come!"

I felt very embittered by the whole thing and tried to make her see the real situation: that my "craving" for the outing had been but a result of her refusal to let me go, that initially I'd asked her in perfectly normal, quiet tones, but she wouldn't acknowledge this and went on claiming that I'd shown a dangerous desire from the word go.

This episode, my helpless writhing in a doomed attempt to break through to her, left a scar on my psyche, one of a whole number I've been carrying along, her legacy.

Finally, feeling totally humiliated *vis-à-vis* the rest of my class, I devised a ruse. On the morning of an outing I got up at five, quietly, so as not to wake her, collected things for the road, made myself a coffee and a couple of sandwiches and soundlessly shut the front door behind me. Surprisingly, when I came back, not only did she not scold me but actually showed off to our neighbors in the kitchen: "Look at my son's inventiveness: I wouldn't let him, but that didn't stop him! Imagine: bent on having his own way, he got up before dawn and outwitted me!"

Her iron grip over my first romances was even worse. I could survive without school outings, but, with my earth-shattering physiological awakening, which had immediately sublimated itself into romantic dreams and poetry, I desperately needed a girl to love and be loved by. Mother cold-shouldered the few girls from my class I'd dared to invite over, so they never came again. She was rude on the phone to those who called me: they complained afterwards. She wanted to pick the girl for me and took me with her on a visit to one of her acquaintances, a widower with a daughter my own age. The girl was very pale and delicate and quite plain, but I liked her father, who had an operatic voice and, at my request, sang many arias, to her piano accompaniment. Mother, while indifferent to the music, went out of her way to be nice to both of them (it has occurred to me since that she may have had her eyes not only on the daughter for me but also the father for herself) and kept calling the girl "sweetie," which, considering they'd just met, I found most embarrassing.

And so my first experience with girls, both romantic and sexual (the two would remain for me inseparable) had to wait till I broke away from Mother for Moscow University.

The dichotomy present throughout Russian literature of the virgin and the whore as a female stereotype took root in me, with a lot of prompting from my mother as to the latter part of this dual image. It was quite ironic that my first sexual experience should have been with a virgin nun.

But again I digress.

"I'd be ashamed of myself if I were you: there's nothing dirtier than women," Mother would say to me, and complain to family friends about what she saw as my excessive interest in the opposite sex. Once she particularly embarrassed me before Joseph Bein, my sister Milla's literary friend, a poet who'd occasionally recite his romantic and musical verses in our room and whom I idolized.

"It's a real shame," she said to him. "The boy trembles all over when he speaks about women."

"Not true," I denied hotly. "Not true at all, that's absolutely libelous!"

"So the accusation's false and you don't tremble?" he gave me a quizzical look.

"No I don't!" I exclaimed. "Not at all!"

"Too bad," he said. "You should tremble. Your blood's young, it should be hot, boiling over at the sight or even mention of a girl."

The more Mother denigrated women, the more I romanticized about and idealized them.

And so it came to pass that all my innocent youthful infatuations and tentative romances, from the age of seventeen on, until I left the country at twenty-one, were inextricably linked with Russian Romantic and Symbolist poetry and the snow, which featured prominently both therein and in the real world all around me. My favorite poet was now Alexander Blok and, just as with Mayakovsky, the preceding idol, I easily learned by heart dozens upon dozens of his poems. (Remembering verses has never caused me any difficulty: if I liked them, repeating them in my mind a couple of times would somehow fix them there permanently—and the same thing happened later with English-language poets like W. B. Yeats and T. S. Eliot.) To complete the picture, I'd also mention a painting that almost hypnotized me in my early youth: Ivan Kramskoy's *Stranger* (or *Unknown*) painted in 1883. Set against a wintry background, it presents a beautiful, sensuous and mysterious young woman in an open carriage on the Anichkov Bridge in St. Petersburg. She's boldly and haughtily observing the spectator. A mixture of her lovely cold enigma and the indifferent, as though estranged, snowy haze enveloping her cast its spell on me.

And my few early dates, at which my shyness masqueraded under the guise of giving lessons, took place late in the evening on the frozen lake in a nearby park where I taught a girl to skate.

(Frozen moonlight pierces the windows of every house and all the windows of all landings of all blocks of flats and remote bittersweet snow breaks forth, again and again, in dream after dream. Whipped up by the wind, it lights my lamps.

Now it continues drifting down, flakes of sky are descending, uncountable and innumerable shreds of cotton wool are endlessly falling at leisure, the moon is transparent on the ice; presently the snowfall is no more, only the crackling in the trees and the screeching of the skates and the sparkling of the ice, and I'm holding her close and stopping her from falling, which she seems bent on doing every now and then; I'm a good skater.)

The skating rink girl was three or four years older than me. She never received my mother's approval because she refused to humor her and show due deference. She was resolute, independent, and feminist—the last thing my mother wanted. Perhaps her being a committed Zionist paradoxically played against her too. It was at that time that Mother began to conceive her revenge against Father: to take all his children away from him, out of Russia to Israel, leaving him alone with his "old hag," as she invariably referred to his second wife. If I got married, it would be more difficult to get an exit visa for two separate family groups than just for an aggrieved mother and her good-for-nothing young son—as she'd try to present me.

But I still regret, however absurd it may sound, not having had any sort of romance with any girls from my own school. They liked me, and I liked two or three very much indeed—and I've painfully learned through the years that liking a woman can be weightier and more to the point than loving her—but I was much too shy to build any friendship, let alone a relationship, with any of them. Those being the years before the so-called sexual revolution, and ours being one of the very best and most proper schools in town—with obligatory ballroom dances, unheard of in any other Russian school—we were all of us innocent.

(The Zionist girl I taught to skate was different: she was part of a group of friends, boys and girls, all in their early to mid-twenties; she was strong-willed and took the initiative. But before anything serious could develop between us I went to Moscow to study, and we hardly saw each other again.)

I've kept pleasant memories of my last two years at school, partly, I guess, because of the usual sentimental regret for "the best years of your life," but partly because of that period's emphasis on music. In addition to the ballroom dances, we had regular visits by singers from the Riga Opera House, who performed songs and arias from a wide Russian and European classical repertoire, after giving us a brief talk putting them in historical and musical context. (One may, if one likes, even see ours as an appropriately humble Soviet analogue of Mandelstam and Nabokov's famous Tenishev school of the early 1900s). The graduation year was also a source of pride for me as I finally learned to fight and stand up for myself, and the school bullies left me alone.

My English was also a boon. Once the sturdiest guy in class came up to me and asked timidly, using my school nickname: "Dubik, can I ask you something?" Puzzled and greatly flattered (I was an A student and he a C minus), I said: "Of course! Go ahead!"

"Know that American 'Sixteen Tons' song?"

"Heard it," I said, "sort of."

"Is it true that what they're singing is:

'Fly your bomber planes, boys, east,

Kill every man, woman, child and beast!'?

Could you check it for me?"

"All right," I said, "I'll try to listen to it next time it's on the radio."

When I managed to catch Tennessee Ernie Ford's classic again, it was clear to me that it wasn't about US pilots dropping bombs on Russia. Of course I could hardly understand all the lyrics—and not only because of my insufficient English, but because of the indistinct way the singer pronounces them—but I still understood enough to get the gist. I don't know where my fellow student got his Russian translation from (most probably from the readily available stock of KGB-spread propagandist rumors), but he must have forgotten all about his question and never came back to me with it. I was glad he didn't, as I would have had to choose between lying and deeply disappointing him. The majority of the country's population—especially the less educated—had been brainwashed into being absolutely certain the United States couldn't wait to attack and destroy the Soviet Union. Still, I think it's quite funny to have turned this song into a militaristic summons. Here's its opening:

> Some people say a man is made out of mud;
> A poor man's made out of muscle and blood—
> Muscle and blood and skin and bone,
> A mind that's weak and a back that's strong.
>
> Chorus.
> You load sixteen tons, and what do you get—
> Another day older and deeper in debt.
> Saint Peter, don't you call me, 'cause I can't go:
> I owe my soul to the company store.

The KGB's spin notwithstanding, there were fresh and daring winds blowing in our school, coming from the young pedagogues. (With my "optimism bias"—something many people have, but I had far in excess—I thought things would go on improving; in fact, freedoms were gradually curtailed in the country after my exit, throughout the 1970s and 1980s.) Daniil Ivanovich, our new literature teacher in the upper sixth (twelfth grade), loved to mock many canonical pieces in the ossified Soviet social demand genre. He was brilliant and exciting but young and couldn't yet wear the mantle of the best literature teacher in town. This mantle—unofficial but still real (you had only to talk to students from other schools)—was worn by our math and physics teachers, Artyom Vasilyevich and Georgiy Alexandrovich respectively. My memories of both are warm and moving. Having made the former angry by attempting to cheat, after which he called me only by my second instead of my first name, I was greatly relieved when after our final school assembly he came up to me and addressed me by my first name once again. Also, what he had to say was friendly and considerate. "As you know, I've given you an overall A in math in your matriculation, which I bet you didn't expect. But I did it only after looking into your post-school plans. Had you applied to any math department at university—like mechanics and math, for example—I'd have given you a B plus or A minus at most, but when I saw it was psychology you were going on to, I thought it was safe to give you an A."

Georgiy Alexandrovich earned my respect and gratitude on two occasions. First, he gave me the only A he'd ever given in any class in our school (he himself admitted as much) for my oral contribution in a lesson. The reason was that I spoke, extemporaneously, on Albert Einstein's theory of relativity, which was not part of our school curriculum. Apparently, in spite of my superficial knowledge of the subject obtained from popular books on modern physics, I managed to impress him. Furthermore, he was the only one among the teachers to give a smile—and quite a long and appreciative one too—at my "Farewell, School!" speech in the Great Hall, which closed our last assembly. I'm still unsure just why he smiled at the words "all things in life come to an end—and so have our school years," but I'm glad he found something in them I wasn't aware of and definitely had not intended. I took that smile, which I still have very clearly in my mind's eye, as a compliment.

By this time I was already writing poetry quite seriously, reading scholarly works on Mayakovsky and the Russian Futurist Movement and corresponding with David Burliuk and Korney Chukovsky, as well as two or three other, totally evanescent reputations, like Alexander Lipovsky, a stolid Soviet playwright specializing in Mayakovsky's life. I wrote a lengthy letter to the head of All-Soviet Radio in Moscow, criticizing Lipovsky's play, which I'd heard broadcast, and to my great surprise received a reply from the author himself. His letter is friendly, although peeved ("I was pleased to receive, among hundreds of enthusiastic letters, your critical one"), and, of course, most Soviet throughout, both in style and content. He defends his work against my unfavorable judgment and signs: "With Young Communist League Greetings!"

Having been inspired with confidence by the *Pioneers' Gazette*, which had commented positively on my poem about Mayakovsky and suggested I submit it to an "adult" publication, I was overjoyed when an older friend who'd been in correspondence with the *Yunost* (Youth) literary magazine in Moscow, offered his good services. This friend—whom I'll call Boris—had written to the editors complaining about his father, who'd abandoned the family for another woman. The magazine published his letter in their letters to the editor section. I don't remember the details of the story, only that it was quite melodramatic and ended with a description of what Boris does when he receives letters from his father, who apparently wants to make peace with his abandoned son: "I tear them up, unopened, into little pieces, which then are thrown to the winds and slowly whirl around as they fall." Boris showed me a reply from a young woman who was one of the magazine's editors:

she'd written with enormous warmth and sympathy. At the time, I was approaching six-teen and had just finished composing the first poem I wasn't ashamed of; my sister Milla, thoroughly educated in Russian Literature, with an excellent taste in books in general and a special partiality to poetry, liked it too and said that, unlike my Mayakovsky poem, this one had "imaginative vision." Titled "The Madonnas," it was about Italian-style caryatids carrying the heavy weight of porticos in wintry northern capitals while dreaming of the sun of their native country. I showed it to Boris, who said he could offer it to that same sympathetic woman editor, with a view to publication. Imagine my happiness! And now imagine my happiness when, a month later, he said he'd visited the kindly editor, at her invitation, stayed at her home and showed her my poem, which she had immediately taken to and promised to publish in the very next issue of the magazine! To cut a long story short, I waited and waited, and he kept saying she'd definitely publish the poem and would write to me herself, until finally I lost patience and wrote to the editor. She wrote back saying that Boris had indeed sent them a poem *under his own name*, about caryatids pining away in the cold north after their old country—and was that poem mine? I didn't know the word "caryatids" and wasn't quite sure just what was meant by "old country" so I wrote back to say that no, the poem about the caryatids wasn't mine, but here's my poem about the Madonnas, which Boris had said they'd accepted for publication. To this she replied, with her customary warmth, that *this* was indeed the poem claimed by Boris as his own, and that he'd lost the magazine's trust, and that although they quite liked "The Madonnas," they weren't going to publish it.

Imagine my anguish, at both this first rejection note of my life and the first example of human perfidy I'd encountered! But I can assure you that life had aplenty of both in store for me.

My next poem, "White Night," was the first I decided to preserve and publish. One of the very first of my verses to be translated into English, it appeared in the *Southern Poetry Review* in the US and the *English* magazine in the UK in the early 1980s:

> I have every reason to fear. I know this agitation.
> At night the flowers' smell is persistent and the light hurts your eyes.
> On the lips a kiss leaves its thirsty trembling;
> To hide from yourself and to keep from the light is impossible.
>
> How to explain and to name this nervously-stammering feeling?
> Sacredly treasured within you, you carry the shame and the guilt.
> At night anxious and sensitive hands descend upon shoulders.
> I stand for hours, pressing my face to the window.
>
> The thought can not break loose from the cage to the wind,
> As feeling is not to be freed from the tightening embraces of verse.
>
> In the dazzling light white branches are swaying.
> Poems born at night bring no relief.
>
> (1967, translated with Chris Newman and Carol Rumens)

It's a truism to say that girls grow up quicker, but looking back, I see how strikingly true this was in our school. Almost all of them were so much more sensible and mature than us boys. They were quick to foresee the problems I'd have with my first name. In the penultimate year of school, when we were fifteen or sixteen, there was a craze for girls and boys exchanging letters during lessons. My first letter wasn't about love at all. Unsigned, it said: "A name is surely not given for Dad and Mom. Think about it." At the ballroom dancing lessons we had to attend once a week in the afternoon, I'd always be late returning to school from home (even though I lived a five-minute walk away), by which time all the stunners had already been invited to dance and all that remained were a couple of plain girls with no partner. It was just as well, in fact, because talking to them while dancing I discovered that looks could be deceptive: the girls were very brainy and exuded a quiet and kind understanding. One of them engaged me in a conversation about my name. She said I should give up my childhood name Zolya and keep only my formal name Yevgeny. I wish I had learned both the lesson of the deceptiveness of appearances and of my name. Failing to do so has resulted in many tribulations throughout my life, both with women and concerning identity.

The history, the peregrinations, and the perturbations alone of my multiple names could fill a separate volume. My mother named me Zalman (a form of Solomon, from the original Hebrew name Shlomo), after her father. Official registration of the newborn being my father's business, he put my name down as Yevgeny on my birth certificate. I never asked him where he'd gotten the name from—there'd never been anybody called that among our ancestors—but my guess is that he took it from literature, most probably from Pushkin's Yevgeny Onegin.

My perception being to a large degree auditory, I like this melodious and euphonic amphibrach of a name much more now than the Zalman with its repetitive spondee and opening hissing consonant, but I had only used it occasionally until I enrolled in the English department of my university in Israel at the age of twenty-two. Till then, my name had usually been Zolya, a diminutive of Zalman, and I saw it as part of my childhood and family identity fighting the impersonal bureaucratic state.

Curiously, the only other Zolya I've come across in my life was our upstairs neighbor in Tallinn, my brother's contemporary and friend. The name being most unusual, no wonder people got it wrong. The mother of one of my school pals called me Zahleh (as in zāle—"grass" in Latvian); the above-mentioned Joseph Bein, Zorya ("dawn" in Russian). Then came the jokes. Zolya sounding in Russian exactly like the French writer's surname, my friend Zhenya Konyaev would occasionally address me as Émile. Once even Artyom Vasilyevich, our math teacher, couldn't resist it, although I must say he looked a bit tipsy during that lesson. Summoning me to his table, homework in hand, he stared at my notebook and said:

"Why are you bringing me somebody else's homework?"

"What do you mean, somebody else's? It's mine, I swear it!" I was beside myself at the groundless accusation. "It's mine, look at my name on the cover!"

"No it isn't: on the cover it says Zolya, whereas in the schoolbook it says Yevgeny! Hahaha!" He found it terrifically funny. I didn't.

My first poetic publications in the country, in the provincial paper *Lenin's Paths* and in the Moscow University weekly paper, had the byline "Z. Dubnov." I missed classes on the day the university publication came out, and my fellow students returning from the faculty to the dormitory told me a number of girls had been asking, "Who is he? What does 'Z' stand for?" (It was mentioned in the paper that I was studying in the Department of Psychology; one of the poems published, "A Fairy Tale," was very romantic.)

After leaving Russia, I began sending my poems to Russian émigré magazines and newspapers in Europe and North America. My poetry, I realized later, was at the time of uneven quality, but in 1971 I had been one of the very first young people to be allowed to emigrate from the Soviet Union, and publications throughout the Russian diaspora eagerly printed everything or almost everything I wrote. And that's where my name came in again. Realizing that the totally unknown and weird—if not nickname-sounding—name Zolya would puzzle editors, I would always sign my poems "Z. Dubnov." The problem was that, in some of these periodicals, it was editorial policy to print a contributor's first name in full, and so they "deciphered" the "Z." Since there are really only two male Russian first names beginning with this letter, Zakhar and Zinovy, some of the periodicals published me as Zakhar Dubnov and some as Zinovy Dubnov. (They should, of course, have asked me first, but I don't hold it against them: both first names are quite rare, so every editor must have been absolutely convinced that the one that came to his mind was the only option.)

In Israel itself it was easier, because here I could use the full form Zalman, which was known and used (take for example President Zalman Shazar), though much less than its Hebrew original Shlomo. Still, there was a catch here too: this name was more of a laughing stock than a respectable moniker. (I'm not quite sure why, but most likely because it smacked of Yiddish and the diaspora; there was even a popular song in the country at the time about some "Zalman who has trousers that fall down to his feet.") So you must understand my predicament when I was mobilized and my army commander—a very sweet and tactful lady—had to introduce me to the rest of the department at the Personnel and Records Division where I was to serve. She knew from my ID that my name was Zalman, but as she was saying, "Here's our new recruit, a nice young man called …" I had a brainwave and announced, "Shlomo." The relief on her face and the happiness with which she repeated that name made me realize just how embarrassing the name Zalman was in the country.

One of my lecturers in the English department here was the American poet Richard Sherwin; confusing me with my ancestor, the historian Simon Dubnov, he always called me Simon, and I didn't disabuse him. By that time I had acquired so many first names that I wasn't particularly bothered. Once, however, an amusing confusion took place when Eliezer Hakak, an army pal of mine, came to visit at a flat I shared with a few university friends. I was in the shower and only heard one loud exclamation of my flatmate on the intercom: "Oh, Eugene! Why didn't you say it right away? He's here, come in and up, take the lift to the tenth floor." It transpired that Eliezer had first asked for Shlomo and been told there was no one by that name. Then he asked for Zalman and got the same reply. Lucky enough to also know me as Simon (the army had allowed me to teach in the department while serving, and on one occasion Eliezer came to my seminar, after which he, Dick Sherwin, and myself had a chat over coffee in the canteen), he tried that name, only to get the same negative reaction. Quite desperate by this stage, he racked his brains and remembered one other possibility—the one that unlocked all doors before him! For now I was mostly Eugene.

For our school leavers' dance (called the "Farewell School Ball") we had the most popular new band in town led by Raimonds Pauls, nowadays Maestro and one of the leading composers of not only Latvia, but the whole vast former Soviet space. He was a young man then, looking just a few years older than us, and must have been earning an extra few bob by playing at various occasions around the capital and most likely throughout Latvia. Following other boys, I made a half-hearted attempt at a sort of fast dance, which required shaking all the limbs energetically and, indeed, the whole body, but my classmate Litovchenko, who was much more streetwise and "with it" than I, made such big eyes at me that I realized something was wrong with my shaking; I retreated in shame and waited for the next slow dance. To this I invited Svetlana, the most beautiful girl in the school. She looked sad, and I asked her why. "Don't ask, just talk to me," she said. "What about?" I asked. "About love," she said. "What do you want me to tell you about love?" I asked. "Anything," she said, "it doesn't matter."

I don't remember what I told her, nor can I tell now, looking back, if it was I she was in love with or some older boy or young man, post-school (somebody had once seen her walking with somebody, if that sort of excited and envious gossip deserves to be taken seriously), but in any case no sooner had the dance ended than another good-looking girl, Irene, waylaid me to inquire if I had any booze with me. She was the opposite of Svetlana: boisterous, noisy, and cheeky; indeed, the only similarity between the two was their equally low level of academic achievement. (Once, at the beginning of a break, when I hadn't been quick enough to put away a draft translation into Russian of Shakespeare's song "O Mistress mine, where are you roaming?" which I'd been working on during a history lesson, she'd snatched it away and read it out loud for the whole classroom to hear, pretending it was my love poem addressed to her.)

All of us boys were drinking throughout the evening, but she must have been the only girl to join in. So she, my friends Zhenya Konyaev, Vladimir Kosov, Vladimir Shkodin, and I had a few sips in secret on the top floor and, when the Farewell School Ball was over, ended up walking throughout the night along the Daugava embankment. A few others came along, one or two other girls for definite, but they must have left earlier, so I remember only Irene, who stayed with us until dawn, when we all went home to sleep the night off. (She was the only girl from the school I'd go on seeing and corresponding with regularly for the rest of my time in the country, but of that more later.)

It was the very end of May, the night warm and beautiful. The stars were reflected in the river and a gentle breeze was blowing. Everything was well disposed toward us and hinting at a kind of future in which nothing—but nothing—was impossible. We weren't drunk, only a little bit tipsy, and talked about everything under the sun—talked and walked and laughed. The bonding and the camaraderie were real and moving, the more so for the absence of any physical contact between boys and girls.

It was unbearably painful for us healthy young males to be so close to the attractive and sexy girls who were our school friends, and yet never cross the border—and I'm not sure I'd recommend this kind of celibacy to any boy in his late teens—but there was so much beauty in that innocence and mutual respect that, as so often, I'm forced to go no further than make a note of the complexity of things.

Of the examination period—both school matriculation and university entrance—only my sitting the Russian language and literature exam remains vivid for me, paradoxically perhaps, because of our former language and literature teacher Antonina Timofeevna coming up to me. Almost every pupil in the school detested her because she had always been full of whims, mostly humiliating for us. (Even now, realizing that she must have been a terrible neurotic, unaware of the harm she was causing our self-esteem yet unformed, I have to call upon all my mature sympathy, insight, and, yes, self-knowledge, to forgive her, as both a victim of her scathing remarks and a spectator of my classmates being put down in class.) Perhaps she didn't really dislike me as much as I thought she did, or perhaps she'd somewhat mellowed since Daniil Ivanovich had taken over from her, but she approached my table with such a huge smile that it made me nervous.

"And what are *you* writing on?" she inquired.

As was the case with all of those Russian language and literature exams, we had a choice between writing on a Soviet literature piece, a pre-Revolutionary work, and a free essay on some ideologically appropriate theme like the role of the Komsomol in raising the virgin lands. I'd chosen to write on Pushkin's *Yevgeny Onegin*.

"The noble classics," I replied.

"What an intelligent answer!" she beamed—and went on repeating, looking around, probably for others to hear: "Remarkably intelligent! Outstandingly intelligent!"

I found her reaction quite amusingly exaggerated—as though I'd just made some earth-shattering scientific discovery—but, still, I was moved by its obvious sincerity and the teacher's pride in me, her former student.

And then, after our last school assembly, Daniil Ivanovich came up to me with the good news. Apparently they'd found a way to justify my not-quite-normative use of a punctuation mark in one instance in my essay on Pushkin, which allowed them to give me a full A instead of an A minus. (The Russian system of punctuation is incomparably stricter than the English: putting, say, a comma where the rules require a semicolon counts is a grammatical mistake.) The teacher looked relieved: "It would have been a shame for our school to give you less than an A for language and literature," he said.

Many factors contributed to my recovery from alcoholism, and one of them was the high opinion my school had had of me. "Your teachers called you 'pride of our school' when talking to us as parents and family members in your final year," my mother and my father and both my elder sisters would say to me, "and look at you now! What would they say if they saw you in this state?" And I began to think I didn't even wish to consider the possibility of it happening—and this, together with my love for sports, inculcated by Soviet education, and a number of other factors, helped me defeat the illness and win.

Chapter 11: The Sea of Youth

And then came the university entrance exams.

I'd applied to the Moscow University psychology department. This department, like a number of others at Moscow University, had quotas for several national republics. Latvia was given two places. This meant that anyone living in Latvia could apply and sit the entrance exams in Riga rather than in Moscow. The competition was also less fierce: in Moscow, there were about fifteen applicants per place, while in Latvia, just under twenty for the two places. So it was easier academically and saved one going to Moscow and back. The only catch was, as I realized *post factum*, that the Latvian Republic was anxious to use those two places for native Latvians rather than Russians or Jews with only weak connections with Latvia, including its history, culture, and language. My parents were born in Belarus, and even I myself wasn't Latvian-born, but had arrived there at the age of eleven. So I saw the point, but it wasn't—and couldn't be—official. Everybody was supposed to be equal in the Soviet Union—Latvians, Jews, Russians.

I was the only one out of the eighteen or nineteen applicants from the Republic to pass the entrance exams with straight A's. Closest below me was a Latvian girl who had A's and one B. The next one down the list was another Latvian with a B and a C. I was obviously the best candidate. My school grades were also all A's, with only two exceptions, both non-academic (PE and woodwork).

The three of us had to appear before the Latvian entrance examination panel and university admission board, which consisted of some dozen members, all looking quite professorial. They accepted the girl, but turned down both me and the other boy, saying they had decided not to use up that year's allocation and to send only one student to Moscow.

Determined to fight the injustice, I talked to the same old family friend I've called Alexander, who'd advised me how to behave faced with the KGB the previous year.

"Nonsense," he said. "They want to send their own Latvian boy, so they'll pretend they aren't using their full allotment and forgoing the second place reserved for them at Moscow University, and then they'll wait for a few weeks until the whole thing is forgotten and you've already enrolled at Riga University instead, and they'll quietly send the Latvian fellow on his way to Moscow. It's clear as daylight."

And so I wrote an official complaint, with either Alexander's or my father's help—I no longer remember whose—which hinted at ethnic discrimination (curiously, Alexander said in this case that it was not necessarily anti-Jewish but more generally anti-anybody who wasn't a born Latvian). My father arranged an interview with the republic's Deputy Minister of education, to which both of us went. The man said the reason the admissions board had given him was that it had been unimpressed with my performance at the interview. I must admit that they had a point. When asked why I had chosen Moscow rather than Leningrad psychology department (the only two universities in the country offering the subject at the time), I'd replied stupidly that it would be easier for me in Moscow where I had relatives. I should, of course, have pointed out the differences in their orientation: in Leningrad, they were more industry focused, while the Moscow department, whose faculty included the world-famous neuropsychologist of memory Professor Luria, dealt primarily with Pavlovian psychophysiology, neurology, and memory. But even so, I pointed out to the minister, I had the best grades and what was the logic of wasting Moscow's gift of a place? Surely they wouldn't hold it in reserve for the next year and then allot three instead of the standard two places for the republic? The man, who seemed quite attentive and reasonable, nodded and said I'd hear from the admissions board again. Shortly afterward, I received a summons to another interview.

This time I was much better prepared, but they must have still thought my obtuseness chronic, for they asked me the following question: "And what will you do if we turn you down again? We can arrange a place for you here, you know, at Riga University, and, with your high grades, in any department you like."

Let them find another sucker, I thought to myself, and said out loud with determination: "I will go on fighting the injustice."

They asked me to go out and wait in the corridor. After a few minutes—among the most tense in my life—I was invited back and told that I had been accepted.

And now Mother started her attacks for real. "How can you abandon your mother—who's already been left by her husband—and live at peace with yourself? Everybody—Nina Solomonovna, Frieda Zelikovna—all my friends are asking: 'How can he do such a thing? Why does he have to go to Moscow and leave his mother all alone? Why can't he take the offer of Riga University?'"

"Because it has no psychology department!" I tried to reason with her.

"Pooh! What nonsense! Who's ever heard of psychology? It's a joke at best. I mentioned it to Joseph Bein himself, the man you respect so much, and he said that when he'd worked in the merchant fleet as a culture organizer there was a psychologist there. Nobody knew just what he was supposed to do, but everybody called him 'Psycho.' You can study anything else you like here in Riga, and be near your mother, and have your customary hot chicken soup ready on the table every day, at any time you want."

When this approach failed, she tried another tack. Soviet education was free, but the grants were minuscule, almost impossible to survive on—thirty-three rubles per month. The majority of students were helped by their families. The few who weren't either had some savings (the older students who'd worked before enrolling) or had to find some kind of night job like unloading goods trains, which made attending half a day's worth of lectures and passing a great number of exams very hard. My father had agreed to increase my monthly allowance from fifty to sixty rubles, which was quite generous. "Of course he'd do it," my mother scoffed. "He'd do anything to tear you away from me! He's afraid of me, of my telling you the truth about him—the kind of father who abandons his own son for an old whore. You could have squeezed even more than sixty rubles out of him, with my advice, but I wasn't going to help you in this case, because I'm against you going to Moscow."

I tried to calm her down by promising to come back twice a year—for a few weeks over the winter break and for a whole three months in the summer. Finally she gave up and bowed to the inevitable. I'd won the battle, if not the war.

The remaining two months of that last summer before university I spent on the beach in the daytime and in the concert hall most evenings. Father gave us his work-subsidized half of a semi-detached *dacha* in the summer resort station of Dzintari, two small rooms a twenty-five-minute train ride from Riga. (It was kind of him but hardly a sacrifice, as there's no doubt that he was also somewhere along that lengthy coastline too, with his new wife, in her *dacha* subsidized by her workplace.)

I stayed there with Mother, and my aunt Fanny from Tashkent and my sister Lena, married and visiting from Tashkent, were renting next door on the cheap—a bargain also, I believe, arranged by Father. (Lena had married, as I have said, thanks to a dog. She'd been visiting our aunt and had been ready to go back home when she'd been badly bitten by a dog. So she'd had to go to hospital, and remain in Tashkent for a while longer, during which time she'd been introduced to a young man—called Slava, but a much more educated and intelligent person than Slava the First, the one who'd been so sarcastic about my God talk. They'd fallen in love and got married in no time.)

Zhenia Konyaev came to see me several times. On Radio Prague, on the Italian Song Requests Program, which I'd come across by chance, one of the most popular songs was Toni del Monaco's "Vita Mia," which had first appeared two years before, in 1965. Zhenia and I liked this song so much that we sang its first lines while walking on the beach:

> *Vita mia,*
> *vita mia,*
> *unica ragione tu*
> *della mia vita!*

I knew some Italian—liking its sounds and rhymes, I'd taught myself a little bit of the language—and it was easy to guess that "*unica*" meant unique. Everything else was likewise more or less clear, apart from the word "*ragione*," which didn't stop me from concluding that the song was about the life of each one of us—the uniqueness of our young lives, so to speak. (In fact it's a love song addressed to a girl: "You are the only reason for my life!")

Another popular song, this time on Riga Radio, was the Bulgarian singer Lili Ivanova's "Morye na Mladostta" ("The Sea of Youth"). My sister Milla and I had long arguments over how to interpret its tempestuous melody (Bulgarian being quite similar to Russian, we could partly understand the lyrics, but they offered no real clue either way—and I still think the words in that song are ambivalent.) My opinion was that, rather like "Vita Mia," the music was expressive of the boundless exuberance and exhilaration of youth. Milla was equally certain that the song's upheavals had to do with one's youth going away and that the music expressed the pain of having to say goodbye to it.

Talking of music, both popular and classical, it was sheer luck that I was spending my last summer before Moscow next to the Dzintari Concert Hall, into which I could usually sneak without a ticket.

My love for classical music preceded my love for poetry. I'm sure I inherited Father's musicality, along with both my sisters; for as long as I can remember, classical records were always playing at home. I don't know where Father learned to play the piano, but he could still play passably well in his late eighties. When, as a young man, he left Gomel for Moscow seeking education and independence, he earned a living as an accompanist for silent films, in the late 1920s and early 1930s.

Music would accompany me my whole life, and most of my close friends and translators would be either professional musicians or, like me, passionate music lovers: Chris Newman, Anne Stevenson, John Heath-Stubbs, Peter Porter. One of the two earliest of my poems that I decided to preserve, written at the romantic age of seventeen (the other being the already mentioned "White Night") was inspired by a musical piece:

Fantasy-Impromptu

She runs, helpless and blind.
Trees fly like flocks of birds.
She runs—and now the sky flies
Like a tear tearing itself from her lashes.
Stop! Shadows run, picking up the trail.
Stop! Clouds flicker past.
How her heart beats, knees weaken,
Blood knocks and tosses through her temples.
Stop! Only one moment! Where are you going?
Only one word … The pedal creaks,
The music arrives like retribution,
The keys tear the grand piano apart.

(1967, translated with Anne Stevenson)

A dozen years later, recovering from a nervous breakdown, I would turn again to music, to Schubert this time:

So The Eyes Are Filling Up

For Stephen Spender

So the eyes are filling up with pain
when on the plains and the mountains
the storm awaits resurrection
and the fear of the sea comes close.

Like the city wind, like the promontory,
like the force of the road, like *Der Strom*,
the thought quickens toward you
and thunder speaks up in the spurs.

(translated with W. D. Snodgrass)

The Dzintari Concert Hall being situated close to the beach (you could hear waves crashing in the musical pauses), it was easy to climb over the fence on the dune side, surrounded as it was by lots of pine trees. Then all you had to do was brush off the sand and walk down the path through the trees toward the hall itself. It was rather like the proms at the London Royal Albert Hall, with cheap tickets for those prepared to stand. I quickly developed a method whereby I'd spot two or three unoccupied seats below, wait till the last minute before the start of the concert and then go down the steps into the Hall and nonchalantly settle into the best of them. For me that meant the closest to the stage and preferably in the center, for I came not only to enjoy the music, but to learn. The concert notes were distributed free of charge, and they were very detailed. I took a pen with me and after a piece, in the interval, would go over the notes, underlying those bits whose truth I had verified during the performance. It went something like this. The program note on Prokofiev's *Piano Concerto in C Major* would mention its varied piano writing and listed a number of things as examples: lyrical cantilenas, virtuoso classical-type and percussive staccato passages, the toccata and the complex passages on the chords, and so on. I'd underline some of those (double underlining the staccato, which was easy to detect), put a question mark next to those I wasn't sure about (perhaps the complex chord bit), and leave untouched those I'd missed (most likely the cantilenas, being uncertain what that meant).

When it was pop music, lots of young people tried to climb the fence, but when it was classical no one did. Most concerts, though, were classical. Once, when an Italian pop group was performing, I tried to pull my usual trick, along with some half-dozen other youngsters, but it proved impossible: the fence was being patrolled by young male and female stewards wearing armbands.

Music and verse were hardly separable for me at this stage. I read voraciously, both poetry and literary criticism, studied prosody and could at one glance (or rather, one scanning-out loud) tell the difference between an amphibrach, a dactyl, and an anapaest, no matter how varied. I also learned various complex rhyme schemes, including the villanelle and the triolet, the Spenserian stanza and the sestina—and, of course, the sonnet, as popular in Russian verse as it is in English. My favorite poet was still Alexander Blok; we had his complete works at home, and I read all his poems (I had no time for his drama, which seemed to me artificial). I also read more of W. B. Yeats, who continued to sound very beautiful and romantic and wistful. The most popular poets in the country at the time were Yevtushenko and Voznesensky; I read everything they published and liked most of it, though they were totally different, the former much more traditional than the latter.

(Little did I know that in the early 1980s, in London, Yevtushenko would help me, a poor student, sell a dozen copies of my first collection of poems, while Voznesensky, chaperoned by his KGB minders, would be touched by and thank me for reciting to him a passage I'd memorized from my favorite poem of his.)

Irene came to visit for a whole day. She'd tried to enroll at university but flunked her exams, which hardly surprised me. She was very pretty and lively, though, and I was terribly fond of her. My mother, fortunately, wasn't on the premises, so it was left to my sister Lena to appraise the girl. Lena had the tact to do no more than cold-shoulder Irene, but afterward she spoke her thoughts to both Mother and me: "I'm sorry my poetic brother couldn't find anybody better than a girl who looks like a mechanic or tinker—a dogsbody, in a word."

"Why 'tinker'?" I was puzzled.

"She walks like one, didn't you notice? Like a sort of unqualified worker or factory apprentice."

She had a point, actually, because Irene could have done with a bit more feminine grace. But I still liked her enormously.

In the evening I took her to a concert, splurging on a standing ticket for her, while I climbed the fence (she'd have climbed too, she said, if she hadn't been wearing a skirt). During the interval, she jumped off the parapet surrounding the hall, which we'd been sitting on, to stretch her legs; I noticed the hungry look on the face of a young man next to me as he was staring at her shapely legs. Although my claim to those legs was hardly stronger than his, I still felt a proprietor's sense of pride and, when she came back, told her about the attention the man had paid to her legs. "I'm sure that's made you happy!" she nodded knowingly, and laughed. I realized I was deeply in love and after the concert tried to put my hand on her bare arm. She slapped my hand: "Don't you ever touch me!" and gave me an intensely hateful look. Terrified, I hastily withdrew the hand. (Quite typically, I wrote a love poem afterward.)

Although I subsequently interpreted her reaction as an immature girl's teasing game, I was also to discover that she had psychological problems and was seeing a specialist. So perhaps I had been right, in spite of my own immaturity, in being so taken aback by her reaction to my innocent gesture.

Irene didn't see me off when I was leaving for Moscow—she was away somewhere trying to get into another university in another city—but one of my teachers did. It was the same young woman—I'll call her Valentina—whom Mother had tried to recruit to bring Father back. Zhenia Konyaev and Yuri Afremovich also came along, and, of course, Mother. Valentina was musical, she hummed the melody of the Beatles' 1965 song "Michelle," currently popular on Riga Radio. Yuri, true to form, immediately said that we should all be grateful for the greater freedom in Latvia, thanks to which we could hear such a beautiful love song on the radio and that I'd never hear it on any radio station in Moscow. (He was right too. Contrary to popular belief in the west, the degree of censorship and jamming of radio signals in the Soviet Union varied between its constituent republics.) When he said the words "beautiful love song" Valentina looked at me lingeringly, making me blush. While Mother was busy complaining to my two friends about me leaving her, the young woman said goodbye to me, keeping her hand in mine much longer than was customary on such occasions. She was the opposite of Irene: graceful, romantic, very bright, and—perhaps the main distinction—composed and mature.

On the train, rolling toward the greatest city in the Soviet Union, I began to sense vaguely, without being able to put this feeling into words, that all that summer's music, both popular and classical, in minor keys and major, stirred me with some inchoate longing that heaved and rose and ran over me, that refused to be quieted, that permeated my whole being, demanding undivided attention and scrupulous analysis. Ignoring that demand could have terrible consequences.

CHAPTER 12: NEVER OUT OF REACH

In Oxfordshire, England

A single leaf hangs in the air
on a spider-thread; at the horizon
a vista of sky and earth is meeting

as we pick our narrow way across
an autumn field of just-sown wheat
and further on along a forest path

to where a reservoir opens.
This, it seems to us, becomes the river
flowing around Muscovite domes

where on a little porch our memory
lies down, as both the wretched poor
stride on cobbled roads and aristocrats

ride slick trotters into the age's storms.
The way there and the passage back
lie along black back stairs and front portals,

sentries cloaked in greenery. Coming close,
we see how clear the evening air is, and
how tremulously a single leaf hangs down.

(1987, translated with Maxine Kumin)

"I'm here to see Father Superior Alexei," I said to the nun who opened the door to me at Moscow's Gate Church of the Intercession in the Novodevichy Convent. It was dark inside and her head was slightly lowered, so even though she was nearly as tall as me I couldn't see her face.

"Follow me please," she said, "I'll call him." And then she hesitated and asked: "What is it about?"

I suspected she had no call to pry into the reasons why her superior wanted to see me and might even be reprimanded for this sort of unecclesiastical curiosity betraying, perhaps, a shade of worldly vanity, but at that point we were standing in the light streaming from a window and the nun looked up.

"I ... I ... He ... He wanted to ... to interview me," I began to stammer, "to teach English ... to a group he's putting together ... of monks and nuns ... nuns and monks ... I mean I've been recommended to him by my lecturer in English ... at ... Moscow State University ... named after Mikhail Vasilyevich Lomonosov ... Department of Psychology ..."

"Dear me, I'm not sure I can take all this in at once," she laughed, "but if you wait here I'll call Father Alexei." Her laughter was warm and musical—and somehow intimate.

When she left, I took a deep breath and let it out slowly. I'd never thought a girl could be so beautiful, and I'd never thought such eyes—blue as the sunlit Baltic wave—were possible. A slight dizziness came over me. Welcome to Moscow, I whispered to myself— and to the crucifix on the wall and next to the window, partly hidden in sharp shadows.

Yes, it all began—like so many things in my life—with the English language.

But first things first.

There's something so exciting about approaching a huge metropolis for the first time by train. A good hour before we arrived in Moscow, little stations began to fly past the train, every couple of minutes. The tension in the air was growing palpably. Some passengers, like myself, were standing by the windows, others were still collecting their things and getting ready. The train pulled into Moscow's Riga Railway Station and I got out with my two suitcases.

The weather on this last day of August (the university academic year started, just like the schools, on the first of September) was sunny and reasonably warm, with just a slight promise of future chills. Though that station was far from the biggest in Moscow, the square in front of it shocked me with its press of people and busy traffic. Daniel Michelson, a friend from Riga and now a sophomore at the Mech and Math Department at Moscow University, had told me that the Faculty of Philosophy with its Psychology Department subdivision was on Mokhovaya Street downtown. I kept asking passersby how to get there, but nobody knew. Finally one who must have been a real Muscovite told me that Mokhovaya was the pre-Revolutionary name of a big thoroughfare called now Marx Avenue and that the various university faculties were right opposite the Kremlin and the Red Square. Impressed, I took the metro to the very heart of the metropolis. An elderly nun was sitting next to me. I had not come across this sector of society anywhere before and so kept stealing curious glances at her out of the corner of my eye.

I reached the department on time. All of us non-Muscovite freshmen were meant to gather at a particular hour, but we had to wait for a long time until somebody came to shepherd us to our dormitory in the southwest corner of the city, at the corner of Lomonosov and Michurin avenues. The area consisted of a number of identical five-story blocks which were in fact an annex of the main hall of residence situated two bus stops, or half an hour's walk, away and part of the huge central university skyscraper referred to simply as the Main Building.

The very next weekend all three of my roommates—students of philosophy I'd traveled with on that first trip from the faculty to our new lodgings and decided to room with—celebrated our first year in higher education by getting totally, insentiently drunk. My previous alcoholic experience was laughable compared to the state they got themselves into. I repeatedly declined their invitations and went to bed, only to be woken in the middle of the night by one of them—one of those "mature students" who'd had working experience and as a result been admitted with much lower entrance exam grades than school leavers—trying to unclench my teeth to pour some aftershave from a bottle. "C'mon ... b-be a p-pal ... d-don't t-try to shirk ... abscond ... p-play truant ... have a go ... for everybody's s-sake!" he was stammering incoherently while engaged in that labor. The other two were bearing witness behind him. I put up a fight without realizing why he should have been doing such a strange thing: I wasn't yet familiar with alcoholics drinking aftershave when they ran out of real booze. In the morning they were all repentant, crestfallen and apologetic, probably afraid I'd complain to the Dean of Students: "We didn't mean any harm, we just wanted to have some drunken fun, it won't happen again!"—but I made a strategic decision to leave them as soon as it was possible to work out new arrangements. Anyway, it would make more sense to room up with students from my own department of Psychology, with some of whom I'd already made friends.

A few days later, our lecturer in English (the subject was obligatory) exempted me from attending. All I had to do now was to show up for semi-annual exams. I was full of gratitude: the exemption from two periods of lectures and practical studies a week would free a lot of time and also save me from the pain of listening to my fellow students making unholy noises. For me, with my obsessions with the auditory values of words, with everything that was phonetical and phonological, this was a real torment, much greater than listening to their grammatical and syntactic mistakes. (To dispel any suspicions of snobbery or elitism, I hasten to say that I would always help anybody who came to me for assistance with English.) Just as I was about to go, thanking her profusely, the lecturer— I'll call her Berenson—asked me:

"Do you want to earn a few rubles to supplement your scholarship?"

"Of course I do!" I answered eagerly. The paltry grant together with my father's help amounted to only ninety-three rubles: quite enough if living modestly but too little if you wanted to have an occasional drink, enjoy a movie or play or concert, and once in a while eat out in a restaurant, to allow yourself a break from cheap but not very tasty university canteen meals. (By that time I'd already acquired dangerously expensive habits which I couldn't afford, copying them from my new friend and roommate whose parental allowance was one and a half times the size of mine.)

"One of the city churches wants an English teacher. Just a few hours a week. Several monks and nuns lodging in a sort of dormitory adjoining the church need to know the language."

"What for—and why ..." I was going to continue "have they come to you?" but she stopped me.

"I have no idea and advise you not to ask them any questions. Their request came to me through my husband who has had some interaction with them in the past."

I'd already heard rumors about Berenson's husband being a native English speaker and a high-placed government or Party official. The mention of him put me at ease, something which, considering the fact that the atheist Soviet state hated the Church, I badly needed.

"Here's their phone number," said the lecturer. "You have to speak to the Father Superior, Archpriest Alexei."

The group consisted of six students, three men and three women, all in their mid- to late twenties and all dressed in their religious garb. My favorite was Father Seraphim because he was endowed with a crazy intensity. ("They say my name means *fiery* in the original Biblical Hebrew!" he announced to me, his eyes burning brightly.) The very idea of monasticism was totally alien to me—and I couldn't get out of my mind the question of sexual abstinence: how could these young and healthy men and women bear living in closed quarters (monastic cells adjoining the church), seeing each other so often, undoubtedly experiencing arousal, and yet never acting on it? As for me, I was going crazy without a woman. Self-imposed opposition to nature seemed to me absurd and masochistic.

I was allowed to call them by their first names only, without the addition of Father or Mother (or, in some cases, Brother or Sister) as is the custom of the Russian Orthodox Church.

On my second visit, in the entrance hall I once again came across the beautiful young nun I'd met the very first time I'd come to the place. She looked slightly younger than the others, probably in her early twenties. She smiled at me and said, as to an old acquaintance: "I know your name's Yevgeny and you're a good teacher. I'm not meant to learn English but I'm going to ask Father Superior to make an exception and allow me to join the group."

I felt the greatest happiness in my whole life—greater even than when I'd been accepted by the Admissions Board. And this sensation of total bliss was also qualitatively different—totally unlike anything I'd ever experienced. I just managed to make a few indistinct sounds and then ask: "But what's *your* name?"

"Anna," she said. "I was named after Saint Anna."

"Saint Anna? What a gorgeous name! Who was she?" I cried out, with real eagerness—not for the saint, God forbid, but for the girl whom in my mind I was already calling "my nun."

"Oh, she was a medieval princess who'd lost all her relatives in wars with the Tartars and was twice canonized by our Church. She's a holy protectress of women who suffer the loss of their nearest and dearest."

With that she was gone.

"I really hope Father Alexei will let you join my group, Anna!" I shouted after her. She reappeared for a moment from round the corner and said: "So do I."

"What a gift for old ladies," was the student's comment on my offering the corridor seat in front of the examination room to a girl. Then he went along the row of students hunched in their seats, heads buried in textbooks, cramming before our very first exam, telling each of them: "Blaspheme! We live in an atheist country. It's part of your ideological litmus test to be able to blaspheme!"

"After the exam," they answered and look uneasily away.

I was interested and approached him. "You didn't think much of my gallantry, did you?"

"My gender education was different," he said. "There was a woman called Pyrda living in our block of flats in Kiev who used to bring men to her flat. Every day a different one, and sometimes a few a day. In an hour or two the man would leave. We children playing in the yard couldn't miss these activities. We were on good terms with her and admired the gap between her front teeth, so it was quite natural for me to ask her about her visitors. 'Pyrda,' I said—I must have been about eight or nine—what do all these men do in your place?' 'Ha-ha-ha!' she guffawed, offering a generous view of the gap. 'You'll find out, boy, when you grow up!'"

I liked the story, and we became friends. I quickly realized Vitaly (I'll call him that) was endowed with superior intellect and erudition. This didn't make me feel terribly inferior, as I was writing poetry that even the most literary-minded and erudite among students considered to be of high quality, whereas his poems, although showing undeniable talent, were but first attempts and did not attract anybody's attention.

(One of my earliest attempts at a longer poem, "Verses on a Journey," merited a real compliment, the more flattering because it came from Gershon Breslav, a second-year student and an expert in Russian poetry. He said that only the great Sologub had written better about railway journeys. I didn't know anything about Sologub but, desperately in need of encouragement, I felt uplifted.)

Vitaly and I immediately discovered we had the same dissident political views. This happened right after the oral exam before which no one would blaspheme. Having passed the exam successfully, a few students took heart and said that God doesn't exist. Their own nerve must have gone to their heads because the very next thing they did was discuss whether the country was on the right track. Then they must have got cold feet, in case one of them should inform on the rest about such subversive conversations—or perhaps they noticed the two of us listening. Anyway, they all started saying that of course our great country was the best in the world and on the best of all possible tracks. Vitaly and I exchanged ironic glances. Later that day we went together to the All-Union Exhibition Centre and there saw the famous statue "Worker and Collective Farm Woman" by sculptor Vera Mukhina. It was monumental and most impressive, with the man holding a hammer and the woman a sickle. Just as I was going to say something about the Stalinesque Art, Vitaly quipped: "We Soviet people have a sickle in our hands and a hammer in our heads." I was won over.

And so I brought him over to my dormitory block to meet my roommates the philosophy students. "One must have pretty mighty brains to study such a subject," Vitaly said with a straight face. Everybody knew that philosophy in our country was the field most permeated by ideology, but my roommates failed to see the sarcasm. With false modesty they began to protest, saying that they weren't really the cleverest of the lot, that many of their fellow philosophy students were brighter. Then Vitaly went even further and said: "Do you start straightaway with Soviet philosophy or do you have to do its forerunners first, people like Plato and Aristotle?" Considering that the so-called Soviet philosophy was no more than Marxist ideology pushed to its utmost limits by Lenin and Stalin, I thought the mockery rather transparent and even got worried for Vitaly—but still they didn't get it. They started enthusiastically explaining that first they had to do the whole history of western philosophy and only then would they come to our own time.

It was just as well for me to move out from their philosophers' dormitory building and move in with my own fellow students, because most students were already living together according to their departments. Psychologists occupied a different block nearby. Vitaly and I started looking for possible roommates—kindred souls. Grisha Vishnyakov was very short, around five foot three, but he turned out to be brighter than any other male student in our year. So we befriended him. For the fourth roommate we decided upon a foreigner rather than one of our own. And not one of the two Mongolians either (that country didn't really count as foreign), but a real Japanese by the name of Yosio Sato. When introduced by our Party history lecturer (aka The KGB Man) as "a scion of Japan's proletariat," he gave a small smile, lasting just a fraction of a second, but we thought we detected irony in it. We had a chat with him, very cautiously, not discussing politics, liked him, and invited him to leave his current roommates and join us.

For any movements after the initial settling in, permission had to be asked from the Director of the Student House Annex. We had to explain and give reasons; I don't remember what we wrote but most likely we mentioned friendship and common interests in a particular field of psychology. Permission was granted: it was probably just a formality.

The Annex consisted of five grey buildings and a cafeteria. No shops, no cinema, no shoe bar or launderette or dry cleaning—nothing. There was a reading room on the ground floor of every block. The dormitory was a place reserved exclusively for study. But for me it all started off on the wrong foot. A conscientious student throughout school, who'd been so much looking forward to hard work at university, I now ceased studying almost entirely.

Vitaly had seized me, was clinging to me, had me in his clutches.

He wasn't liked by other students. He was deeply cynical and manipulative, for all his brilliance and analytical intelligence. He was also genuinely lonely and tended to depression. The latter traits attracted me and made me believe in him as a truly kindred soul.

"When I was six and playing in the sand pit," he boasted, "I'd go up to a boy and whisper in his ear that the other one called him stupid. Then he'd take it up with the supposed offender, and it would all end with the two fighting each other, while I observed them from a distance!"

Or he'd become strangely agitated, as by Grisha's story of a half-crazed schoolteacher who'd called him an opportunist, ready to step over corpses to achieve his goal. "You? *You?* Step over corpses?" mocked Vitaly. "A right cretin that teacher must have been. I'm the one who'll step over corpses—or rather march over them! Give me bodies and I'll march on them! Left-right, left-right! Some make corpses, others turn into them, and still others walk on them!"

Neither I nor Grisha held such stories and pronouncements against him. At the age of seventeen or eighteen it all sounded very funny, surely not to be taken at face value.

Now, through decades of bitter experience in different countries, I've learnt to divide people into two categories: those who are open, sincere, and frank; and "operators" with ulterior motives and a hidden agenda. The first primarily communicate and share with other people, the second mostly take advantage of and use them. In my first university year I was hardly aware of all this, but my older fellow students must have been wiser. About a third of Psychology Department freshers had not come to college straight after school—the way the three of us had—but had first had a job, in some field or other, and their years of work experience had counted in their favor at the entrance exams. Thus, if the overall average pass grade had to be no less than an A minus for school leavers, for those older entrance candidates it could be a B or even B minus. Most of them were in their early to mid-twenties, and a few in their late twenties to mid-thirties. They looked askance at my friendship with Vitaly and occasionally made critical remarks to me which I would dismiss out of hand. Grisha was not taken very seriously, perhaps because of being so short and having comical habits like constantly blowing his big nose into a grubby-looking rag that passed for a handkerchief. My realization that I was quite popular among other students turned my head and was another reason for neglecting my studies.

From a beautiful—and culturally most western—but small corner of the Russian Empire to its center, and from my domineering mother's constant belittling, I was coming into my own. I was judged and found not wanting, but wanted. My poems, which in Riga had the attention of only a few people, were now appreciated much more widely and by a more discerning audience, soon to include literary editors.

My sense of humor was not caustic like Vitaly's or reserved like Grisha's; it was friendly and open. I was elected Floor Representative in our dormitory block and found it surprisingly easy to socialize with everybody around. Shy and self-conscious, I was embarrassed and moved no end when, approaching the dorm after the summer break at home, I heard girls' voices from their first- and second-floors windows: "Look who's there! Look who's come back!" And a few heads appeared from the windows, laughing and calling out to me. It was all very innocent; many of these girls had come from backward provinces with strict family rules; hardly any of them had ever had a boyfriend, and it would take them at least two or three years to grow up; the sexual revolution in the country was still some two decades away. But, just as in school, there was beauty in that guileless spontaneous warmth.

It would have been impossible to imagine Vitaly being met like this; perhaps he himself wouldn't have welcomed it. He'd found his closest friend in me, and a patch of neutral territory in our dorm room, and would go on to marry a brilliant girl in our year who could appreciate his intellect and, perhaps, with a bit of training, even his manipulativeness.

To get her without rivalry from me, he would play a very dirty trick indeed. And even before that, at the very height of our friendship, he'd experiment on me, just to see what he could get away with, given my trust and naivety. Once we were to meet at the entrance to Manezh downtown, near our faculty. The Manezh building is neoclassical, with some ten Roman Doric columns in front of the entrance. I waited for over half an hour and left in a rage. When I saw him in the dorm later, he said he'd been waiting for me in the same place at the same time. Could we have been standing behind different columns and failed to see each other? But the place was so ridiculously small, and the columns not that thick, and I had also gone around them a few times, to make sure! Still, he went on insisting he'd been there and had waited for me. What with my mother's religious indoctrination, and having just clandestinely read the *samizdat* edition of Bulgakov's novel *The Master and Margarita*, I had a weakness for things mystical and so began to wonder if such a weird non-meeting with both of us present could indeed have been possible.

One of my mother's favorite proverbs was "Heaven and earth swore there'd be no thing hidden between them." I don't know about that, but some two years later Grisha came to visit me in Riga shortly before Mother and I got our exit visas, and for some reason I remembered the Manezh episode. "Why," Grisha shrugged, "he had no intention whatsoever of going all the way there. It was hot and he just went to sleep after lunch." (In Vitaly's presence Grisha was intimidated, but behind his back would allow himself to spill the beans.) I wouldn't have held it against Vitaly if he had told me the truth and apologized, but he must have decided instead to explore the limits of my mystical gullibility. As for himself, he was totally rational, a convinced atheist.

It took me a long time to figure out the man in retrospect and to feel ashamed of having swallowed his bait so completely. But there definitely were reasons valid and weighty enough to explain and justify my being enthralled by him.

He was gifted in multiple ways, and some of his later poetry, written when we were in our second year, was remarkably mature for his age, eighteen or nineteen. His interest in philosophy, inherited from his parents who were university lecturers in that subject, made whatever he wrote profoundly interesting. Our reading interests were also similar: the very first thing we agreed on was to put Paustovsky above Ehrenburg as a writer. His antagonism toward the Soviet regime was informed and deep and on an altogether different level from that of my Riga friends. His reaction was swift and contemptuous. Often we'd simultaneously notice the same absurdities and laugh at them afterward.

Here's a typical "political" argument between two of our fellow students at which we had the good fortune to be present.

"Things were really bad under Stalin."

"Oh, no, they were worse under Khrushchev!"

"I totally disagree! Stalin's period was much worse!"

Then they must have remembered they weren't alone.

"But since those days things have been getting better and better, haven't they?"

"Yes, and today everything is really as it should be!"

Back in our own room we had a veritable fit of laughter at both their disagreement and their fear of being taken for dissidents.

Sometimes Vitaly would notice something I'd missed. He elbowed me when our lecturer in Party history said the following about a handful of fearless dissidents: "These brainless young people have come out in Red Square to protest against our troops entering Czechoslovakia! They've forgotten where they live!"

Surely the lecturer was unaware of the unintended *double entendre*—all he meant to say was that they should be patriotic and think of their own Motherland's interests rather than those of another country. But Vitaly picked up the irony: they'd forgotten they lived in a country where deviant behavior could be severely punished.

Yosio Sato was an easy roommate as he spent most of the time in the reading room studying, but he didn't really count as a friend. He was by nature reserved, and his Russian wasn't very good.

So it was usually the three of us who spent time together and talking among ourselves. Grisha also wrote poetry, some of which was very good. One of his poems, about birds returning and people never coming back, was written on my departure from the country and dedicated to me. It moved and still moves me; he managed to get it to me through clandestine channels, when such things could not be done openly, in the late 1970s, and I forwarded it to the editor of the oldest Russian émigré newspaper, New York's *New Russian Word*, where it appeared under the name Mikhail Dvorsky, a pseudonym Grisha and I had agreed on.

Our first university exams were nearing. My new roommates and myself were hardly prepared for them, having spent most of the time talking, writing poetry, and mocking those of our fellow students who were exemplary Soviet youths with the right ideological beliefs. Amidst the verses and endless discussions of literature, philosophy, and politics, as well as the taking apart of our teachers and fellow students (the latter, which we called "time well-wasted," bordering on unhealthy gossip), there was little time left for academic work.

And, of course, there was Moscow—impossibly huge and monumental, *echt* Russian, a shop window of all Soviet ethnicities, clumsy and disorganized, alcoholic, depraved, and stuck up, the nexus of all railroads, the third Rome, the seat of imperial might.

The nineteenth-century poet Vyazemsky, himself a Muscovite, wrote: "There's a delight in the wildness of Moscow too." In my first purely literary dream (my dreams have always fallen, with few exceptions, into two basic categories: imaginatively literary and romantically erotic), a few weeks after my arrival in Moscow, Vyazemsky himself made a tentative, seemingly unselfconfident appearance to make excuses for his home town's "wildness." In my dream, I surprised myself by standing up for Moscow, saying that it had nothing to apologize for and that, on a personal note, it was certainly "a delight" (I used his own word) for me to be in this city, doubly so after the reserve and formality of the Gothic Riga and my mother's grip on my young life. Then another poet, Mei, Vyazemsky's younger contemporary, showed up and supported me. Also a Muscovite, in my dream he blamed St. Petersburg, where he'd moved later in life, for his untimely alcoholic death at the age of forty.

Moscow amazed me with a number of discoveries and inspired an outburst of creativity. Our department and our dormitory block were in themselves a showcase of Soviet nationalities. About half the students were Russian, and the other half, everybody else: Ukrainian, Belarusian, Moldavian, Latvian, Lithuanian, Circassian, Azeri, Uzbek, Tadjik, Kyrgyz, Kazakh, Turcoman, Tartar, Tuvan, Khakassian, and the two people from the brotherly Mongolian Republic I've already mentioned.

Visiting the city's dozen or so railway stations, though, was a real, macrocosmic eye-opener to the vast mosaic that was the Soviet Empire. The world of Moscow taught you everything you might have wanted to know about the grand multinational state with the Russian ethnicity firmly in charge. As for the Russians themselves, here they were quite different from their counterparts in Tallinn and Riga: more "Russian," so to speak: open, noisy, back-slapping, vodka-drinking, absolutely certain of themselves, masters of their universe.

Thinking back to Moscow's skyline now, I see space emptying itself and the distance contracting, contracting, even as I look.

The leaves of the lush trees are translucent in the setting sun. The warm wind of late September gusts enthusiastically, raising patterns of light and shadow all over the welcoming world. The trees are rustling enigmatically, hinting at great things to come. The girls are walking side by side with me, their beautifully colored and patterned skirts and dresses fluttering, rising, making my heart skip a beat at each upheaval of a hem. The traffic lights at the intersection change from red to green to amber and back to red again, but we're lost in talk.

I am coming out of the building and into the avenue. The rain is pouring down, bitter, pelting. The whole city seems flushed away by water. It smells fresh in the rain.

Our dormitory block number five is the last of the Annex, its windows face the highway, all in green lights at night. Bare trees bend before the whistling wind, part of a cold front that has swept in all the way from the Ural Mountains. Standing by the window and listening to the rustling snow and drifting air, I feel a moment of deep aching sadness.

The sun is out in the morning, blinding, shining from the clear blue skies through air that is still and brittle with frost. The streets are a dangerous glaze of ice.

Sunlight and wind. The smell of wet earth and green leaves is intoxicating.

"What's the English for *Khristos*?"—and, before I had had time to answer, she added: "How do you say in English *lyubov k Khristu*? She lingered slightly on the word *lyubov*. She was looking me straight in the eye; her glance was bold and challenging. My first reaction was to look away in embarrassment, but with an extraordinary effort I forced myself to meet her eyes. "The English would be 'love … love of Christ.'"

"Could you write this on the board, please?" she asked.

"Everybody knows the word 'love.'" Father Seraphim had to have his say in the matter. "You can just write 'Christ.'"

"Are you sure you know how to spell 'love' in English?" I asked.

"L-A-V," he said.

"No, no," said Mother Yevdoksia. "It's L-U-V."

"You're both wrong," said I.

"So why don't you write it on the board?" persisted Anna.

Love of Christ, I chalked up.

"Love," she read out loud from the board, looking at me and then, after a small pause lowering her eyes and adding "of Christ."

"What a funny name for our *Khristos*!" said Father Amvroziy, shaking his head in disapproval.

"End of lesson," said Mother Yevdoksia, pointing at the clock on the wall.

Through the stripes of night, with the wind outside now falling to a soft, somnolent whisper, now rising in a passionate gust, I toss and turn and think of Anna.

The street lamp at the corner of the compound, next to the highway, shares some of its light with our dormitory window.

Memory is an abdication of the whole for the sake of a detail. It is never out of reach.

Chapter 13: Speaking Freely

The first year of psychology was heavy with Pavlov's legacies. It was grounded in general biology, physiology, and anatomy, even before we moved to the physiology and anatomy of the brain and higher nervous functions. Some things I saw as superfluous but harmless, like anthropology. Practical biology, on the other hand, I found both unnecessary and unpleasant. I could not skin the obligatory frog and asked a fellow student to do it for me, turning my back while the deed was done. I still don't understand why we had to do this. My impression was that the department was simply looking for things to fill out the curriculum. Psychology was as yet novel in the country; significantly, it was only a sub-department of the Faculty of Philosophy, and so the top heads were still experimenting. Also, there being no Freudian or any of the other psychodynamic approaches—frowned upon, considered "bourgeois pseudo-theories"—a lot of free time needed to be taken care of. All of a sudden an exam in electricity had been introduced, administered by the Physics Department. Having had a rigorous training in the subject at school, I didn't have any problems with this, but for many of my fellow students it was like a thunderclap; they burned the midnight oil and some managed to pass it only on the third attempt. Later we had to do the theory of probability, handled by the Mech & Math Faculty, and apparently on their lofty mathematical level. For many, unsurprisingly, it was the most difficult exam of all. In a "normal" psychology department one only had to do a purely practical course in applied statistics, without any of the supernal theoretical trappings of higher mathematics, as I was to discover when I went on to study in an Israeli university. I forgive the Moscow savants for their quasi-sadistic cluelessness in respect of us the students, but I still bear a grudge about those frogs they made us skin.

Familiarizing ourselves with the human brain was at least the "real" thing, although I found it difficult to hold one, whether whole or cut through the middle, with its terrible odor of formaldehyde, and wonder what sort of person it had belonged to. (Predictably enough for somebody whose early youth had been progressing under the Zodiac of Alexander Blok, my favorite was a beautiful young girl, in her late teens or early twenties, run over by a car or some such thing; in my defense, I can only say that I never imagined her as a suicidal lover: that would come over a decade later, in London.) All of us had strategies to buy time when summoned to show and name parts of the brain, both in Russian and Latin, during rigorous practical studies. I, with a grimace of great fastidiousness, would hold the specimen at arm's length, complaining the while about its horrible odor. The seminar instructor, youngish, in her late twenties, plain and wearing thick lenses, level-headed and with a well-hidden sense of humor, would say gently: "All right, you don't have to hold it, you can put it down: I only want you to point out Broca's area." Overcoming my reluctance, with a great show of self-sacrifice, I'd bring the specimen closer, as if to say that being on the point of fainting was nothing compared with the urgent need to learn about the brain. While doing all this, I was feverishly trying to recall the map of the thing. "No, that's the primary auditory cortex. And this is Wernicke's area. You're moving away. That's the arcuate fasciculus." Finally, by a pure fluke, I may have pointed at the right place and either got my "pass" (we weren't graded in practical studies) if it happened soon enough or was asked to retake the test next time.

Vitaly's approach was different. To show his eagerness, he mercilessly tore at the thing and, while attempting to find the part in question, kept digging at the grey mass so ferociously that soon you couldn't find anything even if you knew where to look for it.

The funniest, though, was one of the Mongols. Among us students were a brother and sister, by the name of Tzoren, from the People's Republic of Mongolia. We weren't sure just how much Russian they knew and suspected they'd played down whatever they did know so as to blame their lack of proficiency in the subjects on their poor linguistic skills. Anyway, the teaching staff must have got instructions from above to treat them leniently. They were most likely in their early or mid-thirties but the sister, overweight, bespectacled, and always covered with scarves and skirts from head to toe, looked about fifty. As if to make up for her dowdiness, her brother looked unrestrained and untamed, like Przewalski's wild Mongolian horse. There was something boyishly showy about him, especially when he raised his head and looked at you askance with his glittering black eye, as he did, for example, when informing you of his first name: "Dah-sh-hoh!" I liked him and had the cheeky courage to tell him he looked like a thoroughbred stallion from the Mongol steppes. Pleased, he laughed; his laughter sounded like neighing. Apparently attempting to win over our instructor by showing that he was undaunted by the brain specimen on the lab desk, whenever asked to point something out, he threw back his head, looked at her out of the corner of his darkly gleaming eye and exclaimed: "Take?"

"Yes, yes, take it," said the instructor impatiently. He hesitated for some time and then asked again, with even greater bravery: "Take?"

By way of contrast, good Muscovite boys from good families, gold medalists and teachers' pets, tried asking for pity. "This is precisely what I did remember," Volodya Deryabin mumbled plaintively, on the verge of tears. "I simply don't understand how those brains could have slipped my mind!"

All these tricks, however, left our instructor unperturbed; she was strict but fair. She gave us some time to get our act together but if we deserved it she would calmly fail us in the end for lack of knowledge. So we ended up knowing the brain map by heart, in both Russian and Latin. And that, unlike any distantly related, roundabout subjects like anthropology or biology or electricity, was the real thing: mastering brain anatomy made us proud.

Drinking was ever-present, as a kind of backdrop. Somehow we in Psychology seemed to get a bit less drunk than students in other departments.

Vivid images readily resurrect themselves before my eyes. Here's a first-year law student, tall, bulky, wearing a long winter coat and attempting to relieve himself into the urinal. He repeatedly fails to hit the target and goes on wiping the sides of his own and neighboring bowls with his coat until they begin to shine. Looking at that needed a strong stomach.

Here are two drunken students of philosophy arguing who was more "progressive" in his contribution to the materialist conception of history, Karl Marx or Friedrich Engels.

"Fuck you," says one finally. "You haven't even read the fucking *Theses on Feuerbach!*"

"No, fuck *you*," objects the other, the more drunk and aggressive of the two. "Fuck you, your mother, aunt, and uncle, you haven't read the fucking *Anti-Dühring!*"

Something gurgles in his throat; he throws up protractedly on the pantry floor and is thus the winner of the argument.

Moscow gave me a number of introductions; the chronic alcoholism in the country was one. Another was people's duplicity and manipulativeness, likewise ever-present and endemic. It's not that I hadn't encountered self-serving falsehoods before—I've already spoken of my classmate in Tallinn keeping my book while swearing he took it back to the library and of my acquaintance in Riga trying to pass off my poem as his own—but those were early and still uncertain examples, from my childhood and mid-teens; all my close friends in those two Baltic capitals had been honest, frank, trustworthy. We'd hardly had any secrets among us and had never told an untruth to one another. Now I was discovering the world of adults, even if mostly young adults, and on a big scale.

In the beginning of our first year, our biology lecturer, whom I'll call here Dronin, an old Stalinist, to judge from his frequent references to "Pyotr Trofimovitch Lysenko" (using the full name, including the patronymics, to stress his admiration), told us to prepare for a presentation that would be graded. We had to split into pairs to prepare a discussion of some problem in biology. One student had to argue a thesis and the other to challenge him. Borovsky, a fellow student a few years older than me, looked and behaved more or less like everyone else, so when he suggested I paired up with him I saw no reason to refuse. We cooked up a discussion. He asked to do the presentation of the topic, and I didn't mind doing the challenges. Dronin gave everyone a pass—and how could it have been otherwise when both the proposer and his opponent had prepared and rehearsed their thesis together, including the four challenges to it and the four answers to them?

Our performance turned out to be a real hit.

To my first challenge Borovsky retorted: "That is not a scientific question at all: biologists formulate it in totally different terms!" He then went on to give the explanation that he and I had prepared together.

His response to my second challenge was even more cavalier: "This kind of criticism is far too elementary—the problem should be discussed in a completely different way!"

I had no chance to get to the last challenge. Already on his third question, Dronin stopped Borovsky as he was saying: "Don't let us get involved in purposeless hair-splitting!" He interrupted our presentation and said: "That's enough: you, Borovsky, have convinced me with your arguments, but as for your partner, he seems not to have prepared his challenges. I'll give both of you a pass, but you, Dubnov, should take these things more seriously in the future!"

After that, Borovsky pretended that nothing out of the ordinary had happened, while I was totally stupefied. I found it difficult to understand why he'd done this, what was in it for him. I discussed this with Vitaly and what he said made sense: inordinately ambitious, the man wanted to show off and make the lecturer single him out. Betraying me—a naïve and gullible youngster—was a ridiculously small price to pay.

Even so, apparently Borovsky wasn't going to have me bear him a grudge and have others—those who had witnessed his caddish behavior—see me taking offense. It would be bad for his reputation. Better to make peace. In the evening of the same day he came to our room and suggested that we should see a film together. It was meant to look like a friendly gesture on his part, offered under the guise of concern for his partner, who now needed something to take his mind off his slight setback. Thanks to my talk with Vitaly, I had the dignity to refuse.

My monks and nuns—including *the* nun whose glances at me had recently seemed to be longer and warmer than before—had to go away somewhere for a few weeks. I felt terribly lonely without seeing her and strangely excited at her every look and smile at me without a hope of being loved. Vitaly, who likewise had no girlfriend, did everything to keep all girls who showed an interest in me away from me. I didn't realize the true reason at the time, because with his caustic intellect he'd immediately home in on their weaknesses until I too began to see them as desperately wanting in intelligence. The true reason, surely, was not even the understandable jealousy of a young man of seventeen or eighteen with no sexual experience and with adolescent acne on his face, but his fear of being left alone in case my love bloomed and led, perhaps, to marriage.

Nothing could be easier—and more dastardly, really—than laughing at those girls, some sentimental, some a tad too simple and straightforward, and most of them barely politically conscious, swallowing the state propaganda. Many were still children, really; a few of them would gather together once or twice a week to read fairy tales aloud to each other; an older girl told us how, upon walking into one of these readings, she'd found them all in tears, having just finished Hans Christian Andersen's "The Little Mermaid." Mocking these girls cost nothing, while being quick on the uptake and catching Vitaly's meaning in half-flight must have let me feel as clever and witty as him. The sad irony, of course, was that in this way I allowed him to keep me to himself and had to remain without a girlfriend. I was stuck with Vitaly.

The half-Polish, half-Russian girl's name was Tania. She was studying Russian philology. Her weakness happened to be over-romantic feelings for me and my poetry. She knew my verses by heart. Trying to appeal to what she must have thought was my poetic sensitivity, she'd say things like: "On New Year's eve we shall all of us be both a little happy and a little sad. We'll celebrate and we'll mourn." Vitaly duly poked fun at her for this the moment she left or when I came back after seeing her off. He'd unerringly home in on every suspicious pronouncement and ridicule it as corny and kitschy. The clichés weren't Tania's fault; she was lovely; her sentimental romanticism came from the heart. Nothing happened between us, but when I was leaving Moscow for good she gave me a beautiful present reflecting, as it now seems to me, her nature, as immature as it was delicate—a doll with rather sad blue eyes and long wavy hair, hand-dressed in a kind of beautiful Indian *sari*. The harmony and tastefulness of everything—face, expression, hair, clothes—were amazing.

Valya was also a philologist. She was tall and energetic, and Vitaly nicknamed her "the bubbly basketball lady." She was a Muscovite and I liked her colloquialisms, open vowels, and direct manner. She quickly cottoned on to Vitaly's subtle ridicule and left. She did everything decisively and with gusto. Although I liked her and sensed that she liked me, I didn't pursue her. Vitaly's mockery of her folksy phraseology and young girl's exuberance had poisoned the relationship.

With Sveta he went further.

Sveta was a first year student in the Faculty of Journalism; she came from the Khakass Autonomous Region, in South-Central Siberia. Khakassians are a Turkic people, a branch of the Kyrgyz. Sveta looked Mongoloid, with stiff, coarse raven-black hair, slightly oblique eyes, and very prominent cheekbones. Her mother tongue was Russian and she was a very gifted poet. The foreign language she took in her department was Spanish, and she liked showing it off: about a third of every note she left on my door or in my pigeonhole would be in Spanish. She had a beautiful figure, and once a Moscow black-marketeer I'd met by chance at an Italian folk music concert, of all places, asked me to "sell" her to a Party bigwig. Well, not quite "sell," although I liked to tease her myself using that word. The man said that she'd be taken care of financially throughout her university studies and perhaps even beyond. The bigwig, he said, loved this sort of combination of an exotic face and a perfect body. I might even get a small present myself for facilitating the interaction by persuading the girl.

Sveta and I didn't take it seriously, of course, but the proposition was hilariously absurd in yet another way: although surprisingly mature as a poet, emotionally she was still a young girl with strict morals and no sexual experience. So we were more like close friends, having poetry as our common interest, with some erotic passion thrown in, up to a limit.

One day, coming back from my lectures, I found a note on our dormitory door. It said, in so many words: "Hey you jerk! That sort of mixing isn't done among us Russians. If you don't chuck the little Oriental, beware!"

I sensed something weird about the note, and in due course, under my interrogation, Grisha cracked and admitted it was Vitaly who'd written it. The latter, when confronted, had no difficulty persuading me it had just been for fun.

He was constantly weaving his stratagems. It takes a particular kind of mind.

I was grateful to Vitaly for facilitating my free speech in a totalitarian state. It was a very great privilege. Almost everybody around was either too brainwashed or too frightened. It was about then I came across John Milton's words: "Give me the liberty to know, to utter, and to argue freely according to conscience," which struck a chord. Having free discussions "according to conscience" with a kindred but intellectually superior soul was all you could ask for. I don't know; perhaps even a woman's love and intimacy could be sacrificed on that altar, especially at the arguably most crucial time of the ripening of still immature minds. My poetry too had acquired a new voice, loud and strong and civic and very different from a typical sensitive and romantic Riga poem like "The White Night". (Indeed, it was on the basis of those Moscow verses that a Russian critic would later say that my poetry's origin was in the "proclamations of Moscow squares.") But by the same token, that was the time of the greatest hunger for a girl's closeness, intuitive empathy, and unquestioning acceptance. Deprived of these, with all my newly found, maturely assured cadences, I hovered on the brink of an adolescent depression. You can say perhaps that this was the price I had to pay for the breaking of my voice as a poet and see my later personal traumas likewise as a payment for artistic metamorphoses and voice mutations. Life and reality were displaced into rhythms, cadences, syllables, duple and triple meters, masculine and feminine line endings.

This idea—Balzac's magic skin in *La Peau de chagrin*, shrinking, diminishing, dwindling away, just as your life force is supposed to do when channeled into art—is tempting but seems to me now too romantic to be accepted wholeheartedly. Too many great artists throughout history have also managed to live more or less "normal" lives while engaging in a creative endeavor for us to subscribe to this "bleeding into art" notion. I think you can have it both ways, so to speak, provided you're intelligent and disciplined and don't have too many psychological problems. Yes, a talented being is basically like a house electrically wired wrongly, but one can learn to live with it, acquire the knack of functioning simultaneously within the parameters of art and those of the real world. Not easy, but possible. And as a result, one's personality and art are enriched. Life's reality always does that.

Yes, I spoke freely then, and I have been speaking freely ever since.

In the winter of 1968 my father happened to be in Moscow. He took me out to the theater and also came to visit me in the dorm. Always disciplined and responsible, he didn't like Vitaly and Grisha, sensing in them a laxity which was foreign to him. He thought they were slackers and a bad influence on me. The first thing he noticed was our dirty floor and their crumpled shirts and trousers.

"Your room needs tidying and your friends' clothes ironing," he said once we were out and on the way to a restaurant. Once inside, the following conversation ensued.

Father: "You should find better roommates. These will drag you down."

I: "They're all right. I can speak freely with them on politics. I know you won't concede this point, because you're always defending the regime. As a communist journalist, you're part of it."

Father: "What a load of rubbish! I don't write about politics. My articles deal with people, their work and study, achievements and failures, marriages and divorces. I'm totally apolitical."

I: "Still, you never forget to mention, when describing a successful man or woman, that they're Party members. And the more successful they are, the more you drive the point home. And if they happened to join the Party at a really early age, it's a veritable celebration for you! You're one of the mainstays of this whole system based on brainwashing the people through the media, habitually lying through their teeth."

Father: "All media lie. Do you think foreign media don't? You think in America or Britain newspapers tell the truth?"

I: "Of course they do!"

Father: "You're silly and over-confident. I'm a professional reporter; you'd do well to listen to me. In every country the media represent somebody's interests: either the already ruling group or the group that would rule. Don't look for truth and honesty among newsmen, especially political ones. By comparison, I do my work with integrity. I write about human beings."

I: "And it helps if they're Party members."

I was to discover that my father was right, generally speaking, about western media. Of course, my congenital inability to keep my mouth shut on politics wouldn't—by contrast with the Soviet Union—have landed me in prison in any western democracy, but still, in a number of cases, speaking my mind was inadvisable in both Israel and Britain.

I spoke freely then, and I shall speak freely now, although this time it involves speaking of myself and acknowledging things I'd rather not. I do not take any credit either for the braveness of doing this in a country where it carried mortal danger, or at present when it involves looking into myself and showing up things I saw nothing wrong with or even used to like but which now embarrass me. The former was just lucky circumstances, living in a conducive micro-world, a milieu and ambience of family and friends all thinking along the same freedom-loving lines and so habitual that I hardly thought of the risks; the latter is a result of having been corrected by bitter experience. And just as then, in a totalitarian state, I spoke freely not to foment dissent but essentially for myself, to keep my mind sane and free, so now I'm speaking freely first and foremost because I owe it to myself. And I do not want to claim an artist's exception or poetic license.

I look at myself as I was then, far away, insouciantly navigating through a bewildering variety of choices, with life ahead forever pregnant with sound, and death a kind of fiction, a bad dream or a horror movie, silent or too distant to be heard.

In 1981 the Georgian Princess Salomeya Nikolayevna Andronikova (Andronikashvili)-Halpern, whom I visited a few times in her apartment in London, often reminisced about the friends of her youth, Mandelstam, Akhmatova, Tsvetayeva (she remained friends with the latter two after leaving Russia in the wake of the October Revolution). One of the things that she told me was how much they had all laughed and fooled around when in their late teens and early twenties, how they hadn't taken life seriously. That information in retrospect conferred a sort of legitimacy on my own youth, which had to a large extent passed amidst fits of uncontrollable laughter, horseplay, and a general sense of fun, interrupted only by exams, impecunious spells, and love affairs, both failed and successful. My careless attitude to many serious things strikes me now as perhaps a kind of compensation for my early and pronounced tendency to depression.

One of the phrases from that period I've been carrying with me throughout my life is a comment made by a fellow student by the name of Ivan Lyagun. He was older and had life experience. Upon hearing me in my accustomed mode—being thoughtlessly flippant about something quite important, a forthcoming exam or a university event where attendance was required—he said: "For you, Dubnov, everything's a fucking joke, but when you're fucked you'll be fucking sure to raise a fucking outcry."

Well … I still feel grateful to Ivan for that saying, even though I hardly heeded it. My two main concerns for years and decades were to remain love and verse. Everything else would become so much less important, even if not always reduced to "a fucking joke."

Over, across, and through the layers of time ever folding in and upon themselves, I look at my youthful self and cannot judge him generously. In fact, apart from the poetry, I'd rather not see any connection with him at all. I feel a certain measure of distaste for his pliability and infantile, self-indulgent ways. Perhaps it's the Spartan, puritan attitude to life I've inherited from my ancestry, parents included, that sits in judgment of bohemianism; perhaps it's the vestiges of my religious ethics still battling the artistic impulse. That may have been one of the reasons—unconscious, surely—why I chose T. S. Eliot as the subject of my doctoral thesis.

Finally, it was getting close to the edge that mattered, the pain bringing me back to reality to tell me that, all art notwithstanding, life was not only here but was here to stay.

CHAPTER 14: VISITING FIREMEN

Anna was still away. The last time I had seen her, in mid-March, it was very windy, with intermittent chilly showers that tore at the trees and shrubbery in the front garden of the church as I walked in through the gate. And then she appeared from around the corner of the church, hurrying, shouting to me: "I have to rush or I'll be late for the lesson!" And then, after the wind's caesura, a sudden thrust of silvery rainy air pushed her black robe back against her body and held it tight. All her contours became sharply delineated: the breasts, the hips, the thighs; I fancied I could even make out her sharp nipples. I stopped in my tracks.

She must have noticed what was happening and intercepted my long look at her below the neckline. She blushed instantly and heavily. "Well, I'd better go in," she said, turning her back on me and approaching the entrance. Just then, as luck would have it, another blast of wind pressed against her shoulders and back, so that her buttocks clearly showed. They seemed perfectly rounded. Throughout the lesson she was strangely quiet, hardly speaking, and I thought best not to bother her. Every now and then she'd look up at me and then again lower her eyes. In the usual boisterousness of the lesson ("They call our own dear Lord 'Jeesis' instead of His real name 'Eessuhs'? Blasphemers! Shame on them!") nobody paid her any attention.

I dreamt of her, once in an embarrassingly obvious erotic way and a few times in a beautifully veiled manner. Having read Sigmund Freud's *Interpretation of Dreams*—not in the faculty library reading room where one required a special pass to be able to ask for half-forbidden books but an old 1920s edition, in a soft cover and dog-eared—I could understand both the perennial sexual symbols and the fluid reality-fed images of those dreams.

I am in the wood at night; the stars are huge, circular and convex, and the nearest tree's black bark reflects their blue light. The tree sways, and I realize it is praying; then its bark slips off and the black leaves of its whole attire blow away. It becomes recognizably female, and naked.

There's a brightly lit house and a lot of light all around. The colors are soft, creamy and pastel. The building's architecture is elaborate and ornate, a mixture of baroque and rococo. It has lots of arched openings and curves; tall towers, domed corners, and colonnades. Spaces interpenetrate; volume and void embrace and oppose one another. The house seems alive, massive bulk and evasive emptiness in a dynamic relationship. I am standing in front of it, agitated, full of eager expectation, my heart pounding. Presently a few dark-clad figures appear and start draping black tarpaulin all about the building. In no time its lively features are shrouded in the hideous black. (I recalled that dream a few years later when writing an undergraduate paper on William Blake and coming across his black-gowned figures in "The Garden of Love.")

Rapid clouds pass by, and the moon's cleanliness is revealed. Shafts of moonlight fall down through trees from the steep sky. I am standing in Moscow's Alexander Gardens, across Marx Avenue from our faculty. There's no one around. Light falls thinly on upright grass and pine needles from the moon and the open door leading into some kind of luminescent tunnel. The moon looks like a human face. It rests on the top of a pine tree. There's a sense of serenity and happiness all around. I wake up strangely optimistic.

Even though Alexei—the Father Superior—had told me he'd get in touch once the group had come back, I took the initiative and called him, in early April, under some pretext or other. I was reassured that the classes would resume as before, but that my students wouldn't be back until September, coinciding with the start of our sophomore year. That meant facing the spring exams and then going back home for the summer break, still without seeing her again. But my emerging love and hope would intermittently light up those weeks, like the flashing neon light of a street sign underneath the bedroom window on a sleepless night.

Money-wise, at least I would be fixed once more for a while by our kind lecturer in English—and in a manner and place I could never have guessed.

"Are you all right financially?" she asked. "I understand the monks are away."

"Together with the nuns," I nearly complained, but at the last moment caught myself and instead said: "Not so good."

"Do you like firemen?" she inquired.

"I wanted to be one," I confessed, "when I was six. But a year later I changed my mind in favor of policemen."

"Well, I can't get you a teaching job with the Moscow Police Department," she gave a deep theatrical sigh, as though grief-stricken, "but you're welcome to teach English to firemen—senior officers of Moscow's central fire brigade, to be precise. For a while at least. They're preparing for some conference in London."

The station commander, Fyodor Sidorovich Vytakin, was short and muscular. He had an agreeable face and friendly eyes. His deputy, Nikolai Borisovich Pyatak, a squat block of a man, balding, with little button eyes and a gallant swagger, presented a figure much more like a commander. Both seemed to be in their late forties. There were also six sub-officers and the station cook. The sub-officers were mostly tall and broad-shouldered, though their noses ranged from pug to Roman and one had funny protruding ears. The cook was small, thin-faced, and shy-looking. They all seemed younger than the commander and the deputy, in their thirties.

For the next month I had to delve deeply into all sorts of fire crew and fire brigade equipment, stored pressure dry powder fire extinguishers, dry and wet risers and fire hydrants, emergency evacuation procedures, chairs on wheels and on tracks, portable fire escape ladders and so on. I'd never thought fires could be so dangerous or fighting them so hard and risky.

Gradually, though, the sub-officers and the cook lost interest and dropped out. I could see from the start that they had resisted the management's imposition. For the higher-ups it had obviously made a better deal: paying me a lump sum and fitting in as many of their employees as possible. Eight for the price of two, so to speak, as only two—the commander and his deputy—were destined for the London Firefighting Conference.

When only two lessons remained before their departure, the class routine unexpectedly took a strange turn. Throughout the first half of the double period (one and a half hours altogether) they paid less and less attention to the material, until, when I asked them to concentrate, Vyatkin said: "Yevgeny" (at first we'd used both our given names and patronymics and they'd called me Yevgeny Leonidovich, but after a while Vyatkin had suggested we stop standing on ceremony), "can we possibly broaden our English conversation beyond firefighting matters? Talk about things in general—everyday things, like our life, family, marital status, children, work, and so on?"

"By all means!" I said. "Actually, I'd welcome this. I admire your professional work, but to tell you the truth, I find its minutiae and terminology …" I was going to say "boring" but caught myself just in time and finished by saying, "involved and complicated. Remember, you're professionals, and I'm new to the subject!"

"Excellent!" beamed the commander. "Super! How do you say in English, *Ya razvedyennyy, so vzrosloy docheryu?*"

"I'm divorced, with a grown-up daughter," I translated, slightly puzzled at why that piece of information should come up first.

I was even more nonplussed when Pyatak asked me how to say he was a bachelor.

After that there was a pause during which they fidgeted, coughed nervously, until, finally, Pyatak swallowed hard and, hiding his eyes, asked: "Yevgeny, could we confide in you? Something very personal. But only if you promise that our conversation stays within these four walls—that you won't share it with anyone else!"

"Well …" I was taken aback. "Sure. My lips are sealed. But what's it about?"

"You know, all three of us are men … healthy males, so to speak, haha! You're of course the youngest here, but we also have our … our desires. And, as you've just heard, we haven't got wives … women … Do you see?"

"Yes, I do," I said, although I didn't. "Quite. Indeed." Curiouser and curiouser, I thought to myself, deliberately in English, having only the day before finished reading *Alice's Adventures in Wonderland.*

Pyatak shifted uneasily in his seat and looked at Vyatkin.

"It's our first trip abroad," said the latter. "I mean to a capitalist country. We've been to fraternal socialist countries—Poland and Romania—but there was nothing going there. We've heard a lot about that Soho place in London …"

"And all the girls there," prompted Pyatak.

"Oh," I burst out laughing good-naturedly, glad to enter into this sort of male bonding conspiracy. "Why didn't you say so right away?! You want me to prepare you for a kind of encounter … I mean for picking up a streetwalker in Soho, don't you? That's easy—and of course I'll never mention it to anybody!"

"Not even to your college mates, right?" said Pyatak.

"Say no more! It'll remain between the three of us. I can only wish I were traveling with you—I'm also without a wife, aren't I—and all three of us could go to Soho and … But what about your … those people … the minders? Surely you won't be allowed to roam about free-ranging?"

They both looked greatly relieved: my guess was the relief wasn't about the KGB on their tails but about my being so quick on the uptake.

"Oh, definitely," said Pyatak, "we'll have KGB people shadowing us all right, but they can't be there all the time, can they? We'll be able to slip away now and then. And we'll be in London for a whole week. Enough time to do it, perhaps even more than once."

"And, Yevgeny," added Vyatkin as the senior of the two and presumably in charge of the ethical aspect of everything, "I do hope you're not condemning us in your mind as immoral. If we were married, we wouldn't seek such pleasures."

"Not at all!" Pyatak echoed enthusiastically.

I'd just struggled with Shakespeare's *Hamlet*, and laughed to myself as I recalled the words "The lady doth protest too much, methinks." A mischievous idea occurred to me to coach them in a sort of Shakespearean—or just old-fashioned English, which anyway I knew better from my literary readings than I did colloquial English. "You go to a place called Soho, see a lady proffering sundry and divers amorous gestures and you address her thus: 'Wouldst thou be so kind as to do a bit of gallivanting with me for a modest reward? I may look only like a poorly-paid firefighting Sergeant from an obscure faraway abode but insofar as it touches noble ladies I'm the veritable King of the Beasts!'" But that was out of the question. For one, I was paid not to have a laugh at their expense but to teach them English—even if not quite its seedier part. For another, I liked both men and felt moved and flattered by their trust. I also admired them for the work they had to do, which could be dangerous. Two men at their station had lost their lives some years before putting out a fire somewhere off the Old Arbat neighborhood. So what I did was teach them how to haggle with a tart over the price, leaving the way to approach her for the next—and last—lesson. I wanted to get a few tips on that from David, an American working on his PhD in Russian philology and living in the main hall of residence in Lenin Hills. I'd met him at some party at the beginning of the first term and had asked him to get me the lyrics of Frank Sinatra's song "Strangers in the Night," which had captivated me and teased me with a couple of words I couldn't catch no matter how hard I listened. He'd gone home for the winter break and had brought me back the full text, pleasantly surprising me: we'd hardly known each other, and I hadn't made my request sound particularly important.

"A special way to pick up a hooker? You must be crazy, man!" he laughed. "There's no special way. It's more likely she'll pick you up herself by saying something like, 'Want to have a good time, man?'"

"It's for a friend, not for me," said I. "I am not going anywhere. And it's not in New York but in London's Soho."

"Don't know about Soho," he said, "but I'd keep it simple and to the point. Let him go up to a woman who looks unmistakably a hooker and just ask: 'How much?' And don't forget to tell your friend to take good care of his wallet."

Some two or three weeks later, toward the end of May, when our lectures were winding up and first end-of-year exams starting, a fellow student sought me out in the faculty refectory. "There's a visitor for you downstairs," he said, "at the porter's. I was just going in when the old man asked me if I knew you and pointed at the visitor. So I said I'd go and try to find you."

"What sort of visitor?" I asked, intrigued.

"Didn't really pay much attention. Ordinary. Around thirty. Tall."

The stranger did look in his late twenties or early thirties and was quite tall. Apart from that—and his eyes, which came into full view a bit later—I hardly remember anything about him.

"Vyatkin," he said, stretching out his hand. "Pyotr Vyatkin. I'm Fyodor Sidorovich's son. You taught my dad English, didn't you?"

"You must take after your mom," I said, shaking his hand warmly.

"How do you mean?" he looked perplexed.

"Tall, I mean," I pointed upward, to draw attention to his height. "Your dad's not half as tall."

"Ah, that!" His tension eased and he smiled. "Yes, Mom's well above average … Zhenia … Can I call you that?"

"Of course," I said. That was the diminutive of Yevgeny; I disliked the intimacy this form implied.

"And you call me Petya. Zhenia, something terrible has happened to my father. Is there any place we can talk? Can we go to a café? It's on me."

"Thanks, but I've got another lecture in half an hour. We can go up to the refectory."

After finding a quiet corner and getting a coffee and a scone, for which he insisted on paying, I asked: "What exactly happened—some kind of accident? But he's alive, isn't he?"

I couldn't see the point of his coming to tell me the news. I had nothing to do with Vyatkin apart from having taught him English language—and for a few weeks only at that. Did his son go around finding everybody his father ever had any contact with in order to update them on his status? Not that I minded terribly—I did like Vyatkin and was saddened to hear something very bad had happened to the man—but I simply found his son's reporting to me rather strange.

"Oh yes, he's alive all right. And no accident either. But he's no longer my father."

Curiouser and curiouser, I thought to myself again. I was feeling a growing affinity with Alice.

"How do you mean?"

"I have renounced him. He's been drugged and abducted by British Secret Services. In London. During the firefighting conference you were preparing him for."

"I'm terribly sorry to hear that," I said. "He was such a nice man. My best student, ever. Great linguistic talent," I lied, not knowing what else to say.

"That's what I wanted to ask you about. What sort of thing did he want to know the English for? If you don't mind telling me. You know, as a kind of bereaved son I'd like to know. I hope you understand."

It was then, at the repetition of the word "son," that I realized in a flash what had been bothering me right from the start. Vyatkin had no sons. He had a daughter. And also I'd noticed an inconsistency: if Vyatkin had been abducted, the son would fight to get him back instead of renouncing him. Something didn't add up. Find another sucker, I thought to myself—and, out loud, said to the "son": "He wasn't different from the rest of them. They all wanted to know the same things."

"What things?" He became alert, vigilant, very much in a secret police way.

"Why, things needed for that English-speaking fire people gathering in London."

He wasn't a total fool, though, and quickly cottoned on.

"Nothing but professional jargon?"

"Of course, what else? That's what they hired me for. Indeed, that's what they paid me, a poor student, for. For fire and workplace safety training modules. For helping employers and owners conduct a fire risk assessment and ensuring their staff receive appropriate fire safety, fire prevention, and risk awareness training. For …"

"No discussions of life in capitalist countries—Britain in particular? No general conversations—like asking for asylum? I'm asking now not only as a grieving son bereft of his father but as a Russian patriot!"

"Of course, of course! I'm a patriot myself! But honestly, nothing outside of their professional interests ever came up. My job, after all, was only to prepare them to communicate with their counterparts from England and maybe other countries on practical matters."

And then I decided that the situation was dangerous enough for me to do a Hamlet-Pasternak on him. This self-defense maneuver needs to be explained, especially as it would serve me well a few more times before my final exit from the Soviet Union.

By that time, my focus of interest (poetic obsession might be more precise) had shifted from Blok to Pasternak, and I had read a couple of the latter's biographies. A translator of Shakespeare—of *Hamlet* in particular—from the early 1930s, it was obvious that Pasternak had immersed himself totally in the play and identified with its central figure who, as he wrote in 1946, was not at all a weakling but rather a princely "judge of his time and a servant of a more distant time." Moreover, as the poem in the *Zhivago* cycle makes clear, Pasternak also saw himself as the actor who had to play the role of Hamlet before an indifferent audience. In 1935 Pasternak traveled to Paris to participate in the Anti-Fascist Congress and then joined the group that went on briefly to England. On the boat from Tilbury back to Leningrad, his cabin partner was their Party supervisor, one Shcherbakov. He was a Writers Union Secretary and in charge of the Central Committee Cultural Section—a literary commissar, in a word. His job on the trip was clearly to be Pasternak's minder. Seemingly worked up, Pasternak talked to him compulsively and frantically on matters poetic throughout the night, till the early hours, when the man begged him to let him sleep. On arrival he would have had to provide a detailed report on his charge's thoughts and behavior. He must have written that the poet was a holy fool not worth bothering with (i.e. executing), because Pasternak survived while all around him major and minor literary figures kept disappearing. According to Pasternak himself, Stalin said: "Do not touch this cloud dweller." While there may be some justification for the view that Pasternak's nerves were indeed frayed (in London, his friends had taken him to see a psychological specialist, who'd found him over-excitable, if basically all right), I tend to think his behavior was in the main acting out that of Hamlet. The latter, after all, was not only genuinely distressed but also using the disguise of being unhinged to save himself from the tyrant.

And so I took up a pose and started spouting from memory: "The early warning of a fire can be life-saving, particularly in the home and at night or in the workplace. By installing a fire alarm or detector you will provide more time for orderly evacuation and the opportunity to deal with the fire before it becomes too large. Once the fire has started, there are ways of fighting it in the fastest time with the least amount of water, causing the least amount of damage. The most common causal factors of loss of firefighter life are a lack of incident command from the first response onwards and an inadequate risk assessment … I can tell you all this in English too. How good is your English, by the way?"

My interlocutor was silent, looking down. I became afraid in case I'd overdone it and he would see it was an act. I wasn't, after all, meant to be a holy fool of a poet but a student, i.e. speaking in a more or less rational manner and to the point rather than raving incoherently off on a tangent. So I added: "But I won't bore you with this specialist stuff: I enjoyed teaching it—and being paid for it—but my subject here at university is psychology, which is a thousand times more interesting. I hope you'll agree with me on that, Pyotr!"

The "son" gave me a close lingering look—and I had a chance to appreciate his pale blue, steel-cold, ceaselessly burrowing eyes. They reminded me of the eyes of that KGB man in Riga who'd pretended to be a Young Communist League secretary. "Well," he said, seemingly satisfied with what he saw, "let this talk remain our secret, Zhenia. Don't mention anything we've said to anyone else. I know I can trust you. And do call me Petya, not Pyotr!"

"My lips are sealed, Petya," I said—and at that we parted.

The very next day I got another visitor. He was waiting for me in the corridor, and accosted me just as I was going out of an exam in mathematical logic. It was none other than Nikolai Pyatak, the firefighter deputy. "Nikolai!" I exclaimed. "Fancy meeting you here!"

Seeming not to appreciate my wit, he whispered in my ear that he had something important to tell me and could we go somewhere private. So I took him out for a pleasant walk in Alexander Gardens just across the street.

"You're likely to be interrogated about preparing us for the conference," he half-whispered, after looking thoroughly around the garden path. "I've come back with herpes, and Fyodor has defected. Don't tell them anything when they come to question you!"

"They've already come," I said, "and of course I haven't made any mention of our … our talks about Soho. Why should I incriminate myself? A fellow arrived yesterday, like you, right in the department, said he was Fyodor's son …"

"Fyodor's only got a daughter!"

"Yes, I remembered that—and anyway the man looked a phony. I just said I'd prepared you for firefighting matters in English. But why should it matter now? He's already defected and you've got herpes."

"They don't know about me. I'm getting private treatment. They have no idea I've been with a whore there."

"But won't he spill the beans? To the local secret services I mean—what are they called now?—MI5 or MI6."

"No, he won't. He was a real, true friend. The staunchest friend one can ever have. Actually, it's not that—I mean about spilling the beans. I'm sure now it wasn't his decision. They must have lured him into defecting by taking photos and then blackmailing him. That whore who approached him looked more like a man in disguise to me, but she asked for such a pitiful sum that he, being a bit miserly, readily agreed."

"Surely British Intelligence could have afforded to employ a woman to have a fling with him for the pictures—even a real prostitute—instead of dressing up a male intelligence officer in female clothes!"

"Doesn't matter. The point is they followed us—instead of our own minders, who we'd been drinking with till they could hardly stand up—and must have seen me. My point is that it's not a question of Fyodor's not telling them about me, but of him making this one of the terms when negotiating with them—that my name isn't dragged into this business, that he was alone all along. I trust him on that. And on keeping you out of it too, by the way. I'm sure he'll tell them you only prepared us professionally and never helped us with a bit extra."

"I hope you're right. He seemed a decent man to me. And I'd never hold that Soho fling against him, on moral grounds. Nor against you, for that matter. *Carpe diem*, as they say."

"Carp what?"

"It's a Latin saying meaning when an opportunity presents itself, grab it. But what really surprises me is that you should've fared so poorly. Couldn't you find a clean tart? I'm sure that most of them get some sort of medical checks every now and again."

"Well, to be honest with you, if Fyodor's undoing was his tightfistedness, mine was being a sucker for pretty nubility. The girl looked about eighteen and was a real stunner. And she even agreed to do a blow job without the condom, for a little bit extra! If my English had been better, I might have even asked her to come to Moscow as a tourist so that we could get married! Just as well I didn't … Perhaps she'd got the disease from her first boyfriend or her pimp."

He walked me back to the entrance of our faculty, and we said our goodbyes warmly. I was later to discover he was wrong on one count and right on another. Some twenty years after, I was to meet Vytakin again, still in his capacity of a fire station commander, although now in a small town in the north of England, and establish the facts. He defected on his own, with no help from MI5, and he kept both his deputy and his English teacher out of harm's way. The way I managed to track him down was most unusual, and I'll describe it in due course.

The third and last visitor who came to seek me out and whom I missed that late May-early June was an alluring enigma—until the start of the new academic year in September, when the veil over the mystery was lifted.

"Some girl was looking for you in the department," said Shestakov, a happily married older student from Gorky on the Volga, as he came back to the dorm after sitting his last exam. "A very beautiful one. I told her she could find you here but she should hurry as all of us who were non-Muscovites were going to leave Moscow for the summer break."

"What did she say to that?"

"Oh, she just asked if you'd be back in September, and I said of course."

No matter how hard I tried to get more information out of him, it was no use. "I was in a rush to get something to eat as I hadn't had a crumb before the exam, so I didn't pay much attention. A lovely face—a brunette I think—and nice figure, sort of average height, seemed young, between twenty and twenty-five." That was all he said.

Two days later, on the very eve of my departure for Riga, the warden of our dormitory block called out to me as I was lugging a suitcase down the corridor: "You had a visitor this morning."

"Who?"

"A girl."

"What did you tell her?"

"That you'd left already."

"But I haven't! I'm still here. I'm speaking to you, in fact. If I'm doing this, in front of witnesses"—I gestured at the hall where a few half-drunk school leavers, come to sit their entrance exams, were hanging about, unsteady on their feet—"how can I have left?"

"She'd knocked on your door, but there was no reply. Then she asked me about your possible whereabouts, and I said you must have already left for the summer."

"I was probably in the showers." There was no point arguing, much less kicking up a row. I wanted to ask her how old the girl was or what she looked like, but thought better of it. This female warden, whose surname we never knew and whom we addressed only by her name and patronymic, Galina Petrovna, was downright unpleasant and a typical example of how small, insignificant bureaucrats arbitrarily endowed with power by the almighty state succeeded in poisoning—and in some cases totally ruining—the lives of countless citizens. (A block warden ruled over some three hundred students. Those little tsars were not academics. The only claim ours had to her mini-stardom was the fact that she'd graduated from the School of Physical Education. She had a particular hatred for our room, which I suspect was the result of having been informed by one of our fellow students that we were engaging in political discussions. The following year, when she contrived a scheme to kick us out of the dorm, we'd have the pleasure of meeting the warden of the whole Annex, a functionary on a different level, of whom more later on.)

I left for Riga quite depressed and composed poetry on the way to the railway station and on the train. This pattern was to continue throughout my life: whenever there was any kind of emotional turbulence, my only way to quieten it was to give it a voice, and any journey, whether by train or boat or plane, had to become fluent, without which its value was in doubt. From about that age—seventeen to eighteen—I would increasingly seek both shelter and purpose in the cadenced arrangement of language.

I stood until late at the window in the passage outside my compartment, which I opened after a couple of other passengers who had likewise stood looking through the glass a few feet away had gone in for the night. The shadow of the train running over the ground, the grass and the platforms of tiny stations flickering by gradually lengthened and finally vanished in the surrounding darkness. Now and again trains going in the opposite direction suddenly erupted out of the gloom, their festive lights briefly brightening the night, after which it seemed more impenetrable still. From time to time, a tiny empty station would slip past with its yellow lights. Occasional locomotive whistles sounded hoarse and sad. Turning sounds and words in my mind, moving through the somber space and its blurred contours back to a reunion with my adolescent past, full of incipient feelings but without a girl's reciprocal love, I felt an unmitigated loneliness. I was yet to discover how destructive self-pity could be, even in minute amounts.

When I finally managed to fall asleep on the overnight sleeper train I dreamt of a long line of people queuing up to visit me in the corridor outside the auditorium in which I was sitting a most difficult exam. The examiner, shaking his head in disapproval, asked me to come up to the door, open it and see for myself. The line was mixed: men and women, young and old. "I love you all," I said, cheerfully waving my hand—the one which still held the pen, the examination paper in the other—"but on this occasion, I'll see only the young ladies." The examiner, apparently pleased, took me by the hand, a gesture I saw as a good omen promising a high grade. And then I woke up to the sight of a fellow traveler trying to push my hand, which had fallen down from the berth and obstructed his passage through the narrow compartment aisle, back onto my stomach. It was very early in the morning. A pinkish mist adorned the horizon. The train reached a bridge and rattled clamorously across. It switched tracks. It stopped a couple of times and moved on again, without whistling. We were about to arrive at Riga's only railway station, a joke compared with Moscow's nine. Having faced new challenges in the very hub of the great empire (admittedly, with only a limited degree of success), having matured (up to a point), and with a (considerably) enhanced sense of self-importance, I was getting ready to pay a visit to the world of my adolescence, which I found suddenly shrunken. I was about to open the door to the old microcosm and re-evaluate the items inside.

The weather had been sunny in Moscow the previous day. It was raining now as I alighted from the train and walked out into the square in front of the station. The warm Baltic summer rain washed gently over me, my novel self—the one I had become after only ten months in Moscow.

Chapter 15: And the Word Was Made Flesh

"I've got a travel pass!" Announce that anywhere on Moscow's public transport, and no one will bat an eyelid. Announce it in Riga's—and you'll get weird looks and even a few laughs. Moscow and Riga. Two capitals and two different universes.

On the train back to Moscow, on the last day of August, I was summing up the impressions and results of my summer visit home. I was still fond of my Riga friends, but I had found them wanting in comparison with the breadth of erudition and interests of my Moscow fellow students, not to mention the depth of character and incisiveness of my closest friend Vitaly. Mother's nagging about my "leaving her, already abandoned by husband," went on. She wanted me to transfer to the University of Riga, even though it had no psychology department. She accused Father of supporting my desire to qualify as a "psycho" (according to her thorough research and the information therefrom, the most popular nickname for psychologists) and even having interceded for me with the Deputy Minister with one aim only—to tear me away from her and her positive influence.

"I know why you went to Moscow," she said. "To be debauched, depraved, and perverted. You father, himself totally carnalized—isn't that why he's left his children to live it up with a whore—is only too happy to see you torn away from the decency and care your mother provides!"

She went on to quote various family friends supposedly critical of me for leaving her alone after the trauma of her husband's departure, until I began to suspect, uneasily, that what had bugged her most was not my absence but her wounded pride, her prestige in the eyes of all those friends, some of them leftovers from before Father left, some her own woman companions, some—increasingly and significantly—members of the city's clandestine Jewish religious community.

I saw my father only a couple of times—not nearly enough, considering he was supporting me financially and wanted to see me more—but such were the consequences of my mother's influence.

I looked up two or three of my classmates—the girls I'd fancied in school—and showed them some of my new Moscow poems. I was surer of myself now, and I could recognize signs of returned affection, and I was flattered that they took my poetry seriously, but there was no dynamic in any of these relationships. Still inexperienced, I didn't press them for more than warmth, especially as the necessary privacy was unavailable. They always had somebody at home, either parents or grandparents, and my own mother, although working now as a bookkeeper (in which she'd been trained ages before as a young girl), was always in from late afternoon on. On a couple of occasions when I invited the girls over, she gave them such a cold shoulder that they showed no inclination to come again. I don't remember if any of them were free in the morning, but anyway the idea of love in the first half of the day, with all the light streaming in through the window, seemed to me, with all the romantic stuff filling my head, quite obscene.

As the train sped toward Moscow, the landscape smoothly moving by as if on springs, I also mused on some of the cultural differences between the two capitals. In Moscow, most passengers on public transport with monthly or yearly passes would announce loudly when getting on: "I've got a travel pass!" They must have felt uncomfortable not buying a ticket from the machine, in case other passengers might suspect them of cheating the system. (Once, being in a particularly bad mood, I snapped at one such announcer: "Have you indeed? A real travel pass? How nice to know!") In Riga, I'd never heard anybody say this. People were much more reserved, minding their own business, unafraid of other people's suspicions, and felt no need to report to total strangers on their own arrangements for travel fares. The Baltic corner was, in fact, the most European part of the empire. Moscow, on the other hand, had long ages before been contemptuously termed "a big village" by the proud dwellers of the then capital, St. Petersburg. Although I could see their point, I was very fond of Moscow. And I would fall madly in love with a girl, typically Muscovite in so many ways, one who came to see me shortly after my return. It was so timely, as Anna and the rest of my church English group seemed to have disappeared, at least temporally. When, the day after my return, I telephoned Father Superior Alexei, he was strangely evasive, saying that they might be back at some point later, when they might resume their English studies, but he couldn't commit himself to any dates or promises. It all sounded a bit fishy to me, and I wondered anew about the very reason for their studying English: what did they really need it for? Surely not for a firefighting conference in London! Nor for picking up a whore in Soho, haha! How about spying for the Soviets in English-speaking countries, then? In priestly garb? No way! More likely they were being groomed as English speakers in order to bear living witness to religious freedom in "the only country where man breathes so freely," to quote the most popular Soviet song.

First item, though, on my return, was the Moscow poetry. It came in the post. In my pigeonhole in the dormitory there was a letter in an official envelope stamped *Literaturnaya gazeta—Literary Gazette*—and my hands trembled as I opened it. Before the summer break I'd sent a few poems to this All-Union publication, probably the most prestigious literary one in the whole country, not really hoping for anything, more out of a sense of obligation. And now the reply, signed by the poetry editor, one Stepanchenko—the name meant nothing to me—invited me over for a chat.

That was another beauty of Moscow: everybody was reading books and everybody was taking my poetry seriously. My Riga friends weren't readers of modern literature: Zhenia Konyaev, if he opened a book at all, would rather reread old Russian authors, while Yuri Afremovich read only books on physics and chemistry. Neither was interested in poetry in general or my work in particular. The overwhelming majority of students at Moscow University, irrespective of their area of study, were avid readers of quality literature: modern Russian authors, translated authors of all countries and all ages—something I would never see again, at either Israeli or British universities. A small minority who didn't read would be too ashamed to admit it, so they kept up the pretense. We always discussed what everybody had read, was in the middle of reading, or about to read. Fewer were interested in poetry, but even so, poetry readership was considerable. Many poets made public appearances in huge Moscow auditoriums, which were packed and would be sold out in no time. (I can console my British and American friends and fellow poets who've always looked with envy on that phenomenon: in today's commercial Russia, poets are as little read by the general public as their counterparts are in the west.) Even in our miserable dorm, which looked like a barracks with bleak walls and four people to a room, those who wrote poetry could always find an audience. Students would cram into a room, listen attentively, and then offer considered comments.

The news that I had been invited to this holy of holies, the office of the poetry editor of such an important publication, instantly spread through the dormitory. Although the invitation could hardly be seen as a promise of publication, still the very fact of it was groundbreaking. Fellow students congratulated me, some—among those who were likewise creative—attempting to hide a bit of envy behind an uneasy mixture of good will and sarcastic teasing.

When I mentioned it to Sveta, the Khakassian girl, she looked so genuinely, wholeheartedly happy for me that I was moved. "Why don't you come with me to meet my friend Marc Andreevich Sobol?" she said. "I'm visiting him tomorrow." I immediately agreed: Sobol (1918–1999) was a well-known poet of the older generation. Arrested in the 1930s for so-called anti-Soviet propaganda (a friend informed on him, as was *de rigueur* in those merry days), he had been sent to a labor camp, then exiled, then had worked at all kinds of jobs—from telephone exchange operator to buffet cashier, forest tree cutter to miner, provincial actor to stevedore—then fought in World War Two, following which he began to publish. A nice and sociable man, he was quite a warm host, but his hospitality began with a recital of his own verse, quite a long one, only after which was he kind enough to ask me to read something of mine. I recited my "Poem of the Journey." I still remember his knowing smile when I finished, the patronizing smile of a maître to a novice. "I wondered while listening what compartment you were traveling in," he said, "and by the end it was absolutely clear to me that it had been first class."

"Well, I'm sorry but it wasn't," I retorted. "I wouldn't have had the money for that. I always travel second class."

"You should always travel third class," he advised, "to meet people and learn about them."

That made me wonder whether he was not right on the whole and whether I had in fact been living and creating in some kind of super-intellectual and over-literary ivory tower. I still had very little knowledge about life and people. Perhaps I *should* travel third class. The problem was, I only traveled between Moscow and Riga, and there were only first and second class coaches on those trains.

A few days later, in mid-September, I took a bus to the offices of *Literaturnaya gazeta* on Tsvetnoy Boulevard. Leaves were already falling. Getting off the bus, I noticed a lovely young woman bending down to pick up one particularly big and beautiful reddish maple leaf out of a few on the ground in the park. While she was doing this, another leaf, a yellow oak one, floated unhurriedly down and brushed her sleeve.

About three-quarters of an hour later, I was walking distractedly through the park, trying to digest what had just transpired in the poetry editor's office. She had discussed the few poems I'd sent in, been encouraging, and predicted I'd develop into a major poet. She boasted about her ability to foretell these things: she'd had an Estonian poet in this very room not so long ago, prophesied the quick blossoming of his talent, and sure enough, he was now being published. (I don't remember the poet's name, only her calling him Estonian, which would have simply meant he came from Estonia—rather than that he wrote in Estonian.) I'd mentioned to her Marc Sobol's critical remark about my choosing the wrong class of train travel, and to my great surprise she'd brushed it off as totally insignificant. "He's one of those belonging to the old era: the war and social-consciousness poets. I wouldn't pay any attention to his opinions." Ironically, having dismissed his views on what sort of thing a modern poet should write about, she herself suggested I redo one poem to meet social demand: turn its artist hero into a young communist one. She said this when I asked what I should do with my poems, in the hope that she'd say she'd publish them. Instead, she shrugged her shoulders and answered: "Nothing." Following this laconic remark, she hesitated, gave me an appraising look, and said: "Well … if you could, a bit … For instance, that is a good poem, the best in the batch. If you could turn its hero, the genius killed by a mob, into a young communist killed by fascist invaders in the Great Patriotic War, then …" I got the message: redact your verses along ideologically correct lines, and the paper may consider printing them. Characteristically, it didn't even occur to me to follow her suggestion. I just laughed it off together with my pals. This would set a pattern: I've always refused to compromise my conscience. It would be temptingly flattering to connect this attitude with the great words Solzhenitsyn put into the mouth of his protagonist: "We get the gift of life only once, but the gift of conscience we likewise get only once" (*The First Circle*), but my attitude was more intuitively psychological than loftily moral. For me, it came down to two things, both selfish. One was self-respect, which dictated that internal, introverted achievement was more important than external, extraverted success. The other was a largely unconscious hunch that artistic talent couldn't survive being violated and tortured in the name of practical gain. So, by refusing to adapt my poem for the sake of a possible appearance in one of the country's leading publications, I was instinctively protecting my personal dignity and my literary gift.

Ancient Slav names for months carried phenological sense; September was called *ruino* or *ruevo*, meaning "all yellow." That autumn in Moscow started particularly early, with cold waves coming in from the north-east. Cranes and geese could now be seen in the sky, about a fortnight before their appointed time, usually toward the end of September. Wild cherries, aspens, and limes were shedding their foliage at twice the usual rate. One windy day in mid-September, when yellow leaves were swishing by ceaselessly in a blur and we'd just come back from our classes to our dormitory, there was a knock on the door of our room. I was the nearest to it, so I opened. A girl came in. She was wearing a light blue raincoat, unbuttoned, and a long dark brown dress. Her face looked tantalizingly, almost intimately familiar, as when waking up from a vivid dream you attempt to recall its images. She glanced quickly around, taking in the surprised looks of my roommates, and said to me: "Hello. Let's go out, shall we?" And it was her voice that made me realize who she was. I made toward the door, but she stopped me and said: "It's quite cold outside, gusting winds. Wrap up warm."

"I looked for you in your department and in this place, about three months ago," she said.

"I know, now," I nodded. We walked in silence for some time, and then I took her hand. "Anna," I said, "what happened to your nun's clothes? Not that I miss them—you look even more breathtaking—if that's possible—in this civilian outfit! I'm just curious."

She didn't answer for a while. I let go of her hand and looked furtively at her face out of the corner of my eye. I'd never seen her so close before. She had an unusual face whose individual features—forehead, eyes, nose, lips, chin—were each very beautiful, but their arrangement on her face seemed just a little bit off, a tad out of shape, and this saved her from being pretty in a conventional and kitschy, Barbie-doll way. Her best features were the full lips, brown hair, and intensely blue eyes.

"Where shall we go for a walk?" she asked.

"How about Lenin Hills?" I suggested. "It's about a half to three-quarters of an hour's walk, depending on how quickly we go."

"I always walk fast," she said.

For a while we walked in silence. There was a strong scent of autumnal leaves all around.

"What happened?" I finally asked.

"I've decided to become a nun-in-the-world and got a blessing from my spiritual father."

"What's a nun-in-the-world?"

"Lay religious, often referred to as spiritual sisters. They were more common earlier on, when the Church was being persecuted: then, there were some very exceptional ones, like the famous astrophysicist and philosopher Dr. Polonskaya or the world-renowned Professor of Medicine Puzik. Now they are rare, but they've let me become one and I have got the blessing."

Since I knew very little about the Russian Orthodox Church and its customs, I found nothing better to ask if this phenomenon was what they called "tertiary nuns" in Catholicism. I'd read of those in some history book or other. She inquired who they might be—quite acidly, adding that she had no interest in any religion other than her own. Undeterred—as I'd always been and would go on to be whenever an opportunity presented itself to share knowledge—I went on to tell her what I knew: that Canon law requires one year of novitiate training called the "canonical year," after which those coming into the organization could become tertiary nuns, or religious sisters, and that today in catholic countries the only difference between a single woman and a religious sister not wearing the habit and living in her own apartment was the vows and the bond to a religious organization. I also added that the Catholic Church frowned on this practice and considered it disastrous for the souls of those involved, as many of them violate their vows and break their bond with the Church altogether. For some reason, Anna seemed displeased with the information I volunteered: she blushed deeply, and I hastily changed the subject. As always when at a loss, I talked about the season and the weather (which, incidentally and unsurprisingly, would greatly facilitate my entry and integration into English life). Showing off, I probably used over-romantic language and, when she didn't react, became embarrassed and held my peace. We walked in silence until we came to the Hills.

It had rained the day before, and the wet leaves were dripping. A dog barked far away, and we stopped, drew apart, then for some reason laughed and drew even closer together. Then I pressed her tight against myself and attempted to kiss her. She fought, broke free, slapped me on the face and immediately exclaimed "Hey, sorry, I didn't mean it!" She brought her hand up to her lips and covered her mouth. She was all flushed. "What do you think you're doing?" she demanded, half in anger, half in self-justification. "You must be thinking I took off my nun's habit because of you! Well, don't you get any ideas: it had nothing to do with you! I had many other … I mean I had other, really important reasons to do it!"

"It would never even have occurred to me you might have done it for me!" I protested hotly. "I'm sure you had your reasons. I'd be grateful if you shared them with me—some of them at least."

She calmed down. I took her hand once again, and we stood there, among trees, branches, and leaves for a while without speaking. Not knowing what to do, I reached for a nearby leaf with my other hand and touched it lightly, but she stopped me, saying: "*Ne poran' etot list: on ranim*" (Do not hurt this leaf: it is vulnerable). That was a perfect three-foot anapaest. Triple meters in English prosody are associated with ballads and comic verses, but Russian poetry works differently, and there they are omnipresent, employed for serious and dramatic purposes. The impetuous and forceful anapaest was my favorite rhythm at the time. I loved the girl even more than before.

Finally she said she had to go, and I insisted on seeing her home. She was renting a flatlet on the Krasnokholmskaya Embankment, between the Taganskaya Metro Station and the Novospassky Monastery (New Monastery of the Savior), the first monastery to be founded in Moscow, converted by the regime first into a prison and then a police drunk tank. She invited me in and made us coffee. I half expected crucifixes on the walls or at least some religious paintings, but, to my relief, there were none. Now I knew better than to continue probing her about changing her nun's status and her clothes. We chatted about this and that and exchanged memories of our childhoods. It transpired we had many in common, including walking along the railroad, collecting little stones, and listening for the vibration of approaching trains.

The autumn evening in the dark room was all webbed and netted by black branches and their shadows. The outlines and silhouettes of the remaining leaves flickered on the wall and the floor. It was the end of September. We'd left the curtains open. Anna was asleep. I was sitting up in bed watching tree shadows tremble down through the window. Presently the sky cleared and moonlight began to stream in at the window. My hand touched the moonlight on her cheek. She didn't wake up. Lots of disjointed thoughts passed through my mind: how beautiful was her Russian, bearing traces of Church Slavonic, and how she'd made of herself a wave which had engulfed me, and how we are born with this hunger for intimacy, both physical and emotional closeness.

We had been to see Claude Lelouch's film *Un homme et une femme*, which had just opened in Moscow. I'd liked it a lot and had been talking about it non-stop, while she'd been unusually quiet. On the bus she'd let me sit by the window—always my favorite seat—but had kept looking through it every now and again, leaning against my shoulder, and pressing her breasts into it—something she'd never done before, although we'd been seeing each other almost every day since she'd come to my dormitory and our walk on Lenin Hills. I made a point of getting off the bus first, so I could offer her my hand to help her off, in the old-fashioned gentlemanly way, and then I didn't let go of her hand. In her small flat, I sat down at the table in the kitchen while she went to make coffee. In the meantime she began arranging things on the table—mugs, teaspoons, sugar, biscuits— and as she was doing this she kept pressing her tummy against my shoulder. When she brought the coffee and started pouring it, she did it again, pressing herself against me even harder. I tried to think if this could have been pure chance, unconscious on her part, but I couldn't concentrate, my ears were ringing, and my arousal absorbed all my attention.

I couldn't take it any more. I jumped up and kissed her, delicately keeping my erection away from her, out of shame. She didn't resist; her lips opened to mine; they were warm, soft, supple, and moist. It was impossible to go on kissing her while holding the lower part of my body back, so I had no choice but to bring it against hers, with a lot of trepidation. I was afraid she might think this too brazen and vulgar. I was, after all, a wild-eyed dreamer with no sexual experience. But she didn't push me away. She pressed her face into my shoulder. I heard the rustle of her blouse over her bra and smelled her hair. Its scent was clean, fresh, flowery, girlish somehow—the fragrance of youth and innocence. I still remember how the word "trusting" as a description of her hair's fragrance came to my mind. (I've always had what I considered to be a hyper-sensitive olfactory perception: I can still with ease resurrect in my nostrils the unmistakable, unique smell of wet wood shavings used in the Moscow metro in winter to absorb the snow melting from passengers' footwear.) My stomach tightened, and my erection grew further and became unbearable. "Anna," I whispered, pleading, begging helplessly. She looked up; her eyes were as serious as I'd ever seen them. She disengaged herself from my embrace and walked into the main room which doubled as a bedroom.

There she drew the curtains and sat down on the bed. I came up to her, ashamed of the bulge in my trousers, even though it was darkish in the room, with only a half-light from the moon through the thin brightly colored curtains. It had been less embarrassing when it could be felt but not seen. Obsessed with the beautiful curvature of the female body, I considered the male body to be clumsy. Michelangelo's graceful David seemed to me effeminate. I was also ashamed of lust. Romantic love, yes; desire and passion, yes, but to be lewd, lascivious? God forbid!

(About four years later, when studying English literature, I would discover the poem by W. B. Yeats—a poet I'd always considered an exemplary idealist—entitled "Crazy Jane Talks with the Bishop" and look with disbelief at the boldness of the lines "But Love has pitched his mansion in / The place of excrement"; it would take some checking of the dates to calm me down, realizing it was written considerably later than "No Second Troy.")

Anna put her arms around the small of my back and pressed her face to the bulge.

I hardly remember anything after that. I loved her again and again throughout the night and fell asleep just before dawn. The creak of trees in the wind must have got into my dream, of which I remembered only some sort of tempest in a forest and a woman's presence. In the morning, when the sword-sharp thrusts of sunlight that had found their way through the gaps in the curtains woke me up, she said: "Go on sleeping. You've slept only a couple of hours. I haven't closed my eyes at all, but I don't feel tired. You just couldn't stop, you know? Of course, I can understand: with all the excitement of a new girl … and a virgin too …"

I didn't have the guts to tell her that she was my first, just as I was hers.

"You're so lovely, so passionate," I said. "How come you became a nun?"

"I may be lovely and passionate—even immodest—but I'm also pious," she said. "Shall I tell you now what you've kept asking me about—why I stopped being a nun?"

"Please do!" I exclaimed eagerly.

"Because I knew you were Jewish and was curious to see what circumcision looked like," she explained, trying to keep a straight face, but then burst into a fit of the giggles and dived under the blanket, head down on my lower part of my stomach.

"I may be uncircumcised, for all you know," I teased her.

"I've read about it and seen medical pictures," she said, momentarily re-emerging from under the blanket. "You most definitely are."

"I take it you had to read this sort of thing and see this sort of picture preparing for your nun's apprenticeship," I attempted to joke, but I choked on the last word and then, only a few seconds later, putting all the love I felt for the girl into the words, whispered: "You engulf me like a wave of the Baltic Sea. You *are* a wave. I can neither measure nor name you."

Still, however flattering it might have been to hope otherwise, I was convinced I hadn't been the only reason Anna had decided to change her nun's status. She never answered my innocent question about what they needed English for, and when once I jokingly called it "monkey business" she laughed and told me not to raise the subject with anybody apart from her. When I complained that there was no point in raising it with her since that got me nowhere anyway, she replied that at least this didn't get me into trouble. So my opinion, for what it's worth, is that there must have been a shady aspect to it—perhaps they were trained for some minor intelligence gathering abroad under ecclesiastical guise. That would also help to explain why they no longer needed my services: their English language training must have been taken over by another department, so to speak. So perhaps Anna had either not wanted any part of that sort of activity or had simply been found unsuitable for it by her superiors.

What surprised me was that she never forgot her religion, even in the most daringly intimate situations. I should have expected this, given her background, which included a priest father who'd died in one of Stalin's labor camps when she was only four and a much older monk brother who'd basically raised her after her mother died a few years later. But it still jolted me when, while writhing and arching her body in lovemaking, she'd whisper words like "the Rock," "Deliverer," "Light of the World," "Emmanuel," which sounded most bizarre but also flattering as applied to me. Since this was my first sexual experience and I had nothing to measure it against, I took it to be just the incoherent mutterings of ecstasy. But when she came up with expressions like "Lamb of God," "Son of God," and "Son of Man," I realized she was talking about Jesus and felt somewhat embarrassed to have such appellations attributed to myself. Later, when she called out the word "bridegroom," I asked her: "Anna, do you see me as a normal lover or as the physical embodiment of Christ?" She laughed but didn't answer.

Her Russian was beautifully poetic, thanks to its Church Slavonic element. On those occasions when we traveled outside the city over the weekend, I noticed that she never uttered the words "forest" and "woods"; instead, she always used pairs consisting of two words which were special expressions for tree clusters (similar to the English collective nouns for groups of animals—*pride of lions, unkindness of ravens, charm of goldfinches*, and so on.). She'd say: *berezovaya roshcha* (birch forest) or *sosnovyy bor* (pine forest).

(I remembered her explanation of the origin of these expressions later, when reading Northrop Frye's *Anatomy of Criticism*, where he introduces his concept of the "Green World"—an adjacent forest to which the main characters of some Shakespearean comedies escape from the city. The English Green World seemed a different planet by comparison with the primeval forest that had nursed the Russian tradition. Anna told me a folktale:

the details sounded remarkably modern, contrasting weirdly with its setting in the huge, timeless, impenetrable virgin forest reaching up to heaven—a contrast that moved my imagination and stuck in my mind.)

And she still inserted religion into the forest, as into everything else. I didn't particularly mind: although it sometimes seemed as if she had come from another language, I'd always fall for hers because it was so poetic. When a bird sang, she spoke about God's presence opening the gates at the end of the song's tunnel. Or she'd say that she could feel the Lord's goodness spreading throughout the forest clearing. Perhaps out of consideration for my being Jewish, at that stage she didn't mention Jesus Christ but spoke of God or the Lord in general terms. Apart from its poetic quality, her language attracted me with its range of folklore. "You're my Arina Rodionovna," I'd joke, referring to Pushkin's nurse. Through the praxis of the night she recited from memory lines from the *byliny*—medieval East Slavic oral epic narratives in verse—especially from my favorite, *Sadko*:

> Sadko set out along the Volkhov,
> From the Volkhov to Lake Ladoga,
> And from Ladoga to the Neva River,
> And from the Neva River to the blue sea.
> Upon the blue sea there sailed thirty ships,
> Thirty righteous souls …
> Many ships smashed on the blue sea,
> Pious people drowned.

(my translation)

I noticed the stress she always placed on religious words like *righteous* and *pious*. Her recital was very different from the way I'd been taught the *byliny* at school, where it was taken for granted that this folk form had paid only lip service to religion and so this element was totally insignificant. Anna dwelled on those words as if she really believed in them—which, of course, she did, and I didn't. I inclined to think that God existed, but I was suspicious of Language's attempt to grope for Him; words of faith and moralistic praise like *righteous, pious, godly, virtuous, devotional, prayerful* (all of them favorites of the *byliny*, as well as common on Anna's tongue) sounded to me sentimental. By that time, I'd discovered J. S. Bach: to me, his undoubted greatness was marred by his pietistic tendencies.

Anna's greatest contribution to my fusion of music and language was her love for the Russian folk song. I shared this love, but couldn't sing in tune, whereas her musicality was complete, and her range of songs beyond anything I'd known. (Characteristically, her opinion of both Vitaly and Grisha, at whom she'd had only a brief look on that first and last occasion of her visit to our dorm, was "no music in them." And she moved me profoundly when once she said, *à propos* of nothing in particular: "your music is really undeniable.")

For almost four months, I managed to handle both my romance with Anna and university studies, until calamity struck in late January. My two roommates and I (Yosio Sato by that time had moved to another room with less highly strung students) were expelled from the dormitory for a whole month. This followed a complaint from our block's warden, the aforementioned unpleasant Galina Petrovna, to the faculty authorities. The block's meeting was held, presided over by the warden, with the floor representatives and some minor figure from the Dean's Office present. It was a kangaroo court: the floor representatives couldn't care less about us but wanted to be in the warden's good books, whereas the youngish representative from our department was oddly passive, either intimidated by the loud-mouthed and brusque older woman or because he had his instructions. Officially, the reason for our expulsion was our lack of discipline. Specific details cited in the warden's complaint were "whistling and speaking loudly in the corridor" and "asking for the showers to be opened late at night." Even to the most hardened Soviet bureaucrat, those would have sounded silly as an argument for expulsion, which was also cruel because the three of us weren't Muscovites, and it was our private luck that we had friends and relatives in the city who were kind enough to put us up.

The real reason for the punishment, though, was quite obvious to us: politics. Somebody or other among our fellow students must have informed on us for holding dissident views and occasionally voicing them openly. The expulsion was to serve as a warning. I base this conclusion not on a hunch but on two facts. One was what happened with our representation to one Devyatkin, Moscow University Hall of Residence Annex Warden, and the other, the reaction of our lecturer in the History of the Communist Party.

The three of us wrote to Devyatkin, briefly explaining the situation and asking to see him. The first thing he told us when we came in was how, during the Great Patriotic War, when a platoon had to get to the other bank of the river, soldiers attempting to queue-jump were court-martialed and executed on the spot. "Perhaps you should shoot us right here for whistling in the dorm corridor," suggested Vitaly. Devyatkin shook his head in pity: "You're Soviet lads but you're fools. I was just making a point. Discipline is important in every field of life. Now, what's all this nonsense about kicking you out for such silly little things? You must be joking!"

We explained.

"Well ..." he frowned in consternation. "Your block warden will just have to have another meeting of your block to reconsider her decision, won't she? I'll give her a call and ask her to do this immediately, before your exile, so to speak, is supposed to come into effect."

We left greatly relieved.

Only nothing came of it. There was no other meeting and no reversal of the verdict. Initially, when we told our warden about our conversation with her superior, she looked flustered and began to mumble, almost apologetically, "Of course, of course," but the very next day her demeanor had reverted to its former unpleasantness. "The expulsion order stands," she said, "and you have to be out by the end of the week."

We went again to Devyatkin's office: I don't remember if his secretary said he was away or too busy, but the bottom line was that we got nowhere.

Then, a week or so into our forced departure from the dormitory, our lecturer in the History of the Communist Party addressed the three of us right at the beginning of a lecture, before the whole auditorium. "What's this I hear about you comrades being thrown out of your dormitory? You should have come to me right away, the moment you were threatened with expulsion. Why didn't you? I would have straightened things out."

One may well wonder what a university lecturer could possibly have had to do with student dorm affairs, but the answer lies in the fact that the man wasn't just any lecturer but a Party man. At the least he was the Party's representative in the faculty; he was likely also connected to the KGB in some way or other. A couple of times, seeing me rush up the stairs (I was often late for lectures and seminars), he'd commented with expressions like "Your energy, Comrade Dubnov, is praiseworthy; our country needs people like this!" or "What an enviable life force you've got, comrade! What don't you come to see me at my office some time, to chat about this or that?" I never went, and I think that it was to show his displeasure that he'd given me a "Good" rather than "Excellent" grade on an oral exam in Party History, when I'd answered all his questions correctly and given all correct dates. Naïve as I was, I was puzzled by what he said after writing "Good" and stamping my exam record booklet: "Although you've given correct answers, there are other issues preventing me from giving you an 'Excellent' grade."

"Don't you understand?" Vitaly then said. "It's to hint at your lack of cooperation in his attempts to recruit you as a KGB informer."

I didn't particularly grieve over the "Good" grade, as I hadn't made any special effort to prepare for the exam: my memory was strong and it had taken just a cursory reading of the material for me to memorize the stuff. Also, although not a single one among us students took the subject seriously, the dissident minority to which I belonged went further and actually despised it. So I just shrugged off his lowering my grade, but the ever-analytical Vitaly noticed something else.

"You don't even see how foul the whole thing is when an examiner openly admits that totally extraneous factors have influenced his grading, things other than the knowledge of the subject he's examining you on!"

Anyway, we were lucky accommodation-wise. Vitaly stayed with distant relations; Grisha squeezed himself into the tiny room in the Main Hall of Residence on Lenin Hills his brother shared with another student. And I was taken in by Anna.

She said three things the day I came in telling her the news, all of which were or would be significant.

The first was the surprised and commiserating exclamation "*Gospodi Iisuse!*"—"Lord Jesus!" —a very pious expression, uncommon in modern Russian speech.

The second was: "I knew something unpleasant was going to happen when I came across the last leaf on the tree across the street just as it was falling. You know that I am prognostic as a leaf!"

Finally, at night when as we lay side by side, post-coital on her folding sofa which served as a double bed, I gave myself a little pep talk. I said that after going back to the dorm I'd start a new life. I'd make sure no official could find anything wrong with my behavior, no matter how critical they might be. I'd stop missing morning lectures, get up at five and jog before classes, spend half the day in reading rooms, drastically cut the time

I spent chatting with my roommates, give up drinking beer, and so on. What she said in reaction to all this struck me as a demonstration of both her depth and her faith; it made me wonder about the connection between the two in general.

She said: "We can start a new life only after our death."

CHAPTER 16: REDEMPTION (ALL WERE SAVED)

At the very end of February, on the eve of my return to the dormitory, Anna and I went skating on the huge rink in Gorky Park. Both of us owned skates, hers were called *snegurochki* (snow maidens) and mine, *dutyshi* (Pectoral Sandpipers, *Calidris melanotos*, small northern birds which they were supposed to resemble). I can't call myself sporty, but I was definitely more so than my roommates. I liked walking a lot; at school in Riga I had made every effort to overcome my unwillingness to get up early by arranging to jog with friends in a local park before school. I couldn't ski but loved skating, which I'd learned while still in Tallinn, at eight or nine. I took second place in the university students' speed skating competition.

Infrequent snow was falling, feather-light crystal shavings coming down indolently, now and then, from the black spaces above the skating rink's dazzling floodlights. Loud music was playing. We held hands as we skated. Her nearness and the smell of her hair intoxicated me, made everything swirl like transparent wind. I missed a turn, failed to maneuver, drove into somebody, and fell. I lay on the snow, heart pounding against my rib cage; she skated back to where I lay. "Come on, get up," she helped me up. "I'm all right, I can get up on my own," I protested. She laughed and we went on skating.

"You know, I've written you a poem," I said. "Composed it, I mean."

"What's the difference?"

"I've composed it in my mind but haven't written it down yet. I'll do that later," I explained. At that stage, I always composed verses in my head, mostly musically, first hearing cadences, then a few words, and then gradually filling everything out. Committing the results to paper was the least of my concerns. Later I would come across Mandelstam's critical attitude to Pasternak's working process ("Now that you've got a flat you can write poetry," Pasternak had said; he had been overjoyed to get a big writing desk and, again, had connected this with improved creativity) and realize my way of doing things was identical to Mandelstam's; it would take me many years to see merit in Pasternak's approach.

"What counts is what's recorded," said Anna, pointing at scratches from skates on the ice.

"Look at the way the snow sparkles on the windowpane," I said when we came in and she switched on the lights.

Her telephone rang. I was making coffee and wasn't listening. Her face was frighteningly set and grim when she came into the kitchen. "I'm going to see my brother in Zagorsk monastery," she said. "He's dying for my sins."

Her older brother Pavel was a monk in the Trinity-Sergius Monastery in the city of Zagorsk (now Sergiyev Posad), some fifty miles northeast of Moscow, the oldest and most important monastery in Russia, the center of Russian Orthodoxy.

"It was the Hegumen himself," she said. "He says Paul is wasting from some unknown disease, something really mysterious, he hinted that it was not natural."

"How did he hint?"

"He said: 'All our illnesses come from Heaven. If we become unwell, we have to examine our deeds.' Then he paused and added: 'Or those of our nearest and dearest.'"

"Does he know about us?" I asked.

"He knows I've become 'a nun in the world.' He may guess it's connected with what he hates most and calls 'lechery.' I'm going to see him, right away. The train's from Yaroslavl Station. If I go now I'll catch the last one."

"I'll see you off," I said.

"No, I'll go alone."

"Let me at least come with you as far as Komsomolskaya Metro. I won't get out to see you onto the train if you don't want me to, I'll travel back to my dorm."

"I have to go alone."

When three days later she came back, she didn't look herself. She was gaunt and pale, and the fanatic implacability of her face reminded me of Feodosia Morozova, martyr of the seventeenth-century Old Believers movement, in Surikov's famous painting.

"I've seen my brother," she said, speaking slowly and sparingly. "He'll die if I don't change my life. Both the Hegumen and the Archimandrite have told me this. Paul belongs to Christ, body and soul. So do I. I'm Christ's."

"You said you were mine," I protested. "Don't you remember how you shocked me—sweetly, of course—I wish you'd go on doing it forever—when you cried out: 'Fuck me, I'm yours!'?"

"That wasn't me," she said, her face a hard mask. "It was the Devil speaking through me. I was possessed."

"Is it because I'm Jewish?" I had my own questions to ask.

"What difference does that make?" she laughed bitterly and contemptuously. "Fornication is fornication, whether with a secular Jew or a devout Christian. It's a real sewer system we carry atop our legs. And now my dear brother has to pay for my sins. When His light has reached us and fallen on our pallor and His obedient snow has destroyed our fields and our sins have been cleansed, Jesus may come again and redeem us sinners … Prayer will lead us to the hereafter … It's not too late to find a church …"

After these words, which sounded to me ritual, came sentences she must have taken from old Russian tales.

"And an old monk from the Andronova monastery encountered Vassily on the bridge over the Volkhov …"

She went on and on like that, speaking as if in a trance. Her words, while very beautiful and poetic, made little sense to me. "What are you quoting?" I asked.

"*Savva Grudtsyn* and *Gore-Zloshchastie*—my poor brother told me to re-read them."

(The very next day in the library I took out those tales and went through them. They belonged to Russian moralistic literature of the seventeenth century; both ended with the spiritual purging of the hero and his entry into a monastery.)

I took out a notebook.

"I've written down, as you said I should, that poem inspired by you and dedicated to you," I said. "Shall I read it to you?"

"Avvakum Petrov, the protopope of Kazan Cathedral here in Red Square—only a stone's throw away from here—said: 'A rhetor and a philosopher cannot be a Christian.' He suffered for faith. He was a martyr. He knew what he was talking about."

"I'll tear it up, then, and throw the pieces away," I said, quite desperately.

"I don't care. I belong to Christ."

That was the last time I saw her. I never bothered to restore the poem (which I did tear up and throw into her wastepaper basket), though I knew it by heart.

(She got in touch a few weeks before I left the country for good. Apparently her brother's mortal illness had been a scam, to bring her back under the aegis of the Church. A monk at that monastery had spilled the beans, uncomfortable with the way the girl had been manipulated. Since then I've seen so many pious people of various religions convinced that the end—religious faith—justifies the means, that I cannot fail to appreciate the ethical attitude of that nameless monk. It's believers like him, perhaps, that stop those who don't believe from being completely put off religion. But anyway, by the time Anna discovered the truth I'd already fallen in love with another girl, a totally secular one, in Riga, and there was neither the time nor any point in going back and opening the wound it had taken so long to heal. She wanted to come to say goodbye, and I said yes, by all means, but I myself heard the unwelcoming note in my voice. She said she would but never did. That was the end of it. A most beautiful and most painful memory, no more than that.)

Depression had set in, coinciding with fierce snowfalls and storms. The wind seemed to me to keep muttering something unintelligible in Church Slavonic. That language even got into one of my most vivid and saddest dreams, full of chill and snow, shades and loneliness. I remembered only a few disjointed phrases of it, which I wrote down upon waking and which strike me now more as an over-romantic disservice to modern spoken Russian than the poetically archaic version of it they had sounded like before:

> Light lies hidden in the shade;
> Inquire about the ritual and how they worship;
> A freezing mist is coming in;
> I am vanquished by the ignorant, not by martyrs.

Images in the dream came and went; I wrote down whatever I managed to remember (that is a pattern I've tried to follow all my life: to have a record of my most vivid or dramatic dreams).

Bright summer light left shadows on an empty seat in a park. Streetlamps came on and caught the profile of a passing woman whose lips moved silently. From the sky grown grey, snow began to fall. Footsteps passed across the glass. I was sitting observing cracks of light around a door I knew to be locked. A solitary girl appeared, with her back to me, wrapped in rags of what looked like moonlit snow. All at once she turned round and, her face in shadows, threw a snowball at me. I couldn't catch it and felt guilty because of this failure; when it fell on the ground it changed shape, began to glitter and appeared to be a crucifix. A naked man wearing a huge cross on his chest came out of his room, closed the door and shuffled down an endless gloomy labyrinthine corridor to the toilet. His shoe laces were undone.

I analyzed those images later when I studied psychoanalysis. Most of them revolved around Anna, memories of her and places we'd been to, and of her religious faith. The last image came from my aunt's communal apartment in Leningrad, which I'd visited as a boy. I realized the reference straightaway, upon waking, although I couldn't understand its relevance. That I would decipher only with the help of Freudian dream analysis, as a student of psychology at a western (rather than Freudo-phobic Soviet) university. The connection must have been sexual: a young woman who lived in a room just across the hall from my aunt and who had seemed very beautiful to me must have forgotten to lock the toilet door; when I, thinking the place was vacant, had opened it, she had been standing facing the door, about to pull up her underwear. I'd been struck and disturbed by the mysterious curly black triangle at the top of her legs. "Just a sec," she'd said, "I'm already on my way out." Coming out, she treated me to a whiff of her perfume (she must have only peed in the toilet, as there were no unpleasant smells), which disturbed me even more.

I found the perfumes Anna used exciting and arousing. She told me that the sense of smell in a woman is much sharper than in a man. When I made an attempt to describe the nature and effect on me of the several perfumes she used she laughed, pleased, and said that it must have been the artistic part of me speaking. She saw creativity as essentially feminine. Pleased myself that she'd been somehow flattered by my sensitivity to smells, I dared not argue. (Although I've never really warmed to Carl Jung with his analytical psychology totally devoid, unlike the Freudian approach, of therapeutic clinical application, I would find his concept of *animus* and *anima* of interest generally and quite intriguing personally.)

With Anna gone, I had to learn the solitary skills of sexual withdrawal. Throughout the seemingly unending nights, I kept resurrecting and painfully relishing lustful images. My formerly insatiable limbs now starved and begged to touch or be touched. By day, after classes—which I couldn't concentrate on—I walked the embankments. The wind there appeared always to be rising from the river, now whirling torn bandages of drift snow, now stripping new snow from the frozen crust and throwing it in my face. I was breathing in the city which felt frostily estranged. I felt it like my own expanded lung but it didn't want to be part of me, let alone console me in my sorrow. When the gusts subsided and great flakes fluttered lazily down and hid the bridges, I felt even more lost, because the black gaps between the flakes suggested to me enormous distances and alienation, zones devoid of music, time fallen off its timeline. Walking the empty, late, solitude-fearing streets back to the dormitory, I was almost hypnotized by the yellow lamp glow of other lives behind window frames.

Poetry could not give me consolation. For a long time I was unable to write anything, apart from this one poem:

Moscow

I hide my face against the tramcar window
Which frost, a whimsical reader, understands:
Just so, a troubled child lays down his sorrow
Held by his mother's mitigating hands.

Love me and open-armed fling wide your gates,
And for my sake unlock your sacral doors,

Walk with me all your alleyways and parks,
Walk with me all your avenues and squares;

Lead me to where the chilling air unravels
My breath in tatters, as a threadbare sheet;
Moscow, I love within your late-night tramcars
Beside the window there, a vacant seat.

(1969, translated with John Heath-Stubbs)

Generally open, this time I didn't reveal much about my relationship with Anna to any of my friends, but all the same the signs of "the end of an affair" must have been glaringly obvious.

"You're confusing the romantic with the profound," said Zhora, an older friend, the one responsible for my first publication in Russia, which I've mentioned previously. He was very brainy. Vitaly disliked him intensely and once they even got into a brawl. "You know, when I worked as a lifeguard on a beach I had to take a special course. They told me something I've never forgotten: that a drowning man or woman will take you down, even though you are attempting to save them. They will drown you, not meaning to, despite themselves. If I were you, I'd re-read Chekhov: a truly great writer, he mentions women, as it were, at a distance."

Vitaly, as always, played a double role. On the one hand, he seemed genuinely sympathetic and repeated a few times that there are other fish in the sea. On the other, he seemed to get a kick out of my weakness and dependence on him. This was combined with his usual tendency to depression. His favorite phrase was "Why is everything so bad when everything could be so good?" Yes, it was meant to be witty—but he was only half-joking. He also liked to quote Alexander Blok's line: "Grey fog is creeping in from the fields, grey gloom is creeping into my breast." I believe that his being ever close made it more difficult for me to recover.

Then one day in March, Lena Tenina, a perky, bubbly, red-haired fellow student, attractive in an unconventional, wild way, came to our room to borrow a book from me; she danced the mazurka, the polka, the polonaise, and a few others besides, and so steered me away from tormenting dead ends and toward a revival of my usual vitality and creativity.

We had been talking about our schools, and, always proud of mine, I mentioned that it had been the only Russian-language school in Riga to have ballroom dancing as a compulsory subject. Upon hearing this, without batting an eyelid, Lena, whose love of music would turn out to be as deep as my own, began to perform a couple of those dances there and then. Then she pushed away the table, to make room, and dragged me in to do figures with her as her male partner. I still remembered the drill from school and didn't do too badly. People came from other rooms to see this rare sight.

Taking a book for her from my shelf, I noticed all the other books there that looked unworried and deported themselves with appropriate gravitas; for the first time I considered my own highly-strung, disturbed state of mind which seemed out of place in their company. Handing Lena the book, I also noticed the way she looked at me. I thought she might be fond of me. I sincerely hoped she was: I liked her a lot and wondered how

I'd never really paid attention to this remarkable girl, full to the brim with life, graced by Terpsichore.

That night I had another long and involved dream. When I awoke, I could recall only two or three sharply drawn images and a few phrases spoken either by myself or by other actors in the dream. I jotted down what I remembered.

Leafless tree branches were wavering ceaselessly throughout the dream. Somebody said: "There are things still to be saved." There was moonlight and starlight; a solitary figure skating out of the light and then returning shouted over to me: "It's better to wait. Keep riding around the edges." And, just before being awakened by Grisha's customary thunderous nose blowing, I answered: "A song will help me do the impossible."

My dreams, full of poetry and imagery, continuing to haunt me, were one of the factors that would later drive me to seek a solution in mysticism and, ultimately, to suffer a nervous breakdown. It is a fascinating paradox that none other than Menachem Mendel Schneerson (1902?–1994), the Lubavitcher Rebbe, that venerable sage of the Chabad branch of Ultra-Orthodox Chassidic Judaism, tried to dissuade me from seeing the hand of God in my dreams. When, during our one-and-a-half-hour private meeting in New York, I, a twenty-one-year-old student still fresh from the University of Moscow, tried to persuade him that my dreams revealed the hand of God, he disagreed and told me that dreaming was essentially regurgitation of daily experiences. I won't go into the other-worldly qualities attributed to him by his followers, but I think now that this exceptionally kind and intelligent man must have seen before him a confused boy, bewildered by his encounter with religion, Israel, and the west in general, and tried to set him straight. He struck me as a born educator, and it wasn't for nothing that the United States Congress proclaimed his birthday USA Education Day. It was also indicative of his astute common-sense approach that during our meeting he, besides all other things, gently and tactfully hinted at the need for a young man of my age to get married. But I'll describe that meeting and our subsequent correspondence in detail later on.

There was a break of a few days in classes, and I decided to visit my Uncle David in Rzhev, a town a few hours from Moscow by coach.

The bus went by the city of Volokolamsk and, my imagination being largely auditory, I at once became excited by the sounds of its name. The three sonorants are truly beautiful, the three O's (which, like all Russian vowels, have the so-called Italian—rather than the English—value) in their phonetically reduced pronunciation both propel the impetus toward the end of the word and anticipate the final stressed A, which Lomonosov himself—in my opinion, the first truly great Russian poet—called the most splendid of all vowels. I composed a poem, there and then, on the rather uncomfortable bus seat. I was also thrilled by what I knew about the history of the place. Every Soviet pupil had to study in depth and memorize countless particulars of the Great Patriotic War in which the battles for that city also featured. For two months, between October and December 1941, Volokolamsk—less than one hundred miles from Moscow—was occupied by German troops pushing toward the capital. It was liberated—and Moscow saved—by the Twentieth Army under the leadership of Lieutenant-General Andrey Vlasov (although we were never told this last fact). Later this truly ill-fated man was executed and the city's military glory recognized and decorated.

That I knew; and I could also figure out from the name Volokolamsk that its history had to do with hauling (*volok*) boats along or over the River Lama. (In fact, its old name was *Volok na Lame*—Haul-upon-the-Lama; Novgorod merchants passed through this town—founded twelve years before Moscow—on their way to the lands of Ryazan and Moscow.)

Volokolamsk

Wring your hands till your arms are a river's
bends; a willow laughs calling me
to where the cranes fly above the Lama,
flooding, epithalamial as young love.

Their luminous path is an Alhambra, halberds,
Calabria, sculptured in those
huge alabaster clouds that back up
into a downpour, like unconscious laughter.

(1969, translated with Anne Stevenson)

I composed this poem on the bus between Volokolamsk and Rzhev; it became one of my very first English publications, appearing (in a different version) in *The Times Literary Supplement* in July 1982 and giving a much-needed boost to my perennial problem of self-esteem.

My uncle worked as a criminal investigator, and his wife Lillian was Party secretary at an industrial complex. Although ideologically we were at loggerheads, they were warm and hospitable people, and we rose above our political arguments. I also liked their two teenaged daughters; both had a sense of fun and treated me with a mixture of respect and teasing. The younger one, Rimma, could play the piano. They all wanted to hear my poetry; following my reading, Lillian said she'd enjoyed it but the kind of verse she enjoyed was simpler, poems about love and little everyday things by popular contemporary Soviet poets. She recited a few of her favorites: they weren't bad at all, coming from the heart, and I said so and was glad I didn't have any snobbish pretensions. Still, for me they were too straightforward, lacking the complex musical gambits and labyrinths of thought characteristic of great poetry.

Seeing me off, my uncle shoved a ten-rouble note into my pocket. I protested (admittedly weakly) to no avail. Since they had also plied me with home-made provisions, which made my suitcase quite heavy, on arriving back in Moscow, I decided I could afford a taxi.

"Can't take you," said the cabbie to a woman in front of me in the queue, "it's the other end of town and only yobs live there. I'll have to drive all the way back downtown empty-handed, with no fare." "You're a fishwife of a man," said the woman. "I'm surprised your wife hasn't chucked you." "I'm a sworn bachelor," said the man, unruffled and, after inquiring about my destination, told me to get in.

"Where shall I put my suitcase?" I asked him stupidly. I was still weak and lonely with depression and I guess that I was ingratiating myself in an attempt to make friends. There was no need to ask: I could have put it on the taxi floor, or on the seat, or in the boot. But the cabbie's answer was remarkable. "Put it on my head," he said.

When we got to the corner of Michurin and Lomonosov avenues, where my dorm was, the fare was four rubles. I gave him my uncle's ten-rouble note: I didn't have any other money. "Haven't you got anything smaller?" he asked. "No, sorry," I said. "Well, I can't break it," he said. "What the fuck, four rubles is fucking nothing, see you next time." Moscow cabbies, I thought and, flattered he saw me as a sort of pal, answered enthusiastically in the same manner: "Sure thing, fucking nothing! Thanks anyway!" He gave me a very puzzled look and I realized that something must have been wrong with the way I had echoed him. The "fucking" expressions which had been perfectly natural on his lips must have sounded false and forced coming from me. Not that I minded them coming from others, it was just that I had never used them myself.

In the evening, the three of us—Vitaly, Grisha, and myself—went to the *Slavyansky Bazaar* restaurant downtown. The middle-aged waitress was quite soulful and motherly, asking us every now and again if we were sure we could take more booze without falling over on our way home. We decided to give her a three-ruble tip. "No need, boys," she said. "I've already added three rubles to your bill."

Moscow again, I thought, and its people.

Next day, our university year's orderly approached us in the department corridor. "You've been taken off scholarship for a month because of your failure to attend," he said. He was the one taking attendance for every lecture (seminars and practical studies took place in small groups, which made it easy for the instructors of each one to check who was present or absent). Elected to this post for being particularly punctual and conscientious (and probably getting a few perks for this), he'd always sit in the front row and turn around just before or at the very beginning of a lecture to survey the students in the auditorium and tick off those present in his notebook.

It was bad news. The only one who allowed himself to wisecrack about it was Vitaly: he could survive perfectly well on his parents' money. "I might just about get by for a month," he said, "but my two chums will not, I'm afraid. One's depressed because his crumpet has dumped him, and the other's so short and puny that with no money for proper nutrition he'll be blown away by the wind."

Our orderly didn't laugh; he had no sense of humor. "I suggest you start attending," he said icily, "otherwise they'll take you off scholarship for good."

I begged my dad to help, making up some fiction or other, not having the guts to tell him the bitter and humiliating truth. He sent me the money without further ado.

It was just as well I had to get back to studies. And I was lucky not to have missed the very first lecture in the Physiology of the Higher Nervous Activity by Chepurnov. It was so absorbing that my analytical mind took over my whole being and dragged me into full concentration. After that one-and-a-half-hour lecture I felt mentally exhausted, as if I'd been swotting for an exam for a whole week non-stop.

Sergei Alexandrovich Chepurnov (1936–2007) specialized in human and animal physiology. The scope of his expertise was huge; his research appeared in *Neuroscience Research Communications*, *Brain Research*, *Physiology and Behavior*, *Neuropeptides*, and many other journals. At Moscow University he taught Physiology of the Central Nervous System and of Higher Nervous Functions in a number of departments.

When I came out into Marx Avenue, the sun was playing joyfully on the melting snow and all around things were dripping and shimmering. The air was nippy and moist. I went into Alexander Gardens. The earth around still-bare trees and pools of melting snow in flower beds smelled delicious with its tang of rejuvenation and dogs' and cats' activities.

I began to walk aimlessly along the river and on Sadovnicheskaya Embankment came across a group of winter bathers. Some of them were rubbing themselves with snow, their skin looking healthily red and raw. A strongly built woman of about forty in a brightly colored bathing costume and house slippers, a towel over her shoulder, winked at me conspiratorially, and a tattooed man in gym shoes just behind her even invited me:

"Why don't you join the club, young fellow?"

"I haven't got any swimming trunks with me," I said.

"I'll get changed in a moment and lend you mine—if you don't mind wearing mine, that is. And I'll let you have my towel too."

"I don't mind," I said. "It's just that I'm not used to winter bathing."

"You'll get used to it, don't worry, maybe just the first time you'll get inflamed lungs, but after that you'll take to it!"

"Leave the lad alone, Misha," the gaudily dressed woman intervened. "One shouldn't start getting used to cold water bathing in early March, the summer's the right time for that. Listen, lad, what's your name? I'm Ninel, nice to meet you. Why don't you write down our swimming club's phone number and give us a ring in about two or three months' time, let's say in May, about starting swimming then. Ask for Misha—Michael Kotlyarov—he's our famous winter swimmer, there was even an article about him in the papers, how he'd been ill but winter swimming saved his life—or ask for me, Ninel, there's no need to use the surname, my first name is unusual enough, it's Lenin backwards, didn't you guess?—we'll take care of you!"

"Thanks a lot," I said—and I really meant it.

An official-looking letter awaited me when I got back to the dorm. It was from *Yunost* literary magazine: another invitation to speak with the poetry editor.

My roommates were out, so I knocked on the door where Natalie, together with Lena Tenina the most intelligent woman student in our year and my and Vitaly's closest confidante among the girls, lived with three others.

"Natalie, I've been invited to see the poetry editor at *Yunost*."

"I've got a bottle of cognac. Shall we go to your room? The girls are all in."

"Yes, let's."

More was to follow.

CHAPTER 17: BETRAYAL

Just as with the *Literary Gazette*, nothing concrete came of *Yunost*. Likewise a prestigious periodical—although a monthly magazine rather than a daily newspaper—it was addressed, as its name (Youth) suggested, to young people. So when I came into the waiting hall and saw about a half dozen men there looking like my grandfather, I assumed they were staff, editors and deputy editors, especially as some of them were speaking to one another in low tones. I was told by the secretary to wait there for the poetry editor. Then a youngish man, perhaps in his early thirties, walked in briskly from the street and asked: "All of you boys to see me? Who's first?"—"Let the lad go in! Let him be first!"—said two or three old men all at once, good-naturedly enough but also, I felt, tongue in cheek.

"Don't give me everything," said the young fellow when I shoved more than half my oeuvre to date at him. "Choose three you think best."

"You are not untalented," he said after looking quickly at the three pieces. "But tell me this. Here you write about being betrayed by a friend. Have you ever been betrayed by a friend?"

"No I haven't," I answered honestly.

"Well, when you are, you'll write about it differently," he said. "Then come again with new poems."

There was a postscript to this. Esther Vilensky, my distant relative in Moscow and a student in my department two years my senior, was friends with one of the poetry editor's deputies at *Yunost*, a young woman in her mid- to late twenties. She showed her my poems and the girl liked them. She was single, and she agreed to meet me—not in the offices in the morning but in town in the evening! This sounded more like a date than a business meeting and raised my hopes both for a publication and a romance. But, as usual, I was late for the date and missed her. She wouldn't agree to give me another chance, no matter how much I begged Esther to intercede on my behalf.

Natalie and Lena Tenina were there to console me.

Their room was a female version of ours.

Students in our department fell naturally into a number of categories. There were the alcoholics-cum-"sex giants," as we christened them: tall, broad-shouldered young men who'd already done their military service, and had work experience, usually at a factory or some sort of other manual job like loading cargoes at a railway station or port. Girls loved them; they were always getting into brawls and seducing married female students. Almost invariably non-Muscovites, they lived in the dorm, hardly doing any studying but drinking a lot. Sometimes they would come, separately or in small groups, to our room and ask me to recite my poetry. Hoping they'd ask him too (which they never did), Grisha was too afraid of their size to say anything. They liked my verses, although on one occasion, having recited a particularly romantic poem, I was asked: "But have you fucked her?"—and told off for writing an idealized romance rather than from real-life experience. (Amusingly enough, that reminded me of Andrei Sobol's criticism that my "Poem of the Journey" had not been written in a third-class compartment; nevertheless, rather than dismissing them glibly, I still think that there is something to be said for my critics' approach in both cases.)

Then there were the well-brought up and ideologically conformist boys, good-natured and usually quite childish. They took their studies very seriously, eschewed drinking and every kind of prank, never risking their grades and ensuring they were in the good books of lecturers and instructors. They were harmless but dull. Another, mercifully small, group included committed ideologues and informers.

A few were something in between, and I saw two of them as friends: Zhora Ilyin and Vladimir Shestakov. Older and more experienced, they were neither drinkers nor ideologues; putting their careers first and everything else second, they weren't interested in dissident political views but would not betray those of others.

Finally, there were a couple of mentally unstable young men, whose disorders must have progressed, as they ultimately left the department for the psychiatric hospital in Kashchenko on the outskirts of Moscow.

The three of us—Vitaly, Grisha, and myself—were difficult to put into categories. We were just different. Perhaps our most important common denominator was an uncompromising political awareness. That was also why we befriended Yosio Sato from Tokyo: as a foreigner, he was also different. It's a sign of our total lack of caution that we talked politics in his presence with total abandon. Although we were certain then that he wouldn't betray us, when I put the question to myself now, I'm unable to answer with the same degree of assurance. I still tend to think he never did, but who knows? Once in one of our classes—most probably Party History—the topic came up of young dissidents demonstrating in Red Square, and he said, in tone with the teacher's blistering criticism of them and in his foreigner's Russian: "Only conscience is needed for such youths." We teased him afterwards, but good-naturedly, understanding his desire to blend in and please everybody. He smiled, a bit shamefacedly. Among ourselves we came to the conclusion that his Japanese friend Kato, who occasionally came to see him, would never play up to an alien ideology. Yosio came from the working class, and to that we attributed his weird habit of always tying his socks around the metal frame of his bed before going to sleep. Whatever his reasons, we thought this rather inconsiderate toward us, his roommates. He himself told us that Kato belonged to the upper crust of Japanese society, with some sort of old samurai connection. The two of them looked and walked in very different ways, reminding me of the two Jews, poor and rich, in Mussorgsky's masterpiece, *Pictures from an Exhibition*.

Yosio finally moved out of our room: Vitaly's rudeness must have been the last straw for him. I now realize that he was not only within his rights but in the right ethically. Older than us and from a poor family, he was on some kind of scholarship and student exchange program; it was absolutely essential for him to graduate. He was also handicapped by his weak Russian. So he spent all his time in reading rooms and when he came in for the night, he wanted to have a proper night's sleep. Our bohemian ways didn't allow this. One night, when Vitaly and I were arguing and quarreling through the early hours of the morning, he finally pleaded for us to quieten down so he could get some sleep. "Is there anything else you want?" retorted Vitaly, still in the heat of our row. After Yosio moved to another room, we asked him, piqued, whether his new, totally mediocre roommates were more to his taste. He answered that it hadn't been better roommates he was looking for but a quieter place—which he'd now got.

His successor was a student with some sort of mental disorder—bipolar or schizo-phrenic—who spent the whole day in bed with his head under the blanket and who in due course had to be hospitalized in Kashchenko.

The women students didn't really drink and there were no great sexual heroines among them. In the main they could be divided into the young and naïve girls and the more mature ones who were either married or hoped to be so, especially to catch a Musco-vite, if they had come from other places. More of them than among the boys were bent on an academic career and studied very hard; also, more girls were mentally unstable, ending up in what we called the "Kashchenko loony bin."

Natalie and Lena's room was a good case in point. They and their more reserved roommate Olga were mavericks in a number of ways and, just like the three of us, they flocked together. But their successive fourth roommates (both called Lidia) one after the other had a nervous breakdown and ended up in the Kashchenko loony bin. (At least one of them was cured: before hospitalization, she'd gone on and on about how the best man to lose one's virginity with was someone like a tractor driver rather than an intellectual; the last we heard of her was that she left Kashchenko pregnant and became a secretary somewhere or other. We joked that she must have found her tractor driver in the bushes around the mental institution.)

Incidentally, one may well wonder why a psychology department had so many stu-dents with psychological problems. My own guess is that there were two main reasons for this, one to do with the subject, the other with the place. Quite a few young people were unstable to begin with and went to study psychology in the hope of dealing with their own difficulties; and Moscow life exerted huge pressures on many first-timers from the provinces, especially girls.

Lena had wanted to study art history but this, like foreign relations, being an elitist field of study, reserved for children of Party nabobs, she had to settle for something where competition was less intense than one place for two hundred or so candidates.

Natalie was tougher, had a stronger psyche and less kindness than Lena. But she was ready to fall in love, and that must have pushed her toward me with my spontaneity and poetry. She had a beautifully thoughtful face (and I think she might well have been the brightest and the deepest of the two) and no self regard. When listening, she'd look down, absorbing and analyzing.

Once, Natalie, Lena, and I had a brainstorming session in order to find out ways for me to earn money through my poetry. The joint effort gave birth to a fascinating idea. All I needed to do was make a kind of blank bar, a template to be filled in according to the occasion the country was celebrating. Lenin's birthday, April 22, was coming up, and I wrote verses describing him standing over the Volga, looking into the distance and seeing far ahead with his eagle's eyes and so on. Then, it was decided, I would just substitute the celebrated occasion for Lenin's name, make one or two other small changes—like standing next to the furnace, or at the helm, or on the Motherland's borders, or over the control column—and hey presto, send it to the appropriate publication, like *Astronaut's Journal*, *Miner's Own*, *Pilot's Weekly*, or *Border Sentinel*. And no doubt money would start pouring in as out of the horn of plenty, because all Soviet publications paid most generously. Alas, the venture failed as soon as it began. The answer I got from the poetry editor of Moscow's *Lenin's Path* newspaper read: "If you write seriously, do send something else in."

"You can blackmail him," wisecracked Grisha. "You can say that unless he publishes something of yours and pays up, you'll forward both your Lenin verses and his reply to the KGB and let them investigate why a man on an ideological job does not consider a poem greeting the Leader's birthday 'serious.'"

(But I, upon rethinking the whole thing, decided that I was lucky to be left in peace. The poem was so obviously bogus that the editor would have had a better case against me than I against him. My return address made it obvious I was a Moscow University student, and it would have taken an empowered official only a few minutes to track me down and inform those on ideological guard that so-and-so in such-and-such department pokes fun at Lenin's memory.)

We had noticed the girls early on, at the beginning of our first year, after a lecture in Party History. The lecturer spoke of the "positive aspects" of Stalin's personality cult and most weirdly explained away Lenin's confirmation of a death sentence pronounced on a group of Russian intellectuals "I welcome their execution" by saying, "Wouldn't you close the window if someone was swearing outside—and at you to boot?" What shocked me most, though, was his reference to the *kulaks*, peasants who through hard work and frugality had become well-to-do and, as a result, had been liquidated with the utmost brutality by Stalin as "class enemies." My mother, in the course of her scathing attacks on my father and his faithfulness to the Party, had described that chapter in Party history with a heart-rending eloquence: "A peasant breaks his back trying to provide for his family, saves every last kopeck—and then those thugs come and confiscate everything and send him with his wife, and more often than not their children as well, to Siberia to kill them there through hunger, malnutrition, and disease." ("The Party denounced the personality cult in the strongest possible terms!" my father tried to argue—weakly, in my young boy's opinion.)

This is how our Party Lecturer put it: "You see a little peasant with a little weedy beard—he seems to be quite ordinary and puny—but no, he turns out to be a *kulak*—and so off he goes. Goodbye and good riddance!"

In the faculty canteen after the lecture we overheard the three girls speaking among themselves about the man's remarks; we asked to join them—and so became friends.

The ever-practical and goal-oriented Vitaly had early marked Natalie as his life companion. But she wasn't really interested in him. When she invited me to visit her at her hometown on the Black Sea during our first summer break, I couldn't go (I felt guilty enough as it was, without "abandoning" my mother for the vacation in addition to the whole year!) but he had shown up at her home instead and seduced her. He told me afterwards that she had thought it was a kind of collusion between the two of us, that I had sent him to test her, sort of. Well, test or not, she succumbed. I might well have done so myself, if I were her, finding his intellect and wit irresistible. The trouble, from her point of view, was that she was romantic—which he wasn't. She was also basically decent—which he, again, wasn't.

Back in Moscow, she'd tried to keep both of us at her side. It was an odd situation.

Seeking a woman's closeness after Anna, I chatted up a lovely student from another department and invited her over. On weekends and public holidays, Vitaly was away. Natalie came by, joined us, got drunk and lachrymose. My guest, a kind-hearted girl, fussed over her. Having brought Natalie back to her room and tucked her in, she saw it was late and returned to her own dormitory. She wouldn't come again. Twice more I plucked up enough courage to speak to strange girls and invite them for a visit—and a similar thing happened, Natalie showing up, taking over the conversation, drinking and sobbing disconsolately. Time would pass and my new guest would depart. Those girls must have concluded she was my girlfriend in distress and, being considerate (I must have intuitively chosen the ethical ones!), didn't want to come between us.

Vitaly's boast to his parents' university colleague has stuck in my mind. "No woman can be unfaithful to me!" he'd announced. "A woman?" she'd queried sarcastically. "A woman can." Zhora, the only person I confided in about Natalie's ways with me, shook his head and said pityingly: "You're a boy but she's a woman."

I didn't quite understand what this was supposed to mean. She was one of my best friends, with similar thoughts, likes and dislikes, sense of humor, ethics, and so on. I saw her as female only physically but not psychologically—so much so that on one occasion following some remark of hers, I burst out exclaiming triumphantly, as though catching her at something forbidden: "See, see, that's the woman in you speaking!" To which she replied, quite sensibly: "But I *am* a woman—so why shouldn't I be speaking like one?"

When Vitaly was about to go away for a few days, she wrote me a note saying, "He'll be gone soon, and I have a bottle of cognac." Once he returned, he sensed something and pressed Grisha, who could hardly have failed to notice at least some of what had been going on in Vitaly's absence, and spilled the beans. "You've stolen the last penny from a holy fool," complained Vitaly. For both his sake and Natalie's, I played down our tryst, but I found his melodramatic accusations dishonorable and undeserved. Even if they were intimate, he wasn't even her steady boyfriend yet, let alone fiancé, let alone husband, and I thought it was terribly unfair to demand of me that kind of restraint, considering she took the initiative. I wouldn't have answered Natalie's call if I hadn't been attracted to her—an attraction which had given me what I still consider one of my best love lyrics.

Natalie was outstandingly bright and sensitive; her appreciation of my poetry meant a lot to me. I think I was in love with her—less obviously, less madly erotically than I had been with Anna, but perhaps in a deeper and more mature way. Still, I never thought of her as a woman by my side because marriage was the last thing on my mind. By then, I was quite seriously considering leaving the country for good. My mother's brother and my cousins had emigrated to Israel two or three years before, and she had started talking to me about applying for an exit visa, risky though such a move was. Poetry had become all-encompassing for me, and I saw clearly that I'd never be able to publish in the Soviet Union without compromising my values first and toeing the Party line at least to some degree. Watching the most popular poets in the country, Yevtushenko and Voznesensky, being tamed and put into golden cages, and Joseph Brodsky, whose poetry had circulated in *samizdat*, tried and sentenced for "parasitism," had sent an unambiguous signal. Being married would have made obtaining an exit visa considerably more difficult.

That was also why I never thought of marrying Natalie's friend and roommate Lena, a gem of a girl, with whom I soon became intimate.

Lena and Natalie were the closest of friends, but they were different. Lena was innocent (I was her first man), sweet, funny, impressionable, open, and incapable of scheming. Natalie's manipulativeness was part of her overall stronger edge. She was very ambitious and totally unsentimental. I've always remembered how she stamped at pigeons in the street to scare them off. "I hate pigeons," she said, quite proudly. I took exception to this: after all, they hadn't done her any harm and hadn't even been in her way. Throughout her life, my mother had taken care after meals to put breadcrumbs out on the eaves for the birds.

When Lena and I became lovers, Natalie must have somehow persuaded her that there could be no long-term harm in her continuing friendship with me, but when later it came to her own grip on Vitaly, she kicked up a row over one perfectly natural trip he and Lena had made to the local cinema when Natalie herself was away for a couple of weeks. I have Lena's letter to me: as usual, without any malice, she jokes about Natalie cruelly interrogating her upon returning to Moscow: "But why did you go to the cinema with him? Couldn't you go with anybody else? With Olga? Even with Grisha? Why him in particular?"

It was Natalie who told me that Lena had aborted my child.

One night, Lena's pubic hair felt prickly to the touch, and I realized it had been shaved off. When I asked her why, she refused to tell me. After Natalie spilled the beans, I asked Lena why she hadn't put me in the picture. "What would I have told the child if I'd kept him and he'd asked about his father? Point at the portrait in a gilded frame on the wall and say: 'Your Dad was a Polar explorer and was eaten by white bears on an ice floe'?"

Her action had been nobly selfless, like everything she did. Going through the abortion (clandestinely, through a private doctor) without telling me had saved me, as it was meant to, pangs of conscience and shared responsibility for the decision. Lena must have also thought that informing me might have seemed like blackmail, as if to say, I've got your child, now you must marry me!

Still, it would take me nearly two years after having seen Lena for the last time to write, in Paris, a lyrical poem addressed to her. When I was with Natalie, a poem created itself spontaneously, as it were, and I read it out to her. Although I found her antagonism toward pigeons puzzling, her tenacity and single-minded drive to get what she wanted must have deep down appealed to me.

In his attempts to get rid of me as a competitor, Vitaly used dastardly methods. Himself basically a teetotaler, he manipulated my weakness for drinking in order to embarrass me before the girl. Thus, once having volunteered to pay for a bottle of fortified wine, while himself sipping only a token amount, he egged me on: "This will be too much for you!"

"No it won't!" I swallowed the bait without much ado, protesting hotly as my manly pride was questioned. "See for yourself!"

After downing a brimming glass, having drunk three-quarters of the one-liter bottle, I proudly showed off my sobriety by walking up and down the room. "Well, one more will surely be beyond your abilities!" he announced with confidence.

"Wait and see!" I gulped down another glass.

"And what about what's left at the bottom? Down the hatch or shall we leave it for tomorrow? I'm not really a seasoned drinker like you, as you know," he excused himself.

So I finished the whole thing, and then he suggested visiting the girls in their room. Half-drunk but seeing myself as an intellectual and witty genius, I must have cut a pathetic figure, which was precisely Vitaly's intention.

But apparently Natalie still wouldn't hold this against me. So then he must have come up with a stratagem as brilliant as it was immoral.

This was against the background of our neglect of our studies. A number of older relatives visited and commented on it. The first was my dad; then came Vitaly's own father. Professor of Philosophy, he was the son of a pig man and had himself been a swineherd as a small boy. Just as with the Pale of Settlement Jews, the Revolution had freed these people and opened for them all doors to education. But this immensely brainy and taciturn man, whom I liked a lot ("Kiss your kindred soul for me," he'd written to Vitaly, referring to me, before coming to Moscow in person), was totally devoid of illusions about the nature of the Soviet regime.

A hard-working intellectual who had achieved everything through his own efforts, he must have been very critical of our attitude to academic work, and I'm not at all sure he liked me. Vitaly conveyed his father's comments to me afterwards: "Dubnov is a poet, so it may be all right for him. But you are not. You must take college seriously, otherwise you won't get anywhere."

Tall and gaunt, he walked even faster than I did (and my walk, which I had inherited from my own father, was almost proverbial), holding his hands behind his back. It seemed that while walking he was thinking incessantly. That aroused both my admiration and envy, as I would more often than not be immersed in memory or imagination than in pure thought.

Then came my uncle David from Rzhev. He noticed the unswept floor and the general disarray and, with his criminal investigator's eye and ear, briefly appraised my roommates. Reserved and tactful, he only asked me about my grades. My average was about a B or B minus, but I told him it was an A minus. "I'm surprised," he said. "I was absolutely certain it was an A, if not an A plus."

The last visitor's judgment was the most scathing. It was pronounced by my elder sister Milla's husband Simon, who was some fifteen years my senior. He already had a bone to pick with me. In order to complete his doctorate in medicine on pancreatic cancer, he needed a bibliography to be appended. The library in Tselinograd where they lived didn't have that sort of information, and he'd asked me to copy down all the titles and authors' names of articles on the subject in the Central Library of Medicine in Moscow. He'd given me some sort of identification card with no photo and warned that I'd have to be at the door no later than seven in the morning, as the library opened at eight and, because it was housed in small premises, people started queuing long before that. To get there at seven I had to get up at the ungodly hour of six, which I had been postponing endlessly, until at last I managed it—only to fail in the task itself. There were dozens upon dozens of relevant articles in the abstracts, and very quickly I got fed up with copying all the details he'd asked for and began to omit the initials of the authors, thinking that surely the surname alone would suffice. Needless to say, my handiwork turned out to be of no use to him, and he had to do everything himself when in Moscow on some kind of mission from the Institute of Medical Research in Tselinograd. So, on his arrival at my dorm to look me up, I must already have been in his bad books. Seeing our room and talking to me didn't make him any better disposed. "Just imagine this," he told my mother later, in front of me, "I come into their room, and what do I see? The three of them lying fully dressed on their beds—at seven in the evening! The room itself is untidy, somebody's sweater on the floor, books in disarray on the shelves. Your son at least jumped up promptly to greet me, and one of his roommates had the courtesy to stand up and say hello, but the other one [Vitaly] remained lying there on his stomach, with his shoes on and his bum pointing at the ceiling—without saying a word. Those are his friends! It's difficult to say this to a mother, but the truth, however bitter, must be told: this young man here may be a complete good for nothing!"

I had considerable respect for Simon and understood his attitude, even though I was terribly hurt by his complete dismissal of me offered to my mother in front of me. An ambitious and dedicated physician, he had always worked hard to achieve his goal and had no patience with slackers. He wasn't interested in literature, and my poems meant nothing to him. But still I had always thought his stubborn overconfidence to be a flaw, and it would, in fact, lead to his untimely death, when he misdiagnosed an internal pain as a gastroenterological problem, whereas it was to do with his heart. Neglecting to be properly examined by a medical specialist, time and again telling my sister that he was a doctor himself and knew what his own problem was, he died of a heart attack.

All the criticism notwithstanding, we never really changed our indolent ways (when I happened to phone the dorm from downtown at two on a Sunday afternoon, I was told: "They're sleeping in their beds and neither wants to come to the phone, as yet," that *as yet* nearly making me die laughing), and managed to get by with a minimum of work, mostly through our natural aptitude or by sheer luck. One example of the latter I find both amusing and flattering to myself.

Our regular instructor in applied psychology being on a sick leave, I was told to submit my paper (a practical assignment) to one Filonov, who taught in the Forensic Science Department. I handed him the sheets.

"Why's everything here crossed out?" the man, quite young, probably in his early thirties, seemed over the moon.

"It's not crossed out," I said. "It's my handwriting."

He grew serious and began to look closely at the first page.

God forbid—the thought flashed through my mind—that he should start reading it attentively and see what rubbish I've written.

"Very unusual." He finally tore himself away from my handiwork. "You think in images."

"Mmm," I hummed contentedly, to humor him, not knowing how best to react.

"Come again another day, your handwriting is of interest to me. I have to go to a symposium now," he said, returning the sheets.

"And what about the pass?" My heart sank.

"Oh, I've quite forgotten. You want an A?"

"No thanks, there are no grades. Just a pass."

"Curious way of writing: developed ability to think in images," he said while signing my exam booklet.

There were two exams that presented a real problem: English for Vitaly and higher mathematics for me. He knew he'd never pass the English test without my help. So he made an arrangement with me. I was to prepare him for English, and he would bail me out at the test in probability theory by sitting next to me and solving the problems and matrixes I got from the examiner. I had no doubt he was able to do it: the high school he had gone to had a particular strength in mathematics. We failed to sit these exams (I was exempted from English anyway) on schedule with everybody else as he wasn't ready for the one, nor I for the other; we needed time for me to coach him to re-sit English. I should have felt ashamed of myself for taking the easiest way out instead of making an effort and studying probability theory myself (my school was also pretty good for math, in which my final grade had been an A), but I had been putting off serious college work for too long and didn't feel up to the challenge.

He passed English all right but he didn't help me with probability when it came up a week after, and so I failed. I've always remembered his little smile when he told me he couldn't solve the two problems I had on my exam sheet.

The plump and kindly examiner, our lecturer in probability theory from the Faculty of Mech & Math, was in tears sending me away with an F: "If you didn't have it in you, then it wouldn't be so terrible, but you have, you have! I remember some of your answers from the floor at the beginning of the semester."

"It's all right," I mumbled, consoling her. "I've just neglected the course a little bit—but I'll retake the exam in September and get an A."

"Yes, I am sure you will!" she exclaimed, brightening up a bit but still looking let down.

Lena, who was in the same examination auditorium, told me how, after I'd been sent away with an F, Vitaly had stayed and helped a few other students with their difficulties: "presumably to make himself popular," she said. She also made sure other students knew about the episode: with her usual refusal to keep quiet about injustice, she was most vocal telling everybody she could collar about how my supposed staunchest friend had passed the English test thanks to my tutoring and had now violated our trust and betrayed me. I don't think anybody was interested: they had their own problems, and anyway it was the very end of the academic year and people had to prepare for the summer break. So did I. Back in the dorm, Vitaly told me that he honestly couldn't have solved the most difficult problems I'd been given; as for helping others before his own—successful, needless to say—presentation of his exam sheets, he said Lena's report was hysterically overblown. He had helped only one person sitting next to him, who'd begged for assistance and whose matrix was very easy—but that was all. Anyway, he said, surely there was a limit to cheating without being caught and reprimanded even in this exam, where examiners were quite lenient and took into account the difficulty of the subject. You could surreptitiously and quickly help solve a tiny elementary problem for somebody riding shotgun, but surely not for anyone else in the auditorium!

I return again and again in my mind to that episode. Calling someone a liar is a serious accusation. All of us sometimes allow ourselves a little falsehood, hopefully harmless; psychological research shows that children who always tell the truth are maladjusted. A *liar*, however, is someone who specializes in the art of artifice; someone to whom lying is a natural recourse. Vitaly was such a one. I had no talent for deception and could be no match for him.

He was the closest friend I had in the Soviet Union. I liked his sharp mordant wit and his fortitude. I still cherish many fond memories of these. Once, in an obvious attempt to ingratiate himself with the instructor, at a seminar a student declared that longevity could not be greater than in "our country." Vitaly loudly objected: "Methuselah lived longer, even though he didn't live in our country. The Lord God doesn't live in our country either but lives eternally!" (Even if no student, in a country where all were supposed to be out-and-out atheists, would have taken this seriously, the lecturer might have; the episode was typical of Vitaly's audacity.) His typical sayings were bitterly cynical: "God created woman so that man should not become cocky and forget he's an animal. The moment he wants to tear himself from the earth and soar high above, a woman appears and he again becomes a beast. There are two things which do not let him grow arrogant: lice and women." Or: "A thinker is a eunuch in life's harem." Or: "Don't blame life: all's well that ends well."

Basically a humanist, I couldn't really share these attitudes, but I saw and sympathized with this frustration of a widely read young thinker surrounded by intellectual inferiors and dependent, at his hormonal peak, on a woman's favor. (For me it was fondness, warmth and regard—if not outright love—for the girl that gave intimacy its meaning, though I did make allowances for his attitude.) It was a rare pleasure of male bonding, of a conspiracy of dissident views when nothing needed to be said and we'd just exchange brief glances as the Party History lecturer referred to "enemy poets." I loved his story from his childhood, when he'd taken literally a speaker's imaginative metaphor about the red walls of his hometown's university "being painted with the patriots' blood" and, amazed, had tried to calculate how much blood would have been required to paint such a huge building. And I had a veritable fit of guffaws when I happened to be a witness of Vitaly's generous offer to two partners at cards who'd just lost money to him. He suggested that he cancel their debt if they danced, holding hands, naked, in the light of the moon somewhere outside the dorm, away from the view of the authorities. I could see they wanted to agree: one was blushing heavily and, like a fish, opening and closing his lips silently, while the other kept sighing heavily and making weird movements with his head. But they must have been embarrassed to accept the deal in my—and perhaps even each other's—presence.

I was never to see, speak, or correspond again with Vitaly after leaving the country. Following the test on the theory of probability, we met twice: once when I revisited Moscow and the second time when he came to see me in Riga. On that last occasion, when I was down with depression, he demonstrated subtle verbal cruelty, thinking, as was his wont, that I wouldn't cotton on. That finally convinced me of his character. People are obviously complex, but still I think they may be weighed on their negativity and positivity—the measure of light and darkness in them. With all his excellent qualities, there was a preponderance of murk in Vitaly. I do not regret having parted ways with him.

As it turned out, I would never have to retake that exam. Instead, two years later, to the day, I would leave the country for good.

CHAPTER 18: LIGHT BEYOND THE WINDOW

One morsel of luck came my way on the eve of my departure for home: a three-and-a-half ruble honorarium for my translation into Russian of a long poem by a Tuva poet whose name I no longer remember. I did not know the Tuva language—a Turkic dialect with many Mongolian words (the Tuva Republic lies in the extreme south of East Siberia and has a long border with Mongolia)—but a fellow student by the name of Artyna was a Tuvan and he had given me a literal crib. It had actually been his idea to begin with: students from national republics were as a rule proud of their cultural heritage and wanted to bring it to the awareness of Russian speakers, and he had approached me as a sort of unofficial "poet in residence." However, the poem had a passage with the obligatory glorification of the October Revolution, which I simply couldn't bring myself to translate. So I'd made a deal with Grisha, offering him the ideological bit and half of the future payment, while keeping the other sections, about the nature, seasons, and landscape, for myself. (Grisha hadn't minded in the least and did a decent job.)

The translation was printed in some Russian-language publication in Tuva's capital, Kyzyl: it must have been a magazine as the poem would have been too long for a newspaper. I do remember the letter from its editor, which accompanied the honorarium. It praised the translation and said that the poet—still young and a good swimmer—had since drowned in the strong current of a local river.

Having diluted my sorrow at the failed exam in booze, which I had asked Lena to share with me, I had only two rubles left for the rail ticket back to Riga; the cost was about ten rubles. So I begged Grisha to let me owe him half the money and keep the three-and-a-half rubles toward the ticket. He was kind enough to agree.

Now I was faced with the difficult task of negotiating with a train conductor at Moscow's Riga Station. I sent Lena to do the job. The woman conductor agreed to take me in for the five rubles as a ticketless passenger, provided I knew my place. So I sat on my suitcase by the door near the lavatory, where I was to spend the rest of the journey, from evening until the following morning.

Before Rzhev, the conductor came to me: "That's your lot, next stop off you get, can't go further."

"How do you mean?" I couldn't believe my ears. "My girlfriend made an arrangement with you, didn't she? I've given you five rubles for you to take me to Riga, haven't I?"

"The situation's changed; there is a danger of ticket inspectors coming aboard in Rzhev. I'm not losing my job because of you."

"What do I do now?"

"How should I know? Buy a ticket like everyone else."

"If I'd had the money for the ticket, would I have given you five rubles?"

"Well, arrange it with someone else, then."

"I have nothing left! I gave you everything I had!"

The woman shrugged indifferently in reply: "If you don't leave on your own, I'll call the police."

I got off the train and walked along it. The stop was five minutes. If the worst came to the worst, I could surprise my Rzhev relatives, spend the night with them, and ask for money, but I hated the idea. All I wanted was to get home. At an opportune moment, when the conductor of another carriage had gone inside—for no longer than a minute, as all of them had to stand on the carriage steps signaling with their lanterns when the train was about to move off—I climbed the stairs and hid in the lavatory.

Two hours later, the pounding on the door became unbearable, and I had to get out. I was dropped off by the conductor at the next station, Velikiye Luki. It was the middle of the night and, despite the summer, terribly cold. But I was lucky once more: three cars down another woman conductor was handing a drunk over to the local police.

"I'm-m … among other things … m-mistreated b-by fate," protested the drunk. "I've been, b-by the way, b-beaten up, v-very incidentally."

"No one here will believe your stories! It's you have beaten up others," she was pushing him out. "You've drawn blood from two innocent passengers for nothing! And all because of the booze." She turned to the policemen. "He's drunk two bottles of vodka and broken six glasses. Who will compensate me?"

"Don't panic," said one of the policemen, moving away slightly to let me in, "we'll write everything down in a moment, you'll sign, and I'll countersign it, and those six glasses will be written off so you won't have to worry … But tell me this—where do you live?"

"Moscow—I'm a born Muscovite," the woman brightened up. "Oh, I don't know how to thank you, I was afraid I'd have to pay out of my own pocket. And everyone knows what miserable pay we conductors get!"

"Why don't you come to visit us some time? I could show you around the place. Velikiye Luki isn't Moscow of course, but there are also things to see. There's a hotel which isn't bad at all."

"But where will I find you?" the woman blushed. She must have been no older than thirty and quite good looking.

"What's there to find? Nothing could be easier! Police Department, Senior Lieutenant Selivanov Vladimir. And your name?"

"Irina."

The end of the conversation I never heard, for I was once again hiding in the lavatory. There were no more stops before Riga.

Upon my arrival in Riga, I was met with Daniel Michelson's negative report on me to my mother.

But I shouldn't have worried: my mother couldn't care less, as my carrying on with my studies at Moscow University formed no part of her plans. It would take me many years to realize that her primary purpose was to get revenge on my father for having left her for another woman, by taking his three children forever away from him. While I'd been in Moscow, she had hatched a plot to apply for an exit visa to Israel for both of us and later to persuade my sisters with their husbands to follow. As a result, my father would remain alone with his "old rag" and her grown-up daughter, who cared nothing for him.

After my haphazard but still rational and more or less structured life in Moscow, Riga greeted me with—and would soon totally engulf me in—a dim, surrealist world. Moscow was creativity, intellect, and attainment of general and academic knowledge. Riga quickly became a mix of unbearable physical longing and incipient and only vaguely defined religious faith.

The first salvo and harbinger of things to come was my reunion with Joseph Bein. My friendship with this gifted but mentally unbalanced older poet would accompany me for many years, his emotional support and, vicariously, his talent encouraging me, but his chaotic, anarchistic ways undermining all my scholarly aspirations.

I traveled to see Bein at his home on the outskirts of the city. He never let anybody into his apartment, where he lived with his wife and six children: it was part of his many superstitious hang-ups. Not that I minded: I admired him as a poet, loved his wonderful sing-song way of reciting his verses, and felt flattered that somebody much older and already a local celebrity—albeit minor—would befriend me. Also, I actually preferred, as I always did, to be outside, in the fresh air and in the park. There I met him and his friend by the Latvian name of Gegermanis, older yet than Bein, stooped, sad-looking, a drop constantly hanging from the tip of his crooked nose.

I went nearly gaga from their spontaneous witty exchanges. Bein's friend, whom he called Geger and who seemed to be quite a learned man, quoting freely from Greek philosophers, asked Bein to help find him a job as a lavatory attendant and to buy him a drum. Bein made a counter-proposal offering to buy a regimental banner in which to wrap Geger's mortal remains. Then he said he had a present for him and unfolded a pair of white stockings. I guessed that he'd bought them for his wife or daughter, and I burst out laughing. But Geger didn't even smile: he examined the material and said they weren't warm enough because autumn was approaching.

Bein suggested that I recite a few of my poems for his friend's benefit and evaluation: "Geger knows a lot: don't be misled by the way he looks."

I felt very shy reading out my verses to strangers—unless I was inebriated and the stranger was a pretty girl—but Geger encouraged me, quite gently: "Yes, I'd like to hear some of your work. Joseph has told me you're gifted."

I recited four or five poems. "From Russian song through Mussorgsky to Stravinsky," he said. "Visually, Čiurlionis, Goncharova, and Kandinsky."

I was mystified. "I hardly know anything about Stravinsky—and I've seen only a couple of paintings by Goncharova and Kandinsky!"

"Don't worry, everything's in good time," he nodded sagely.

"Geger doesn't only diagnose the present: he also predicts the future," said Bein.

I was stupid enough not to ask about the man's background and education.

As we walked around the hilly park, Bein occasionally addressed various people there.

"Tell me, uncle," he said to a woman sitting on a bench rocking a baby in a pram, "surely it wasn't for nothing that Moscow, burned by the fire, was surrendered to the French?" He was, of course, quoting Lermontov's famous "Borodino" poem; put to a contemporary woman, a total stranger, the question sounded hilarious. At this time of day, most people on the benches were women with children or infants; they all seemed to enjoy his tomfoolery. Perhaps some of them even fancied him: with a huge forehead, penetrating, immensely intelligent eyes, and a thick red beard, he looked like a Biblical prophet—or at least like Walt Whitman.

"Can I and my two friends carry on walking?" he asked another woman.

"Why, certainly," she answered good-naturedly.

As we climbed the path, he sang a few lines of a popular song over her head and, upon our descent back to the path's lower reaches, asked her: "Who was it singing up there?"

"It was you!" she smiled.

"No it wasn't. Not me."

"Who was it then?"

"Why, the First Secretary of the Communist Party Comrade Brezhnev!" he explained matter of factly, as you would a common scientific phenomenon to a small child.

I envied his total lack of embarrassment, self-consciousness, and self-regard, which I could never hope to attain. But throughout his pranks, Geger was muttering under his breath: "I have nothing and no one. Nobody owes anything to anybody." He cut an almost tragic figure in his loneliness. Despite his unkempt appearance, he seemed endowed with a kind of stern nobility.

This was to be my world—part of it anyway—for the next two years, one of the most difficult periods of my life.

No sooner had I stepped down from the train than Mother began her well-thought-out and prepared assault on me. Her aim was to persuade me to leave university and apply for the exit visa—a move involving very grave risks to a young person's future in an authoritarian state.

She insisted I come along when she was visiting her friends, and I found it difficult to refuse, much as I hated those visits. Her fierce pride demanded an escort, and I felt I owed it to her. Her friends fell into two categories, of which the first, religious, was by far the preferred one. The second, passionate secular Zionists, were only tolerated, as temporary allies and an aid in the task of helping me reach the decision she wanted.

Ironically, at least half of the latter group went on to use Israel as a transit station, ending up in the States, Canada, or Germany, but I don't want to judge other people's lives and values. I was quite willing to be persuaded, and only a little Zionist and religious indoctrination was needed. In fact, unbeknownst to all of them, my main reasons for emigration were neither nationalist nor metaphysical but political and artistic. I dreamt of living in a free country where people were not imprisoned after demonstrations and where dissidents were not put in mental institutions to ruin their psyches for life; in a country where one's art had a chance of becoming appreciated without the need to praise the Party. Having said that, I was also caught up in the resurgence of Jewish honor and self-assertion all over the USSR, which followed the astounding Israeli victory in the Six Day War. The Soviet media had openly sided with the Arabs it had armed, and had appeared to look forward to the annihilation of Israel. I noticed, too, how valor and daring elicited the respect of not only Latvians, who'd cheer any small country's fight for freedom against overwhelming odds—especially against Russian interests—but also many Russians, who admired military prowess and resented their money being sent abroad to support various tinpot dictators (especially of what they considered to be inferior peoples).

The risks in asking to leave the country, however, were huge; the gamble could really involve life and death. The state knew what it was doing when it demanded that a character profile from an employer—or Dean's Office for a student—be submitted together with a visa application. This character profile had to be addressed to the relevant authority, i.e. the Visa Department of the Ministry of Internal Affairs. You had to tell your employer or Dean what the paper was for, i.e. emigrating to a foreign country. Lying could only make things worse, as the Ministry or KGB officials always contacted the office issuing the character profile to make sure the applicant had been adequately punished. Employers and Deans had no choice but to dismiss or expel the applicant. Not only that but they were obligated to record the reason for this in the applicant's papers: "Employment terminated as citizen so-and-so wants to emigrate to another country" or "Student so-and-so is expelled as …" Now imagine that your application to leave the country has been—as in most cases—rejected and you need to go back to everyday life, to earn a living or take a course of study. Wherever you go, they ask you for your papers; after they read why you've been sacked or expelled, they show you the door. The only job you can find is menial: sweeping streets, cleaning lavatories, shoving coal into furnaces, or washing dishes in cafeterias. As for higher education, forget it. So your future prospects in the country were basically ruined. And even all this wasn't necessarily the worst fear of a would-be applicant. The worst fear in an authoritarian state which had already once been totalitarian was that it would revert back to absolute tyranny—to something like Stalin—and your life quite literally ruined. We grew up in the shadow of the autocratic Khrushchev, who was replaced by the more or less equally autocratic Brezhnev; no one could promise us that the latter might not be replaced by somebody with ruthless dictatorial ambitions. In such a scenario, the first candidates for prisons and labor camps—if not summary executions—would be those wishing to exit the Socialist Motherland, Paradise on Earth, people automatically branded as traitors.

Still, the pull of liberty was powerful enough for me to cast my lot with those willing to risk it.

I decided there was little point in getting expelled, that it was preferable to quit on my own. In that way at least my university record would be unmarred and, if refused the application, I could try to enroll elsewhere, perhaps the University of Riga. Of course, the first question they'd ask is why leave and then attempt to restart college when anyone in their right mind would arrange a transfer, but I would cross that bridge when I came to it. And so my mind was made up to return to Moscow for the new academic year, not to study but to drop out.

Meanwhile, there were, as usual, matters of the heart to attend to. I was nineteen, the Baltic summer was wonderful, the girls wearing miniskirts.

I felt so much more at ease with those I mentally christened "typical Soviet girls" than I had with Anna the nun. A Soviet girl was secular and apolitical. My friend Yuri Afremovich introduced me to a salesgirl in a store where he'd taken a summer job. Her name was the female version of my own official name—Yevgenia/Eugenia—and she was my age. It took me a long time to realize she was an alcoholic. I didn't really know what that was. My pals and I had often joked about it but had hardly understood the phenomenon. I liked her a lot for her openness and sense of humor, but we didn't have much in common and she always drank whenever I came to see her. I got used to joining her in the boozing, often bringing a bottle with me, and to leaving her place half-drunk. There was something vaguely disturbing about it: you began to feel the drink was ousting conversation, discussion, exchange of opinions.

More momentous was my reunion with Irene. Like Eugenia, she was lacking in education, though Irene managed to graduate from high school, whereas Eugenia had dropped out at fifteen and during that summer was taking a course for adults wishing to complete their school record. Irene also drank, but only socially, at least at that time, although I was no longer sure it was merely social when I last saw her, a year and a half later.

Irene had been my first love and the inspiration for my first love lyrics. She was a pretty girl but what attracted me most was her folksy language, with such pieces of popular wisdom as

> Once long ago we'd reap and sow
> And give birth on the good earth—
> Now we're much too fine for that, you know!

(this and all other verses in this chapter were translated with John Heath-Stubbs)

I was also fond of her mischievousness bordering on wildness. Moscow helped me lose a lot of my timidity and come out of my shell, but I still envied her seemingly total absence of hang-ups. I didn't realize that she did have some—just different ones. She was unbalanced. Looking back later, I could see that the excessive anger and spite with which she'd hit me whenever I attempted sheepishly to caress her arm or hold her were more than just a teenage girl's pretenses or a flirtatious game: they were signs of incipient mental disturbance.

Like Eugenia, she had a good sense of humor, and we used to tease each other: she, about my poetic ambitions (even though she had recited my poems at a literary evening at Leningrad Polytechnic, where she'd managed to enroll the previous year) and I, about her superstitions. (It had surprised me at the time that one could be both irreligious and entertain beliefs which are not based on reason, but later I discovered that no less an intellectual than James Joyce had been such a one, and so I calmed down somewhat; as for me, I managed to evade superstition even at the height of my greatest religious craze.)

Irene believed in the significance of black cats and lucky and unlucky numbers; in harmful and protective colors and in touching wood; in not walking under a ladder and in never going back to the apartment after having left it, even if only in order to pick up something forgotten; in avoiding sitting at the corner of the table on big occasions so as not to forfeit her chances of getting married, and so on.

In August she came back from Leningrad Polytechnic, from which she had now been thrown out for failing most of her exams. That had been her only year of higher education; her parents now demanded she find employment, and she was preparing to become a secretary of some sort. She rang me and said that "the ancestors" (the word for parents our generation commonly used) had left her a bit of money before going away for a few days and that we could go, as we usually had done before whenever one of us had a few rubles, to the bar in the basement of the Riga Hotel. The place was cozy and comparatively inexpensive; you could just have a coffee, a piece of cake, and a little glass of cognac or liqueur.

We sat there and I reminisced about her school pranks.

I had had a habit, when a teacher called upon me, of standing with my hands behind my back. While giving my answer, I would often be so nervous as not to notice that Irene, who sat at the desk behind me, put various odds and ends into my hand—pens, pencils, a pencil sharpener, screwed up bits of paper, even notebooks. I would mechanically put all of them on my desk. When I had finished and sat down, she would thump me on the shoulder and say: "Now give me back everything you've taken and stop making passes!" Or worse still, she would put up her hand and say: "Alexandra Ivanovna, Zolya has taken my notebook and all my pens again—that's his way of showing interest in a girl!" And before I had time to open my mouth, the teacher would say, not without indignation: "Dubnov—give Pyshina all her things back at once! You ought to be ashamed of yourself! At nearly eighteen it's about time you thought of another way of making an approach to a lady!" I would stand up, red as a beetroot, and stammer out: "Not making an approach, Alexandra Ivanovna, I've no idea how they got there …" But Irene would already have interrupted me in a martyred tone: "This always happens—he clears out my entire desk as a romantic gesture!"

Once in the Great Hall, when our class was rehearsing a selection of songs for May Day, she had talked all the girls into singing, in the refrain of one stupid song, *Zolya is my love* instead of *Cuba is my love*. The music teacher couldn't make out what had gone wrong—in mass singing, words get blurred—but she sensed that something was amiss and asked them to sing properly. I was so embarrassed I didn't know where to look.

She burst out laughing when I remembered all this. "Yes, I liked you a lot," I said. "I can tell you this now, because I'm no longer in love with you, like I was before."

"You were in love with me?" she exclaimed—as usual, she didn't seem to be worried that people might overhear. She was answered by a stout elderly waitress. Brandishing a dozen or so beer mugs in the air, she addressed Irene in a loud and reassuring voice above the hubbub: "Yes, he was, dear—and don't you worry, he still is!"

People at the neighboring table applauded. I went red.

"Back at school I loved you a lot," I said softly, trying not to look around. "Didn't you realize? I was sure you knew."

"I hadn't the faintest idea!" Irene shook her head, tossing her hair wildly. "How could one possibly tell with you when there's always the same look on your face:

> For our happy childhood
> Thank you, Motherland so good!"

I saw her home. She lived not far from me. "My parents are away," she said. "You can come in for a drink, but don't get ideas."

She sat me down in an armchair by the window in the sitting room and went to the kitchen to brew some coffee. We drank it with the celebrated Riga Balsam liqueur. Soon I began to feel slightly tipsy.

"Would you like me to sing something?" she asked.

"Please do," I nodded, grateful.

A rich contralto welled up, filling the whole place.

> Little light beyond the window,
> White the snow is falling, falling,
> And my mother won't allow me,
> Will not let me kiss that boy—

She sang with a teasing half-smile for me. She drew out the song—already a slow one—so much that it seemed to me it would never end.

> It will pass, and you'll forget him—
> Mother warns—if you enjoy
> Sliding downhill on a sledge,
> You must haul it up again.

She was now looking not at me but through the window. Not only her voice but her whole bearing seemed to me to be that of a true artist.

> Gravely speaks my mother to me,
> And the courtyards deep in snow;
> Days and years have passed away
> Since that still remembered time.

She was now singing as if for herself alone—or else for someone very far away. She had, with a movement of her hand, tossed her hair backwards; her hands were clasped together at waist level.

> And I don't at all repent me
> When I look around—long since
> Down the hill my sledge stopped gliding,
> Now I only haul it up.

Could it be that she still remembered that "Little Light beyond the Window" was my favorite song and that once I had even done her homework in return for her singing it to me? She was already singing "You'll recall many long-forgotten things" from the old setting of Turgenev's poem—the song for which she had gained the second prize at an All Riga Schools Competition. I could not take my eyes off her.

"When did you start wearing glasses?" she asked. "You didn't wear them when we were at school, and you were better looking for it."

"I don't remember, probably a year ago; I'm shortsighted but only a little."

"Let me see what you look like without glasses."

She came and knelt on my lap, clutching my shoulder with one hand and removing my glasses with the other.

"Get off, that hurts," said I, but she stayed where she was, scrutinizing my unspectacled face.

I put my right arm around her neck, drew her close and tried to kiss her on the mouth.

"How dare you!" She furiously slapped my hand and pushed away from me.

I sulked, offended. It had been just the same at school: you never knew what she would do next. And now how are you supposed to guess what's in her mind when she scrambles onto your knee and takes your glasses off, and her face is only an inch or so away from yours?

The clock on the wall struck twelve. I got scared: I'd told Mother at home I'd be back by ten.

"Can I phone home from here?" I asked.

"Is it your Mummy—to inform her that you're in good health?" she asked sarcastically.

"I told her I'd be home earlier," I began to explain, but she cut me short: "Go on then, phone."

A terrible whisper was waiting for me on the other end of the line.

"The whole apartment's asleep, you'll wake everyone up, where are you speaking from?" Mother asked ominously.

"I … I'm speaking … from … from Zhenya Konyaev's, I won't be long …" I stammered.

"Come home at once—and don't ring the bell, you'll wake the whole apartment. Just knock, I'll hear. I'm not going to bed: I'm waiting up for you."

"All right, I'm coming," I said and hung up.

I hesitated. From where I was, I could see that in the bedroom across the flat Irene was opening cupboards and laying out fresh sheets, just as if she were at home alone.

"Is this for us?" I tried to be jocular, coming into the bedroom and watching her deft movements.

"Off with you, home to Mummy!" she cut me short without even turning round.

"Well, if you want to get rid of me like this," I said with some relief, "I've no option. I'll call you."

I went out onto the landing and started down the stairs. I had hardly got as far as the entrance when her door opened and her voice rang out for the whole building to hear: "Off with you to your Mummy!" Then the door closed with a bang—probably the loudest slammed door I've ever heard in my life.

Shortly after that, I left for Moscow—to drop out of university—and from there for Moldavia, to see my sister and be blessed by a holy man.

CHAPTER 19: EARLY FAREWELL

That autumn in Moscow was breathtakingly lovely. The weather seemed to me a metaphor of beauty and energy. Everything was a youthful green. I rubbed my shoulders on the gleaming trees, breathed in the silky air, and gazed at the luminous mystery of the sky, lost in reverie.

I realize now that all this was a manic spell—a relatively mild one—part of my bipolar tendencies.

Lena Tenina and I were walking south down Vernadsky Avenue. The sun, as it set somewhere behind Nikolskoye and Ochakovo, cast long shadows on the sidewalk and endowed her cheeks and forehead with a delicate pink glow.

My head was spinning all the time; the gentle breeze was a clear harbinger of freedom.

The giddiness of flight was starting to get hold of me, a bird's free soaring and an escape from a prison-like country.

In the Dean's Office, I explained that my father was gravely ill and I had to go back to Riga to take care of him. I said that once he got better, I'd come back and ask to be reinstated in the department. I don't think my story fooled anybody. For one thing, people in such situations don't drop out but arrange an academic leave of absence: instead of ceasing to be enrolled—and having no guarantee of a future reinstatement—they remain students who can by rights resume their course of study whenever they like. For another, it's more than likely—considering the well-developed network of informants, that someone had told the department authorities about my real plans. Only a few of my closest friends knew about them, but we all know how a careless word gets around.

I said to Dean Kulakova—a tough woman who was always smoking and always wore a leather jacket (perhaps she had a whole assortment of them, but to us it had always looked like one and the same jacket)—that at home in Riga I'd have to find employment and for that purpose needed a character profile from her, in addition to the usual academic transcript. She said all this would take some time. Doesn't matter, said I, I'd got lots of other things to arrange and I'd come again in a few weeks to collect all the papers.

From Moscow I traveled to Beltsy in northern Moldavia to stay with my sister Milla and her husband Simon.

He turned out to be a marvelous host, but the boredom of a provincial town—small in comparison with Riga and Tallinn—not to mention Moscow—was getting to me, and so I was glad when my mother phoned and said that her religious friends in Riga had told her that, being already in the area, I should not miss the chance to visit a holy man living around there.

"I'll give you the money for the trip," said Milla, "but don't breathe a word about it to Simon: he's militantly anti-religious. We'll find the time when he's got to go away."

The journey remains one of the most surrealistic events of my whole life, generally not short of the bizarre.

First I had to fly from Beltsy to Camenca, and from there take a bus to Rybnitsa.

After two hours of waiting and drinking bad coffee at Beltsy's minuscule airport, I witnessed a weird scene. A drunk, unsteady on his feet, was being escorted by the police, a man and a woman, both in uniform. As the posse passed my table, snatches of conversation reached my ears and I realized the drunk was a pilot and the "police" only local officials wearing airport uniforms. They were trying to persuade him to fly. The woman was humoring him, like a mother humors a rebellious son: "Why won't you consider taking off?" The man sounded more assertive: "The passengers are waiting, you know, some have already complained! What if they complain to the higher-ups? You may lose your license!" The drunken pilot quite sensibly replied that first he had to sober up, as his life was dear to him. He didn't mention the lives of his charges. At first I found the whole thing funny, but then a dark thought entered my mind: my plane was late, and this pilot was being cajoled into taking off. What if he was meant to fly me, among others?

They seated him two tables away from mine and brought him a pot of coffee and a jug of water. After his escort left, I went up to him.

"Excuse me, can I ask where you're flying to?"

"Camenca," he said. "Why?"

"Because that's my destination."

"So? I'll get you there."

"But ... But ... they said you were a bit, er ... the worse for wear. You look okay to me—quite okay, in fact!" I added hastily.

"Don't you worry, lad, I always fly drunk. Well, half-drunk, to put your mind at ease. Somewhat inebriated, as you students might say."

"What makes you think I'm a student?"

"It's written all over you. Give me half an hour and I'll be in perfect condition to get you to Camenca. Although what anybody in his right mind would be going there for is beyond me. It's even worse than Beltsy."

"I'm going to Rybnitsa, actually. Taking a bus there from Camenca."

"To see that Jewish fellow, the holy man? Well, that at least makes some sense. I knew you were an intellectual. Ask him to bless me too; Ivan Nikolayevich Shevtzov's the name, born in 1941."

I wasn't sure the last detail was all that important, but anyway I promised to mention his name and pass his request to the Jewish miracle worker.

"Tell him I'm a good pilot—but don't, don't tell him I drink!" he added. "I may be able to stop, with his blessing."

"Don't worry, I'll attest to your good character," I said.

The man was as good as his word and got me and the other half a dozen passengers of the tiny plane to Camenca. There I discovered that the bus to Rybnitsa had just left and I'd have to wait two hours for the next one.

I went to the local newsagents and bought a cheap paperback: Simon Lipkin's translation of the *Mahabharata*. Then I went to a wine merchant's opposite and got a one-liter bottle of equally cheap Moldavian wine. Lipkin's rhyming version of the ancient Sanskrit epic was so engrossing that I didn't even notice I'd finished the bottle. Then the bus came and I got on.

The sunset over the steppes was astonishing: this alone would have made the trip worthwhile. Huge crimson stretches were drawn over the sky, over the distant horizon; every few minutes the coloring seemed to change, and I no longer knew whether my head was spinning because of the wine or because of the resplendent landscape.

"Where can I find ...?" I began asking a passing yokel in Rybnitsa—a real village, even smaller than Camenca—but then couldn't recall the holy man's name. "Just a sec,"

I said. "I'm a bit potty, but I've got the name written down somewhere here in my note-book."

"Never mind," said the yokel. "It's the second gate on the right."

"Are you sure we're talking of the same man? Here, I've found him, Chaim Zamvl."

The yokel burst out laughing and told me that I wasn't the first fool who didn't know what he was talking about. This Transnistrian town (his words: to me it looked a village) had been blessed by a righteous man, to be blessed by whom KGB people brought their whole families from the farthest corners of the country. Even the Germans, he said, hadn't laid a finger on him when they'd occupied the place and murdered all the Jews. He told me that the holy man immersed himself in a river several times a day, which in the brutal Moldovan winters required breaking through thick ice. With this introduction I trudged on, swaying slightly from the effects of the alcohol.

(Just the other day I told this story to my friend Gabriel Levin, who had been trained, and used to work, as a psychotherapist. His first reaction was noteworthy. He drew attention to something I considered unimportant: to my need to turn to drink when feeling under pressure as early as the age of nineteen. That had surely been a weak point and a soft spot; unfortunately, so many people around me drank and considered it perfectly normal that it seemed so to me too, and there was no adult around who'd point it out as danger-ous. There's another lesson in all this: time and again, the nonchalance of youth conceals, behind its charming face, the seeds of future traumas and disasters. A Serbian proverb which I came across many years ago and which has stuck in my mind says: "Sow a deed, reap a habit; sow a habit, reap character; sow character, reap destiny.")

Unsteady on my feet and now with a dull headache from all the wine, I approached a little gate. The door of the simple one-story house—more of a shack, really—was open. There were two people inside at the opposite sides of a long rough wooden table. One of them asked me to come in. He looked to be in his sixties and had amazing light blue eyes, clear and innocent, like a child's.

I sobered up, somewhat, sensing myself in the presence of someone unique.

"I want to go to Israel with my mother," I said, "and I want to have your blessing."

The man asked me a few straightforward questions—my age, occupation, where I lived, inquired after my parents, their divorce, my mother's age and situation, and then gave me his blessing to leave the country. The whole interaction—lasting probably half an hour—impressed me as something totally guileless and pure. He hardly ever raised his head high enough to look me in the eye, which gave the impression of extreme modesty, and he was very kind, but what impressed me most was, again, the almost child-like inter-est he showed in people (surely I wasn't exceptional in that). I hadn't expected this degree of unpretentiousness and genuine human curiosity from somebody of his renown and religious stature.

And I even remembered to ask him to bless Shevtzov! I said he was a nice, decent, and kind man—which was perfectly true, because he hadn't crashed the plane but instead got me to my destination in one piece.

Chaim Zanvl Abramowitz (1902–1995) was a follower of the immensely influential Has-sidic Master of Shtefanesht, who had been revered by Jews and Christians alike, and was known as the Rybnitzer Rebbe; he too had a reputation as a miracle worker. In dealing now, as an agnostic, with the two prominent figures of modern Hassidism I've met (the other being Menachem Mendel Schneerson, already mentioned), I'm happy to take my cue from my distant ancestor the historian Simon Dubnov. Although himself an atheist, he treated the Hassidic movement and its leaders with a large degree of sympathy, both in his monumental history and in his autobiographical *Book of Life*. He was moved by their poverty and authenticity, by their love for simple folk. Having researched the movement's past and present and gotten myself acquainted with many among both its rank and file and its senior members, I realize how fortunate I was to meet perhaps its two most exceptional modern leaders. In many ways different, even diametrically opposed, they shared humility, disregard for personal possessions, kindness, and deep humanity, and in that way were worthy successors of the movement's founders whom Simon Dubnov had written about with singular respect and warmth.

Back in Beltsy, I tried to read Moldavian poetry. I had started learning Italian and been amazed to hear Italian words spoken by simple Moldavian folk. I asked my brother-in-law why they so often used the Italian phrase *mamma mia*. He laughed and said it was Moldavian and not *mia* but *mea*. If Italian and Moldavian were closely related, Moldavian and Romanian were, I was told, basically one and the same, though some saw the former as a dialect of the latter and the Russians, who'd flooded Moldavian with Russian words and replaced its Latin script with Cyrillic, insisted it was a separate language.

Then in a cheap cafeteria I overheard a conversation between two men at the next table. They were speaking in Russian and arguing over which of them had the harder job. From what I could gather, one was a herdsman and the other a woodcutter. They were chaffing one another good-naturedly. Then somehow the argument moved to national culture, and the woodcutter said that the locals were sorely wanting in this, that they had never produced anybody even remotely rivaling that great Russian genius Pushkin. The herdsman became agitated for the first time and accused his friend of talking nonsense, of not knowing what he was talking about (that phrase stuck in my mind because I found it amusingly self-contradictory). I realized then he must have been Moldavian. He proclaimed one Eminescu to be Pushkin's equal and there and then started reciting out loud, from memory, a poem which sounded to me magically hypnotic in the original. He then proceeded to explain to his Russian friend what the verses meant.

My brother-in-law was a busy doctor not interested in poetry, so I went to his parents, who'd been trained as physicians at Alexandru Ioan Cuza University in Iasi in Romania and spoke the language fluently. The retired couple were eager to return to their school years when Mihai Eminescu (1850–1889) had been on the curriculum. I told them about the poem I'd heard in the cafeteria; they recognized it as "La Mijloc de Codru" ("In the Middle of the Forest") and went over it with me. I then asked them about more recent Romanian verse and was introduced to Tudor Arghezi (1880–1967), whose modernity and experimentation—and spirit in speaking both against the German occupiers and the communist usurpers—impressed me. They also praised Nicolae Labis (1935–1956). It was the openly dissident Labis, who died so very young (according to one not easily dismissible version, murdered by the *Securitate* secret police), who captured my imagination; his poem "Death of a Deer," written only two years before his own death, stuck in my mind.

The elderly couple then became really enthusiastic, going on to tell me something of the country's recent dark past. My sister and her husband were about to move to Tselinograd (now Astana, capital of the Republic of Kazakhstan), where job and research prospects were much better than in the European part of the country. The name Tselinograd in Russian means Virgin Land City; that whole area used, not long ago, to be a place of exile for minor dissidents (major ones were sent to labor camps). Under Stalin, between 1940, when he grabbed Moldavia, and 1941, and between 1944 and his death in 1953, thousands of Moldovans had been deported to Kazakhstan. "Why should my son go to Siberia?" my sister's mother-in-law kept complaining and appealing to me (she was right about the geography, as the city was situated along the southernmost reaches of Siberia and had in fact been founded by a unit of Siberian Cossacks from Omsk). "He's no thief, he's committed no crime against the state; he's a bona fide citizen!"

Her husband told me that when the Russians had come to annex Moldavia from Romania in 1940 they "made sixty lei equal one ruble and so emptied out all the stores." I asked: "And before that what was the rate of exchange?" Thirty years had elapsed, but the laughter with which he greeted my question was still angry and bitter, as if it had all happened only recently. "Rate of exchange? Before those thugs arrived, nobody considered rubles to be of any value at all!"

There were no tickets for the express, but I was so fed up with doing nothing in Beltsy—Romanian poets' company notwithstanding—that I decided not to wait but take a slow train to Kiev, from where through trains to Moscow were frequent. In a way, the trip was worth it, as I had had yet another glimpse of the "real" as distinct from the "educated" component of the country. You could classify all the carriages of that train as "third class." There were only rough benches around tables, all of them taken. People jostled, sweated, and hated one another.

Passing through the train in search of a vacant seat, I came across two drunks lying on the floor by a queue for an occupied toilet—of all the places to pass out! After a fruitless search through several carriages, I suddenly noticed that one big fellow's backside was taking up two seats.

"If you just shifted a tiny bit to the right," I offered tentatively.

"And what?" he asked, genuinely puzzled, in Ukrainian.

"Then I could have a bit of room to sit down," I said. He burst out into multiple layers of imaginative swearing whose mainstay was the word "fuck" in its various forms, declensions, and inflexions.

After the next stop, I did find a place to sit, at a table whose three male occupants were drinking vodka. They were making a lot of noise but seemed not to mind me joining them. "A bit of the healing drop, lad?" the noisiest and drunkest suggested, pushing a bottle in my face. "No, thanks," I said and, half disingenuously, added: "I've got a meeting with my Dean of Students, so I have to stay sober!" (My mother had taught me never to lie, if I could help it; later, in London, the English poet John Heath-Stubbs, my older colleague, co-translator, and close friend of quarter of a century, liked to repeat jokingly that you shouldn't spend your falsehoods on small things as you never knew when one would be needed; throughout my life I've always tried to steer as close to the truth as humanly possible; I did have to see my Dean of Students, even if only a few days later.) Anyway, at that point vodka wasn't one of my drinks, and I wasn't used to boozing up in a company of strangers, at their expense to boot.

A woman conductor (actually, this is superfluous: all conductors in the country were women) came over. "What kind of folks are you?" she demanded like a scolding mother. "There's a ticket inspector in the next carriage, and he asks me, 'What have you got next door, a zoo?' Haven't I asked you people to keep it down?"

"Yes, we are folks—and you are a woman, ha-ha!" guffawed one of my fellow travelers. (There was a deep undercurrent of misogyny in Slav culture; the man could have taken his cue from the Russian proverb: "A hen isn't a bird, and a woman isn't a human being.")

At the next table, populated by four men speaking Moldavian, something else, equally of note, was going on. They were having a real feast, not just with many bottles of Moldavian wine but also with big chunks of meat and lots of fresh fruit, the latter quite cheap in that southern republic. Two tall, broad-shouldered Ukrainians were passing by; they stopped by the Moldavian table and, uninvited, helped themselves to the food. Not only that: while guzzling, they seemed to be openly mocking the food's owners—laughing at the tops of their voices, praising the quality of the meat and the juiciness of the fruit in Ukrainian. The Moldavians looked puny by comparison with these two, and so they suffered their mortification in silence, the deep redness of their faces and necks alone betraying their feelings. Having cleared most of the table, the guests—belonging to a rival ethnic group—moved on.

Upon arriving in Kiev in the evening, I discovered that a train for Moscow was leaving in an hour's time but with only third-class tickets left. The next one wasn't until the morning, so I got what was available and boarded the train.

"Is that the Moscow language you're speaking?" a young fellow asked me in amazement when I apologized for accidentally pushing him. He was about my age but, with his Bogdan-Khmelnitsky-Hetman-of-Ukraine seventeenth-century mustachios and traditional Ukrainian clothes, he seemed to come from another world. The question puzzled me for a moment, but then I remembered that *Moscow* for Ukrainians simply meant *Russia*. This was an old historical contradistinction between the Kievan Russia and the Muscovite one. He then proceeded to tell me about himself and this, his first trip outside his own town to some sort of Young Communist League activists' get-together in Moscow as part of the delegation from Ukraine. Then I heard people quarreling across the passage over a seat. "Don't fuck with me, you baggage!" said a man to a woman. "It's you who are fucking with me, you hoodlum," replied the woman and added politely: "if you don't mind my saying so."

All that was more than I could take, especially after my traumatic previous third-class carriage experiences. I went to find a conductor to ask if there was a second-class place available and how much extra I'd have to pay. Yes, there was a place, and the difference in the price of the ticket (which she must have pocketed, as I was issued no new ticket) was only a few rubles. So I moved up the social ladder, to a four-passenger compartment with a closing door and a quiet passage outside. I was also fortunate in that this compartment had only two occupants. (It occurred to me afterwards that perhaps there had been a secret arrangement between the ticket office and the conductors whereby the former would announce that all tickets had been sold out and the profits from the subsequent shady deals—of which I was sure mine was far from being the only one—would be split between the two sides; otherwise, the fact that the whole tickets and seats thing didn't add up could simply have been attributed to a lack of coordination, a countrywide phenomenon.)

One of the two passengers in the compartment was a man, the other, a woman; both probably in their early thirties. There was no interaction between the two, and they kept themselves largely to themselves; it was only toward the end of the journey, when the radio in the passage came to life and started playing patriotic songs about Moscow being everybody's beloved capital, that the man cracked some kind of risky joke about this capital sucking resources from the whole country. The young woman then went out, taking her makeup bag with her, presumably to the toilet.

"You'd better be careful with pronouncements like that," I said, nodding toward the passage she'd just disappeared along.

"What—her?" asked the man. "You think young women can be informants?"

"Everyone can be an informant," I said, my Moscow University experience behind me—and we both laughed.

In Moscow, I stayed with my distant relatives—the family of the sister of my uncle Meir's wife. The Vilenskys were very hospitable, ready to put me up for as long as I needed. They had four children, of which the middle one, Esther, whom I've already mentioned, was not only a fellow student in the same department (although two years my senior) but a real friend and a confidante. (Whenever I shared my affairs of the heart with her, she would invariably query my attitude to her own sex, thinking I was putting too great an emphasis on the physical part of a relationship; I see her point now, that of a young girl's dream of romance and her inability or unwillingness to empathize with a boy's hormonal tidal wave.)

"What are you so proud of, Dubnov?" asked Kulakova.

"I'm not proud," I said, "I just want my character profile—to get a job in Riga, you know, to be near my sick father. You promised—you said it would be ready when I came again in early December."

"We're all so busy now," she said, "with the end-of-year exams. Come again next week: I should have it ready by then."

I could have kicked up a row about all that bureaucracy and feet-dragging and complained to the higher-ups—the Soviet Union of my time was not a lawless country as long as politics weren't involved—but I decided it wasn't worth it. So I said I'd return in a few days' time. Anyway, I wasn't in any particular rush to get back to my mother and low-level job hunting. I didn't have a diploma or any sort of training to help me get a qualified position.

I saw all my student friends, who had now moved from the Annex with its four people to a room to the Student House, or Main Building, with its luxurious conditions of two to a room and lots of amenities situated in the building. I no longer had a student card, so somebody needed to sign me in and I wasn't allowed to stay after ten. I felt humiliated by the procedure and envious of my friends: we'd all suffered the iniquities of the Annex together, but now they were reaping the fruits of their patience and I wasn't. I was also saddened by their reports of the new courses, new lecturers, and coming exams. It was no longer my world.

Although my academic transcript showed that almost all my grades were As and Bs, with only one exam failed, Kulakova's character profile said I was "an unexceptional student." I had no doubt she knew about my future plans. Paradoxically, her unflattering characterization may ultimately have helped to get the exit visa: my mother, who was the main applicant, used Kulakova's attestation as evidence of my being totally mediocre—bordering on retarded—and of no use to anybody in the Soviet Union.

With all my official university papers in my bag, for the last time in my life I walked from the Faculty to Alexander Gardens on the other side of Marx Avenue. It was late afternoon in December, and already dark. The weather was dry and frosty—I remember the radio said it was twenty-eight below zero on the Celsius scale—with no hint of snow: an anticyclone wave coming from the Northern Urals. There were few people around, three or four solitary figures all wrapped up against the cold and wind, hurrying on. I wandered along the paths in the Gardens and then stood by the Eternal Flame on the Tomb of the Unknown Soldier. We in the postwar generation had no symbol more sacred than Red Army soldiers who gave up their lives for the homeland. Dressed lightly, I was freezing, especially my feet, but I didn't want to leave, not yet. My breath hung white, then was shredded, then taken away by the air to vanish into the rawness of time running on and time remaining immobile. I felt like I was saying a final farewell—and not just to Moscow University and not only to Moscow herself, but to the whole country. Inner music began to play in my mind—always a sign of verses being formed—and a poem almost gave birth to itself, from word upon word hoarded somewhere under the fiercely beautiful freely stretching sky, me acting as a kind of conductor of an orchestra that knew the score by heart. When I managed to write it down with my numb fingers, it seemed to me to have been written in some catatonic language reflecting the state I had been in. Here it is, translated, as almost all my Russian poems have been, in close collaboration with my literary friends:

Alexander Gardens

Where the snowless December like rarefied air
    in the mountains is burning the breath, once again
Into the Gardens at random I've come: it is here
    that I go through the names, outwaiting the waiting, reliving the pain.

The black midnight air is dissolving to blue
    over the quivering flame in the heart of the thick granite stone;
At the train's window a double is standing, to view
    the tense and impassive reflection it dares not acknowledge its own.

How the harsh Russian frost, unremitting, prepares
    your breath and your spirit for the rigorous course of existence;
The freezing of the soul turns into the stares
    of the white-eyed Muses and word of farewell to the land in the distance.

And with my lips seeking sounds for our destiny

under the tall Moscow sky I forget what to say;
Farewell rises up to a scream but it chokes in me,
 air like packed snow has amassed in my mouth, and my breath's forced away.

(Moscow, 1969, translated with Chris Newman and John Heath-Stubbs)

As I was about to leave, a man came up to the Tomb. He looked youngish, perhaps in his mid-thirties, and was dressed even more lightly than I, wearing a thin—although stylish—leather coat over a worn-out jumper, a fur hat with its ear flaps up, and no gloves. I was wearing gloves and wished I had thick woolen mittens, the kind children wear. My ear flaps were down.

"Aren't you cold like that?" I asked, my teeth chattering.

"Cold?" he laughed. "Young man, in Irkutsk we have a saying: 'One bottle of vodka is not yet a drink, two hundred miles is not yet a distance, and thirty below zero is far from being a real frost.' When we have real frost, lorry engines must be left running day and night—or we light fires under them. Your spit freezes before reaching the ground. Steel shatters like ice. Truck tires burst."

"Is that where you come from—Irkutsk?" I asked. "What are you doing here?"

"Getting married. Tomorrow. My fiancée's a Muscovite. In the meantime, I've decided to come here to pay my respects to the Unknown Soldier. My parents were in the military and died in the war. My father was a lieutenant and my mother was actually above him in rank, a captain. Both were killed in April 1945 during the attack on Berlin."

"Are you going to stay in Moscow after you've got married?"

"Oh, no! I'm taking the girl back to Irkutsk. As a lorry driver, I earn at least three times as much there as I would around here."

"What does your fiancée do?"

"She's a school teacher. She'll find work there easily. And what do you do?"

"I'm a student," I said. "Here at Moscow University." I felt anguished saying this: I was no longer a student. "Goodbye and good luck to both of you."

"Same to you," he took his naked hand out of his pocket to wave at me in the freezing air. "You look scholarly. I'm sure you'll be a professor one day!"

Chapter 20: Parents

In Riga, I was greeted with alcoholic updates from my close friends. Zhenia Konyaev, now a student at Riga Polytechnic, had become his year's orderly; his job was to monitor attendance and collect money for various initiatives. (He explained to me apologetically that he'd agreed only in order to be in the good books of the Dean, because his grades had been so poor that the man had threatened him with expulsion.) Having collected subscription money for some relevant local paper—something like *Latvian Technology* or *Soviet Engineering News*—he had found the temptation to spend it on booze—with our mutual friend Vladimir Kosov—simply irresistible. Then, faced with the obvious problem, he stole fifteen rubles from his parents. The theft was discovered, his folks wept bitterly over what they called "bearing and raising a thief" and threatened to throw him onto the street.

The second piece of alcoholic news was more surprising, concerning as it did Yuri Afremovich, who hitherto had never touched a drop. He too had had to collect money, to buy a skull specimen for his year at the School of Medicine, where he'd enrolled the previous September—and he too had spent it on booze. (To me this was the first sign that something wasn't quite right with my friend, whose self-discipline and pedantry I'd always envied; indeed, the very next year he would fail a number of exams, be expelled, and drafted into the army. I suspect all this had happened as a result of the inescapable hormonal attack and Yuri's unwillingness to even acknowledge, let alone face it.)

The next item on my own agenda was getting permission from my father to apply for my exit visa. That was easier said than done. The state wanted to have it both ways: to show it respected its own laws regarding the "humanitarian reunification of families" but not to let its citizens out, even those it didn't particularly need, so as not to encourage others. The parental permission requirement had been designed as yet another barrier. Ostensibly, it was intended to avoid financial claims by parents against their children outside the country. In theory, a father could demand that his son living elsewhere should support him in his old age, but since the Soviet Union never paid any pensions to those who left and didn't allow them to take out more than a derisory amount of their own money, you had to be naïve to believe anybody at the top was concerned about international law or old parents' well-being. Parents who gave their progeny such permission could expect to face difficulties at their work and obstacles in their careers. For somebody employed on the so-called "ideological front," this permission could be particularly risky. My father, as both a communist and journalist, was an ideological worker *par excellence.*

"Not to worry," said my mother, "he'll be only too happy to oblige—I'll threaten to ruin his whole career!"

Father flatly refused.

"Get ready," Mother said. "We're going to pay him a visit."

He lived with his new wife Raisa just a few streets away. Mother knew their address because one of her cronies lived nearby and was acquainted with "that woman." (She also described the manner—totally banal, aimed at undersexed dolts, I must say—in which Raisa had seduced him.)

Raisa turned out to be quite plain indeed and, though she was slightly younger than my mother, she looked much older. Spectacles in thick black frames hardly helped.

(To my mother's half-credit, perhaps, she would always use my father's example as a stick to beat me with, saying that in choosing a woman who was neither young nor pretty—even though with his good looks, his way with words, gentlemanliness, and social position he could surely have found one who was both these things—he showed a praiseworthy maturity and intelligence, whereas I supposedly chased after young girls who were as silly as they were pretty. "Why did you have to take after your father in all his bad qualities and neglect to imitate his few positive features?" she demanded, time and again.)

"I won't give my permission," he said. "I'm adamantly against his leaving the country."

"You won't?" my mother's voice rose quite a number of decibels. This surely embarrassed the couple before their neighbors: the block of flats was genteel, elitist, in a street of foreign embassies.

"Please, keep your voice down," he begged. She didn't.

"I saved your skin when they wanted to expel you from the Party and fire you from your ideological job: I said you knew nothing about the religious goings-on in the family. Well, I can tell them the truth now. In fact, there may be no need to delve into the past: the present is surely scandalous enough. It's known as immoral behavior and it goes against your Party's principles. You publicly betrayed and shamed your wife of thirty years, who'd sacrificed her whole life so you could pen articles in praise of your Party's high moral ground—and you left her without a kopeck!"

"I divorced you and married Raisa," he retorted.

"People saw you long before that, in city parks, in broad daylight, walking with her arm in arm—a married man, father of a family! You know me. I'll make sure the story of your life circulates widely through all Party headquarters and editorial offices of the city."

"Shall I give him the permission—what do you think?" my father asked his new wife. Such a momentous decision, I thought, and he asks her advice. She had more dignity. Shrugging, she said: "It's your call."

(Mother would remember his behavior again and again in the coming years and rub it in: "True to form, he had to ask his second wife about his own son—she was to decide your future!" There was nothing I could say to that, even though I was sure that whatever she said, he'd give this much more thought later on. Father had always been a docile husband ruled by Mother. I felt hurt that he'd had to consult somebody who was a total stranger to me.)

Mother shook her head in pity. "You're asking *her*? You disgraced your children, you left your little boy when he was just a child, traumatized by the tragic death of his older brother, and now you think you can stand between him and his future? We'll see about that—and your Party will have to look into your whole life story!"

"Stop trading in your son's 'tragic death'!" Raisa intervened.

"You—you say this to a bereaved mother?" said my mother. "You have a child too: aren't you afraid to make such pronouncements?"

At that point, my father showed some character and said to Raisa: "Don't—don't get involved in this, it's between us."

And then, to my mother: "All right, I'll talk to a couple of people who are in the know and discuss it with them. I'll have to find a way to phrase the permission so as not to harm myself."

I have mixed feelings about my father's second wife Raisa. In fact, I have mixed feelings about my parents. I think I'll conduct a kind of trial of them—Father and Mother and, if only by implication, Raisa too—and let the readers' jury make up their minds. I promise that no one will come out of this either white or black. The whole idea may sound obsessive, but we are never finished with the dead, are we? I don't think we can be, really, either culturally or personally:

> We are born with the dead:
> See, they return, and bring us with them.

> (T. S. Eliot, "Little Gidding")

FATHER, LEONID

Prosecution:
The man was a lightweight, pusillanimous philanderer. Despite the fact that his wife Adele possessed a great and unusual beauty, he'd never been able to let a pretty girl, however young, pass by without opening the door to her or complimenting her or picking up something she'd dropped. He knew that proud Adele felt humiliated; knew there'd be a scandal each time she witnessed this behavior, and yet he seemed unable or, more to the point, unwilling to restrain himself. Once a handkerchief of his daughter's girlfriend fell out of her pocket—the girl must have been in her late teens—and he, *paterfamilias*, bent to lift it from the ground and restore it to her—"huffing and puffing and groaning," in his wife's words, because he was no longer young and it must have taken rather an effort. On another occasion, Leonid helped a young woman he hardly knew to get off a bus by offering her his hand; while he was busy doing this, his own wife, coming next, was ignored. His conduct prompted their son Vladimir, a boy not yet twenty, to cry out in protest: "Enough—stop tormenting Mom!"

During the Great Patriotic War—admittedly, not the easiest time to keep faithful at the front line—his infidelities were so singular as to merit this comment from the wife of a fellow officer: "All men betrayed their spouses in the War, but no one went further than that bald-headed degenerate."

We don't know for certain, but there are strong indications—and his eldest daughter Milla's strong suspicions—that he had an affair with somebody, probably a secretary, at work in later years. This was long after the war and before Adele, his wife, stopped sharing a bed with him, due to the trauma of their son's untimely death. And his conduct during the period leading up to his departure from the family was that of a cad. With Adele still mourning, his eldest daughter Milla still unmarried and close to thirty—disastrous for a girl at that time and in that place—he was seen walking arm in arm with his mistress in a central park of the city at mid-day. Of course, that woman must have put pressure on him to do this, for her own dishonorable reasons, but weakness of character has never been an excuse, either on ethical or legal grounds.

Nor can timidity and spinelessness excuse his performance when, before his very eyes, his son Vladimir was being denounced and expelled from the polytechnic. The young man was fuming after that kangaroo court, his anger directed not at his judges—for it's a waste of breath to complain about the morally corrupt—but at his own father: "He kept socializing and smoking with them during the break in the proceedings!" Leonid even lacked the guts to use his position as a communist and journalist and declare that he'd hold accountable all those involved should they discriminate against his son. He failed to muster enough intelligence and presence of mind to make them think twice and hesitate in fear of retribution. He had all the cards in his hands, but didn't use them because of his deeply ingrained avoidance of all conflict. Since when has cowardice been an acceptable, legitimate defense? When the conflict with the neighbors, which had led to his son's expulsion and ultimately his death, had only started and that thug of a neighbor had given the young man—half his age—a sharp slap in the face, any other father, in Adele's words, "would have killed on the spot, without thinking, the man who had dared lay a finger on his son." The rhetorical exaggeration aside, had Leonid reacted in any forceful way, at least by lodging a complaint with the police, the whole tragedy might have been avoided. Instead, he chickened out, blaming his own boy for the altercation in the kitchen. As Vladimir lay dying, he said: "Let him not come to my grave!"

A shallow man, he substituted easy sentimentality in the world of books for the harder task of building bridges within his own family, of finding a way to the hearts of his own children. You may say shallowness is not a moral failure, that it's genetic. Perhaps. We won't accuse Leonid of this, however absurd the spectacle of seeing him enthuse over both Beethoven's Fifth and the most meaningless of silly pop songs, or grow equally lachrymose over great works of literature and cheap tearjerkers. But what about a moral obligation, a sense of duty to his children? He was cold as a father, not just to his eldest son but to all his children apart from Milla. She was his favorite because she'd taken after him, both in character and professionally, as a journalist. Confiding in everybody, friend or foe, he said to a colleague at work about Vladimir: "I don't really love this son of mine." (And indeed why should he when Vladimir once said to him: "Dad, you're behaving like a guilty schoolboy!") To another colleague he complained that he wasn't particularly fond of his daughter Lena because she'd "taken after her mother." Even with the youngest, Eugene, admittedly his second favorite after Milla, he remained rather remote, and the fact that while exercising with dumbbells every morning he never made a move to ask the boy to join him speaks volumes.

Escaping into the fictional world of *belles-lettres*, his family and its problems had always been of limited interest to him. He was never emotionally involved. When Adele would ask his advice on something concerning family affairs, he'd blurt out, unthinkingly: "Do such-and-such." When she complained: "But that makes no sense!" he'd blurt out: "Why, then, do the opposite!"

One of the last acolytes of a murderous, corrupt ideology—Soviet-style communism—he had never taken the trouble to examine it and had never made an effort to show respect for the beliefs of others. Adele's brother, upon hearing she'd come to visit with her husband, exclaimed: "I'm glad she's here, but why has she brought the communist—the pagan—with her?"

The saying of Socrates, "The unexamined life is not worth living," fits him one hundred per cent.

An educated man, a veritable bookworm and an avid theater- and classical music concertgoer, he had nevertheless not taken the trouble to think for himself but had gone on toeing the Party line. His snapped reply to Eugene made only a couple of years before his death, "Don't you say a word against Lenin!" shows no attempt at analysis.

Perhaps the man had the inglorious finale of his second marriage coming. It certainly gives one pause. He cared devotedly for his wife Raisa, who'd developed Alzheimer's disease, washing and cleaning after her, until her daughter and son-in-law had decided to put her in an old people's home. Then, while Raisa was still alive, the two of them told him he wasn't needed any more. He was entitled, as the owner's husband of over three decades, to at least his share of the flat, situated as it was in one of Riga's most upmarket neighborhoods, but the sharp couple had already taken care of that. While he'd been stricken with grief upon discovering his wife's incurable illness, they'd convinced him to sign his rights away to their own daughter, Raisa's grandchild. And so the man was thrown out, without a penny to his name, to the mercy of his children in another country. (In an epilogue, Raisa's daughter, still a young woman, died soon after, in terrible pain, of cancer.)

You can put your own interpretation on all this, but before admiring his selfless behavior toward his sick wife, perhaps two quotes would be apt. One is from Bertha, his brother David's second wife. She said to Eugene: "I hope I'm not speaking out of turn, but your father was always under Raisa's heel, she did with him as she wanted." The second is from Adele. She said: "Your father is a type who'll always be an appendix to his woman. He's unthinking, like a beast. When he was my husband, he did my will, and you can bet he'll do exactly the same with his second wife."

Defense:

Leonid's attitude to women is attributable to his old-fashioned gallantry. Those manners were derived from books, especially nineteenth-century Russian literature, which was notoriously romantic. At worst, perhaps he was a bit of a ladies' man. A more intelligent and sensitive woman would have turned a blind eye to such trivia. What is of real importance is that he never stopped loving his wife, from the early courtship (when he nearly killed himself thinking she wouldn't marry him), through the war when he wrote her passionate letters from the front, and indeed up to and after the tragic death of their eldest son. Eugene, their youngest, can testify to the fact that as he was growing up the relationship between his parents was no less normal than an average married couple, with both quarrels and times of happiness. A hard-working man, all Leonid's thoughts were of providing for his family. Even his wife always acknowledged this. Following their son's death, when she let herself go berserk, made no effort to pull herself together, and wouldn't let him near her, he totally immersed himself in work, sometimes staying overnight at the offices of his newspaper, sleeping on a cheap camp bed he'd bought. His grief may have been no less great than hers, but he didn't have the privilege of abandoning himself to it: he still had to earn money to feed the family. In sharp contrast to her, he was not a performer; whatever he felt or did was never for show. Even in Adele's most deeply felt emotions, there would always be a theatrical element.

He was fifty-two when his wife stopped sharing a bed with him. It's a testimony to his love for her that he, a healthy man in his prime, went on suffering and waiting for her to resume normal marital relations. When that didn't happen, who can blame him for looking for somebody else five years later? When she had not only dismissed him as a husband but humiliated him before their children, hurling abuse at him and throwing things in his face.

As for that report of his alleged amorous doings in the war, is there any independent evidence of them? Assuming the words about his infidelities had in fact been spoken by another officer's wife exactly as quoted by Adele, without being embroidered by her enviable imagination, can one rely on their truthfulness? Who was that woman and why did she say what she said? There could be many reasons that have nothing to do with his actual conduct. What if she'd tried to seduce him—a dashing captain, educated, well-read, · behaving like a gentleman, popular with women—and had been rejected? Don't we know that "Hell hath no fury like a woman scorned"?

His tactics over the threatened expulsion of his elder son were surely designed to win over the accusers through friendliness and reasonableness. It didn't work out, but that was a miscalculation, not a dereliction of duty. Leonid was cerebral and knew that emotional outbursts of the kind Adele was known for can occasionally win the day, but are risky.

Reserve can be mistaken for coldness but it shouldn't. Just because Leonid never paraded his feelings, one shouldn't assume he didn't have them. His son's death touched him profoundly—but he carried his grief inside. His heart-rending loneliness within his own family cried to heaven. The only child who understood and sympathized with him was his eldest daughter Milla; it would be cruelly unfair to begrudge him his communication with her. Not only were the other children still too young, but they had already been turned against him by their mother to varying degrees.

His supposed lack of involvement in family affairs can be put in proportion by reminding ourselves that he was the only breadwinner among six people. He never turned down an offer to write an article for a newspaper or magazine, no matter how uninteresting the subject matter or close the deadline: every line was a few more kopecks that went toward feeding and clothing the children—or, indeed, buying another pretty garment for Adele, to satisfy her pretty woman's vanity. He often had to write his articles through the night to meet the deadline; spartan in his lifestyle, he made do with very little; work and family were his whole life.

As for his inability to accept denigration of Lenin, how many old men can renounce a cause they've given their whole life to? It is too harsh to expect them to erase their past. Eugene can testify in his father's defense. In the early 2000s, the former corresponded with the late American author Arthur Miller and saw what he interpreted as the writer's avoidance of the topic of the Soviet Union. This is not to criticize Miller, an honest and fearless man who could have been mistaken, as indeed can all of us, but to stand up for Leonid. Old men are explorers only in fiction; in real life most of them want to justify their life's deeply held beliefs and resulting deeds. Yes, there have been some who had the fortitude to completely reconsider and renounce their past, but it would be unfair to hold everybody to the standards of the few.

Leonid was proud of the way he'd lived his life serving his homeland honestly and wholeheartedly. A few months before his death in 1999 he wanted to show the many medals and orders he'd got in the Great Patriotic War to his son and the latter's friend Sasha Glot, who were visiting him. Eugene said he'd already seen them, but his friend expressed an interest. Watching his father enthusiastically explain the history of his every military decoration, the circumstances of each and every award to an eager listener, perhaps the son felt ashamed of himself for his indifference. Perhaps he even reconsidered one or two of his past and present attitudes to his father.

And so one shouldn't rush to blame the father if there was a distance between him and his children. Adele and the children themselves had a hand in it. We should be reminded of Leonid begging his son not to drift away from him following his departure from the family: "An affectionate calf sucks two mothers."

Equally wrong would be to reproach Leonid with having never examined his life in general, apart from its communist context, in which, as we know, he was only one among many millions of Soviet citizens. Unlike Adele, he never wore his heart on his sleeve. Who knows his old man's thoughts when fate slammed the door on his life with his second wife and brought him humiliated back to his children to be taken care of?

It is immoral to see the end of his second marriage as somehow deserved and fitting. He was fortunate enough to have had his share of happiness with a woman who genuinely respected him and whom, in return, he loved deeply. His daughter Milla would always remember the opening of one of Raisa's letters to Leonid—a letter he showed her to make her understand his feelings for his second wife. The letter began with the words: "My dear husband." Adele had never shown him even a minimal degree of regard. In addition to their mutual esteem, Raisa and Leonid also shared a sense of belonging to the country and its history—something at best only half-present in Adele. Raisa had paid dearly for what were euphemistically called "excesses of the personality cult"—her first husband, unable to withstand torture, threw himself out of the window of his interrogation room. In many cases, such personal tragedies only strengthened the bonds one felt with the state. Jean de la Bruyère wrote that "the subjects of a tyrant have no motherland"; both Raisa and Leonid would have disagreed vehemently.

Finally, the charge that he made Adele suffer is false. Theirs was a more or less average, reasonably happy family, as many friends and neighbors can testify, and Adele wasn't particularly religious. The rift and accusations began only after Vladimir's death. It was Adele who, instead of keeping her family together in the face of the tragedy, made all of them suffer.

With all the pain it caused, her behavior was inexcusable, self-indulgent, unbridled, wild, destructive. And if we're going to hold one person accountable for an excessive lightness of character, why not hold the other one accountable for an excessive heaviness—bordering on a mental disturbance?

MOTHER, ADELE

Prosecution:

It takes a very special woman to destroy a love as strong as her husband had for her. The children can testify that Adele called their father names in front of them (including "old fart") and on at least one occasion threw his shaving things in his face. There were many things worthy of admiration in him—his second wife was quick to find them—but Adele never appreciated them. A gifted and pretty girl married to a man who doted on her, she quickly got used to playing the role of prima donna. Later in life she told her son Eugene how she'd enjoyed turning the heads of all her husband's friends. Admittedly, the coquetry—if you can even call it that—had been most light, but still it had been part of her character of a beautiful and willful young woman. She would have been happier perhaps with a dominant man, but she'd had her own reasons to marry Leonid. He was handsome and a man of the world, with a promising career, who'd take her away from her small town and stifling family atmosphere. And the fact that he was madly in love with her and quite pliable was not to be sniffed at either. Their children, on both sides of the parental conflict, always concurred that the best man for her would have been somebody like her own elder brother and their uncle Meir Stambler—that is, an absolute tyrant.

Adele had always put Meir's will before that of her husband and his interests before those of her family. In one heart-rending instance, she brought herself and her children close to starvation because of her fierce loyalty to him. This story is worth looking at closely.

The year is 1943, the height of the Great Patriotic War. Leonid Dubnov and his three brothers are in the Red Army pitted against Hitler. One of them, Lev, will soon die what was called "the death of the brave" on the front line. Leonid's family and his in-laws have been evacuated to Kirov, a medium-sized city in the Northern Urals. Relatively speaking, they don't suffer all that much: Kirov has many officers' families, is supplied decently, and Adele and her sister Faina have jobs as bookkeepers. We don't know what the third sister Hannah is doing, but all of them appear to be safe and sound. Then their young brother Zoussia dies of leukemia and soon after their old father dies of typhus. Their mother, having lost both son and husband, is near a total breakdown. Their elder brother Meir decides to move to Tashkent in Central Asia. There are a number of reasons for this decision, some to do with keeping the year of mourning properly according to religious ritual, others to do with his position, which has now become more precarious. Still only thirty-three, he should be away fighting the Germans, but he isn't. He is a deserter. He's got forged ID showing him to be in his early fifties, past the age of military duty. Sometimes people who look like they're the wrong age in the wrong place are stopped by military patrols, their papers checked. Deserters are summarily shot when caught. He'll stick out less in a huge multi-ethnic city like Tashkent. (We're not judging him, and we'll leave aside the question of morality—why he thinks his religious practices and his hatred of Stalin's regime are more important than taking part in the battle to protect his co-religionists from Hitler's death camps. The proportion of Jews in the Red Army, relative to their proportion in the population, is higher than of any other ethnicity. So is the percentage of the fallen among them.)

Meir Stambler leaves for Tashkent, and so do his mother, his two unmarried sisters, and Adele, with her three children, Milla, Vladimir, and Lena (Eugene is yet unborn). For his mother, he, the eldest son and the Torah prodigy risking his life to carry on the family tradition, is now the only reason to go on living; his sisters follow so as not to leave him unprotected, vulnerable with his counterfeited papers. In Tashkent, flooded with evacuees, Adele cannot get work and is, like so many in that place, on the brink of starvation. She becomes bed-ridden with pellagra, an acute vitamin deficiency. Her youngest, Lena, a child of four, is begging in delirium: "A little piece of bread, please, a breadcrumb!" Her sister Hannah is last seen on a stormy winter day, rain and snow intermingled, begging for food on the outskirts of the city.

The postal services during the war being unreliable, it takes time for Leonid to locate his family at their new address; he brings his generous military rations—heavy with chocolate—and money to buy fruit and vegetables on the black market, and saves his wife and children. Adele has said that if he had come a few days later, most of them, if not all, would have been dead. (Typically, she blames him for the situation, accusing him of whoring on the front line instead of getting food to his family.)

In a brutally manipulative manner Adele usurped—or attempted to usurp—their children, aggressively molding them, turning them against their father and everything he stood for. A born manipulator, thinking only of herself, she did everything to deny both her sons a normal boyhood. There is evidence that with Vladimir she succeeded. When her younger son Eugene tried to date, she would time and again try to shame him, quoting his late older brother as an example he'd fallen short of. "I don't need girls," Vladimir was supposed to have said. "There's only my Mom for me in the whole world." You can put a mother's appropriation of her sons in psychoanalytic context—as indeed so much else in Adele's conduct—but this would hardly diminish her failure as both wife and mother. Who knows what sort of emotional wreck Vladimir would have developed into if he had survived? In addition, she'd taught him her own kind of inflexibility, her inability to compromise, which renders life a hundred times more difficult than it already is, especially in a dictatorial state; it may well have been fortunate for him to die when he did.

Following that death, she took her grief out on her youngest and most vulnerable. Eugene was eleven. She kept asking him: "Where's your older brother, your protector and deliverer?" and answering herself: "He's no more, your brother; you've no protector and no deliverer." She'd tell him off sharply when he laughed at something or other: "Your brother's dead and you're laughing?" She didn't miss an opportunity to point out to him how little he showed the admirable qualities of his brother.

At night he'd be woken up by her hysterical cries: "My son, my son, why have you left me?"

You can make allowances for people in these situations, but can you make just *any* allowances? The impression one gets is that she wanted her children to be her co-sufferers. As for her husband, here she knew no bounds whatsoever. She would scream at him in front of the children: "Murderer! You've murdered your son! Your own son, dying, said, 'Do not let him come to my grave!'"

He bore all this with an admirable patience but the only thing she remembered was his timid request a year later to come with him to a film. "Barely a year has passed—and he's already forgotten his child!" she fulminated. "There are many fathers whose mourning in such cases is even deeper and longer-lasting than that of mothers!"

Adele's heredity and warped upbringing were to a large degree responsible for her shortcomings, but family background cannot absolve people of their neglect of marital and parental duties. Most of us, religious or not, believe in free will and the will and capacity of people to change.

Defense:
Any court of law takes into account the defendant's family background. From the first stages of her life, Adele was crippled by her own parents and her older brother. In patriarchal families of that period, girls were not taken seriously and invariably put down, whereas boys were doted on, praised, and spurred. This was especially the case with Meir, exceptionally gifted and brave, seen by his instructors in their clandestine religious school

as a prodigy. Both Stambler parents—the harshly authoritarian mother and the more easy-going but uncompromisingly pious father—saw their fulfillment in their eldest son only and would totally ignore their daughters the moment he entered the room. No wonder the girls had developed very similar and deep-seated feelings of inferiority.

Adele was in many ways a child who never grew up. Sexually timid, despite all her boasts of young coquetry, it was not accidental that she never remarried. When her neighbors wanted to introduce her to somebody or other, years after her divorce, a half-crazy woman friend of hers told them off: "Adele lives only for her children, she'd never consent to get married again!" As usual, Adele herself was too proud to declare otherwise. He burning desire not to remain alone in her old age showed itself poignantly when she was already in her seventies and a very distant male relative from Leningrad appeared on the horizon. A couple of years older, he was all she wanted to be—religious but also worldly, a professor of economics interested in theology. It was he who'd found her address in Israel while he was still in Leningrad, he likewise who'd phoned her upon immigrating and suggested they should meet. Blushing like a teenager, she discussed the likelihood of marriage with her children and spent a long time choosing what to wear for the meeting, which she clearly saw as a date. She asked advice on her clothes from both her daughters and her son.

It turned out the man was happily married, with many children and grandchildren; he just wanted to meet a distant relative, no more than that.

Adele's emotions bring to mind a little animal, innocent, harmed by her environment, unable to understand why she is made to suffer.

She can hardly be charged with unquestioning love and admiration for her brother as though these were crimes. We must also understand the sacrifice that religious people—whether Jewish like Meir Stambler or Christian like the well-known Irina Ratushinskaya—made for the sake of their beliefs within the Soviet Union. Religion was the only thing they had to pitch against the state's onslaught. Attempting to define abnormality as deviation from the norm of the majority, psychiatry has a problem with such individuals. Were the few Germans opposing Hitler abnormal? And Meir Stambler, who hated—and taught Adele to hate—Stalin's dictatorship viscerally, perhaps with a kind of hatred only an orthodox believer can have for the devil come to destroy his faith—was he abnormal?

Yes, her decision to follow him from the safety of Kirov to the unknown and dangerous waters of Tashkent can be seen as mistaken, but, fearless as ever, she did indeed save her brother's life in Tashkent—just as she had almost certainly saved their father's in 1937 by being brazen enough to threaten his interrogator with her husband's invented journalistic powers of retribution.

This is what happened in Tashkent in 1943.

Meir Stambler, who goes everywhere chaperoned by his sister, is stopped by a patrol. He produces his forged ID. One look at it—even with his beard, this man of thirty-three hardly looks fifty-three—is enough for them to take him to the military police headquarters. She follows him there. He's arrested. She asks to speak to the officer in charge and is shown in. She goes out of her way to explain to the major that her brother is indeed as old as his papers show him to be and that he's very ill and that they've just lost their father and younger brother and that he, the major, should show compassion, and that her own husband is also a major and war correspondent, and so on. He listens for a long time and looks at her without saying a word. At the end of her speech, he gives orders to release the prisoner and return his ID, endorsed by the headquarters. As she's leaving the room and already in the doorway, he calls back: "Comrade Dubnova!" She turns. "Good luck to you and your brother, ma'am—and don't think others fools."

Selflessly brave, a woman like this deserved a man who'd be her equal, and her life was only half-lived in his absence. You can blame God or fate or chance, but, if anything, Adele is to be pitied rather than censured.

Nor can she be so peremptorily accused of hurling abuse at her husband for no reason. She called him names—and indeed threw things in his face—in the wake of his flaunting his mistress in public, the father of grown-up and still single daughters, a married man walking arm in arm with that hussy in the central park, for the whole city to see. And some did see, in fact: two family friends told her about it. How many women would restrain themselves from making a scene under such circumstances?

His conduct also explains why she was angry that he had found his family in Tashkent only when they were already at the brink of death. Leonid was a womanizer—if not an outright philanderer. He was extremely handsome, and the war situation was a paradise for sexual liaisons. In fact, they were tacitly fostered by the state—for the warriors "to let off steam"—just as the state would later turn a blind eye to the Red Army's massive rapes in Germany. It's not beyond the realms of the possible that he was in no rush to get back to his family, assuming they were more or less all right. You can't blame Adele for being jealous and wishing he'd come sooner.

Blaming a mother for excessive grief over the tragic death of her firstborn is easily done by those who haven't been through such a disaster. Who can tell what grief is appropriate and what over the top? Many decades later, when she was in her eighties, Eugene gave her a beautiful birthday present: an old photograph from around the early 1950s, enlarged and framed. The picture, taken on Pirita beach near Tallinn, shows her, Vladimir, and Eugene in Vladimir's arms. The mother and her firstborn look exceptionally attractive and intelligent; the little boy seems to have noticed something interesting and is trying to get out of his brother's arms. The picture is shot through with an uncanny bliss and tranquility. "Did you like it? Do you look at it now and then?" Eugene asked his mother, noticing after some time that the photo on her table was turned backwards. She hesitated, and he realized his mistake. "It's painful for you, isn't it?" he said. "Yes," she answered, relieved she didn't have to explain.

As for Adele's supposed manipulation of her children, you can call saving them from being brainwashed by the Party and the state "manipulation," but not everybody would. Considering that Leonid once called himself a "mouthpiece" of the Party, perhaps counter-cultural influence was badly needed. Whatever their disagreements with their mother on other issues, all the children sided with her side in that ideological confrontation.

True, Leonid worked hard—but so did Adele. Shopping, cooking, washing and ironing took up all her time and strength. Her husband was a stickler for meals being on time. She boasted that not once throughout their married life had she failed to put well-cooked and tasty food—the dishes he liked—before him when he wanted it. At the age of sixty, in Israel, in order to pay back a private loan taken in Riga for her and her son's needs associated with their exit from the Soviet Union, she went to work on a conveyor belt. There she was quicker than young girls working next to her. When she had paid off the family debt and wanted to resign, her employer begged her to stay. He called her his best worker. Free at last of financial burdens, as a pensioner she would master Hebrew to perfection and go on to explore what interested her—religious thought and Kabala mysticism.

A woman of total integrity, she turned down an offer by a school principal to use her new immigrant's tax exemptions to buy heavily taxed electrical and electronic equipment for the school. "We'll split the tax difference fifty-fifty," he said. "The school will save badly needed money, and you will get a few bob. You won't need this sort of stuff anyway, and it would be a shame not to make use of this loophole." Adele looked at him and said: "It is not for wheeling and dealing that the state has honored me with the new immigrant's status and privileges."

She was penniless and in debt when she said this. Many would call her refusal stupid. For her son it has been a source of great pride.

The Verdict:

We move between Philip Larkin's "They fuck you up, your mum and dad / They may not mean to, but they do" and childhood memories engraved on our minds and characters.

Father: "Don't jump over your whole body by leaps and bounds: use the loofah consistently, step by step; first wash this part, then move to the next one."

Mother: "Don't be afraid, you're doing it too slowly! Bolder, bolder, pour the milk in one quick go, then you won't spill anything."

You've stumbled and fallen, and your Dad's worried face is bending down to you. You're ill and have a headache, and your Mom's rocking you and singing to you. A few images will always be with us until the ultimate, the irreversible migration.

CHAPTER 21: CHICKEN SOUP

Autumn

The world is a house
As cold as ice—
Impossible to keep warm.

Behind the wall
A sick old man trembles
Between white sheets.

I am slowly freezing
In this crypt of a house.
Can he survive?

I hear his rasping cough;
No medicine can help him now.
Winter is closing in.

(I am grateful to Derek Mahon for suggesting some changes to my own translation of this poem written in late 1969)

Father granted his permission, carefully worded. It didn't say he'd given me his parental assent to leave the country. Instead, he wrote: "This is to say that I consider myself legally bound never to ask my son for financial assistance irrespective of his domicile." We applied to the authorities, worried the formulation might not be acceptable. It was. The last four words must have done the trick. The principal applicant was Mother; she referred to me as of no use to anybody anyway, a boy who had to drop out of university due to his weak mind.

Our application to leave the country on the grounds of "humanitarian family reunification" was refused within a few weeks. The reason given was that the family reunification was seen as *netselneso'obrazno*—a cleverly chosen word with a wide variety of meanings, including inappropriate, inadvisable, inexpedient, unfeasible, unreasonable, unwise, and imprudent. *Refuseniks* could take their pick.

According to the rules, you had to wait at least a year to apply again.

Father told me that the Deputy Education Minister of Latvia had summoned him and had been quite angry. "We sent him to Moscow," he said, "we did so following your personal complaint to me, and now he's let us down by breaking off his studies."

I didn't think it probable that the man had been informed of my application to leave the country by the foreign visas department of the Ministry of the Interior where we'd applied; it was much more likely that Moscow University had informed the Latvian educational authorities of my departure. I don't know what reason my father gave him for my dropping out—I hoped he pretended to have those health problems I was supposed to be helping him with—but I was immensely grateful to him for not making an issue of it. I felt terrible enough as it was, imagining the furious Deputy Minister telling my humiliated Dad off and the latter having to take it all with no arguing back; his mentioning this to me as if in passing, in one brief sentence, was an example of his characteristic reserve and the kind of understatement I later came to identify with the English. (The innate reticence of the poet John Heath-Stubbs, who would much later be almost a paternal figure for me, often reminded me of my father's.)

Now all I could do was wait—and, of course, get a job.

At least with employment I was quite fortunate. Zhenya Konyaev's father used his connections to get me a job at the State Latvian Institute of Urban Construction Planning. I started work on January 5, 1970, as a Technician and on August 5, 1970 was promoted to Junior Engineer. I was to be a member of the Scientific Organization of Labor unit comprising only myself and my boss, the engineer. Now, in our faculty at Moscow University there had been a track specializing in Industrial Psychology where you were taught this scientific organization of labor, but we didn't take it seriously. Only one student was preparing to take it up because his father-in-law, director of a big factory anxious to create a sinecure for him under his own wing, had told him to do so. We dismissed industrial psychologists as people who told workers what color their walls should be painted. As for the scientific organization of labor, there were lots of jokes going round about it. Here's a typical one.

A customer coming to the restaurant observes that the waiter is attired rather unusually. A tablespoon sticks out of his top pocket and a little chain is seen below, disappearing into his fly zip.

"What's all this about?" he asks, pointing to the two new features.

"Why, don't you see," says the waiter, "we've got this scientific labor thing now."

"I've heard of it," says the customer. "It's supposed to be very progressive, but what has it got to do with the spoon and the chain?"

"Well," the waiter begins to explain, "before this scientific organization thing came, whenever a fly got into the client's soup, the waiter, according to instructions, had to take the dish back to the kitchen, remove the insect, and then bring the soup back. Now I'd just take this spoon out of my pocket and get rid of the fly, on the spot. Valuable work time is saved in this way."

"Oh, I see," says the customer. "That makes sense. But what's the chain for?"

"In the old days, when the waiter took a leak, he had to wash his hands afterwards, according to instructions. Now, thanks to this scientific labor thing, I can simply use the chain to take the object out, without touching it. So I don't have to wash my hands, which, again, saves time."

"I can understand even that," says the customer, getting agitated. "But how in God's name do you get your object back into your trousers without touching it?"

"Why, with the spoon!" beams the waiter.

My job was very low-paid and really invented, but to get it I had to tell them that once my father got better I intended to go back to Moscow, get my diploma in Industrial Psychology and come back to them as a fully qualified specialist.

Now, instead of lectures on brain structure and higher nervous functions, I had to sit through talks, obligatory at every Soviet institution, raising public political and social awareness.

The visiting lecturer would say: "In the west they wonder how we can think Lenin's words 'Every kitchen maid should be able to administer state affairs' are still relevant today, in the second half of the twentieth century. But we know just how relevant these words still are!"

Mysina, head of the printing section—and the one who later got me into my final tangle with the KGB—commented from her seat, with a mixture of smarminess and subservience: "Nowadays we no longer have kitchen maids. We have specialists in the culinary field!"

"Do you want to hear a talk next time comparing the position of women in bourgeois Latvia with that in our Soviet Latvia today?" asked the lecturer after his talk.

"That would be very interesting!" Mysina again volunteered on behalf of us all.

"Why's he always got his nose in a notebook? What's he writing there?" my fellow workers asked my line manager, the engineer, about me. (Throughout my life I have always used boring official events of this sort to fill out my diary or compose poetry.) Soon enough, I got an anonymous note bearing these words: "We're struck by your disregard for our collective body."

In fact, my attitude to my fellow workers was nothing of the sort; the note was unfair and I suspect it was written tongue-in-cheek by some girl or other present at the meeting and curious about my unusual conduct. I was fortunate with this "collective body." As with all other difficulties in my life, this too could have been much worse. Apart from Mysina, who, local rumor had it, was a sort of liaison with the KGB, all the people I knew at our institution were intelligent and pleasant. It was perhaps representative of the best in the Soviet Union. Yevseyev, head of the Planning Section, the one who had given me the job, was Russian; my immediate supervisor Aaron Shlomovich, Jewish; the planning engineer Milch, Latvian; two clerk-cum-graphics girls Russian and one Latvian. I've retained very warm memories of all of them. The overall head of the Institute, Nartysh, was Latvian, but he was too distant for little people like myself, and I was privileged to meet him only when he summoned me for a KGB-initiated interview. But that was still to come.

Aaron Shlomovich was an orphan. His parents had been killed in the Great Patriotic War, and he had been brought up in an orphanage. In his mid-thirties, short and compactly built, with intense black eyes, he exuded tension and readiness to fight back. It took him a while to lose his habitual suspiciousness—yet another quality he must have learned at his orphanage—and open up to me, but when he did, he gave me his friendship with no reservations. We confided in one another; he too would have liked to emigrate to Israel, but couldn't do it because his wife feared applying in uncertain circumstances. The funniest thing about my position was that not only had I nothing to do in my line of work but I had little idea what his duties were. (A friend who had left the USSR much later in life simply laughed at my puzzlement and said that half the country had functioned in that way.)

Aaron got a camera for our section (an avid amateur photographer, I was glad he'd asked for a good one) to photograph objects useful in our task of improving productivity. He talked about getting a tape recorder, presumably to record our colleagues' ideas. From time to time, he went to other institutions dealing with construction planning and sometimes took me along. The purpose was to share experience and projects, but discussions there seemed to me just a way to pass the time pretending to work toward achieving something. Occasionally I had to bring our camera with me to photograph well-organized workplaces or successfully colored walls.

(As a conscientious employee, I'm still proud of my refusal to comply with a request to use government equipment for pornographic purposes. When an engineer at our industrial counterpart, the State Latvian Institute of Industrial Construction Planning, asked me to take a few photos of his girlfriend with no clothes on, I politely declined. I have to say she was quite plain-looking, with no figure; considering my permanent state of being starved of sex, I wonder if I'd still have refused if she's been slim and gorgeous.)

Sometimes I'd simply walk about the city taking pictures of people and parks with this camera, which was vastly superior to my own. My interest in photography had started at the age of about fourteen or fifteen. Father had just left and Mother had found a temporary part-time job running a youth club. It had two simple cameras that could be borrowed and a dark room with all the necessary equipment. I learned enthusiastically about bracketing exposure, viewfinder systems, metering the light and exposure, lens and depth of field, aperture and perspective. I began developing, fixing, and printing films on my own and experimented with all kinds of photographic paper of various contrast grades and emulsion types, with different printing techniques and methods of processing the print like toning and hand coloring. It excited me in a way discovering a new land excites an explorer. Photography was to remain one of my greatest passions.

For the first months at work I was housed in a big empty room-cum-office on the top floor under the roof and was privileged to witness the way a typical Soviet institution functioned. The heads of sections and departments must have made an effort to produce results, but the lower-ranking employees had plenty of time to spare. My room became a place of pilgrimage for bored workers who welcomed an opportunity to get away from their own office and to have some company and even a reasonably informed conversation. The taciturn Latvian engineer Milch came; as with Aaron, I gradually won his trust, and he complained about the Soviet occupation of Latvia. Lena came, a graphic designer and gifted artist, to chat about this and that and to show me her drawings and paintings. (I still have an illustration she did for one of my early short stories.) And, of course, Aaron would visit me very often, two or three times a day. When one of them came and saw another already there, he or she would quietly depart and return later. I was hardly ever alone. It began to weigh me down, at least with the two men it did; I felt like a receptacle for other people's loneliness. I had plenty of my own, but no one wanted to hear me out.

Vladimir Deryabin and Alexander Sled, friends from Moscow University, came to visit; I showed them around. They went back to study, getting closer to their degrees with every passing day; I remained in my limbo.

I liked to refer to those one and a half years until my exit from the country as a "passage through torment" or the "way of suffering," to use the title of Aleksey Nikolayevich Tolstoy's trilogy (usually translated as *The Road to Calvary*, a mistranslation which anyway would be misleading in my case). This time, ending in a peak—or abyss—of "malignant sadness" (the title of Lewis Wolpert's book on depression), was a mixture of interminable quarrels with Mother, the onslaught of religion, and the unbearable poignancy of love begging consummation.

Mother started to take me around to see her cronies. By that time she'd induced so much guilt in me that I found it impossible to refuse, even if every now and then I'd try to. She was too proud to show up on her own, and I was a substitute for a husband. After two years among my peers, young well-educated men and women at Moscow University, I found myself visiting people my mother's age or even older, some of them backward, some half-senile, cracking jokes at the sight of me, like, "We extend our welcome to the working classes!" or—inviting me to their family table—"Wash your hands—we aren't proud!" That was the husband speaking. His wife explained to my mother and me: "I've been told by the doctor to bring a sample, so I've already peed in a bottle and tomorrow morning I'll take it to the clinic."

It got worse when Mother began dragging me to semi-clandestine religious meetings at the end of every Sabbath. These took place at somebody else's place each time. I admired the fortitude of her friends and the Orthodox Jewish community's general persistence in sticking to their religion in the face of the state's harsh disapproval—if not persecution—but there was absolutely nothing for me among them. Those gatherings were warm, with friendly chat and exchange of news, and discussion of matters of faith, but all that was of no interest to me whatsoever. The youngest person present was the physicist Prof. Herman Branover, now seen as one of the world's leading scientists, a pioneer in the field of magnetohydrodynamcs—and he was almost twenty years my senior! In keeping with the old Hassidic tradition, stemming from bitterly cold Ukrainian winters, those gathered every now and again had a little drink of vodka, which was supposed to "release the soul." Those drinks were the only thing I enjoyed there. (Later I'd heartily wish I hadn't.) And so, drinking vodka, tucking into hot potatoes and hardly paying attention to the conversation around me, I'd either compose poetry or regurgitate in my mind the book I had read most recently, or think of girls, more often than not erotically.

Once I couldn't take it anymore and refused. I said I had a headache. Mother's attempts to make me change my mind were of no avail. Then, as I was in the middle of reading a book, Herman Branover's call came. Solicitously, he inquired into my headache, suggested I take a pill and said they all would be most happy if I joined them, as my customary presence was sorely missed. "I'll come," I said. Now, Herman was a remarkable man, and I admired him for his spirit. (He was to go on with his fifteen-year struggle to leave the Soviet Union, constantly harassed by the KGB, later becoming the first Jew with a Doctor of Science degree and the title of Full Professor to receive an exit visa.) But at that moment I hated his guts. I vacillated for a few minutes and decided to ignore his approaches, for which I had my own name: an iron fist in a silk glove. And then, just as I was going back to my book, Mother herself phoned. "They're all waiting for you," she whispered threateningly—and I put on a raincoat (it was pouring outside) and trudged miserably to the tram stop. That particular meeting was at the opposite end of town; I had to change trams along the way. I both despised and pitied myself throughout the journey.

Mother was now firmly ensconced in that religious community. "Why are you clinging to this life?" she asked a woman friend of hers who wasn't a full believer. "This life's just a dream."

The other's reply, "Better to dream a good dream than a nightmare," was, in my opinion, eminently sensible. But that woman, widowed and still carrying vestiges of prettiness from her youth, made me feel embarrassed by frequently reminiscing in my presence about the time of her life when she had been "so vibrantly, so adamantly young."

Then there was also the growing secular Jewish awareness; a few times I went to Rumbula with other young Zionist dissidents to clear and maintain the place and feel part of something, especially when standing and singing the Jewish partisans' song by the monument to the victims of German occupation.

Rumbula (or Rumbuli) was a small railroad station in a forest twelve kilometers south of Riga, where in 1941 the Nazis had killed all the Jews imprisoned in the Riga ghetto. In 1964, local Jewish activists had managed to overcome Soviet government barriers and erect the Rumbula memorial stone, with the inscription "To the victims of fascism" not only in Latvian and Russian, but also in Yiddish. (The memorial sculpture, designed by Sergejs Rizhs, would be inaugurated on November 29, 2002, and I'm glad that the memorial stone from Soviet times, by which my friends and I had stood many times between 1969 and 1971, was preserved.)

I was connected to that part of the Holocaust in two ways: my distant ancestor the historian Simon Dubnov was murdered in the Riga ghetto, and Frieda Michelson, the mother of one of my best friends, Daniel Michelson, miraculously survived the liquidation in the Rumbula Forest. In fact, at that time, in the late 1960s and early '70s, she was working on her book *I survived Rumbuli*, but I was already thoroughly familiar with her story, both from her own lips (she was a close friend of Mother's) and from her son Daniel's retelling of it.

Another center for Zionist youth in Riga in the late 1960s was the home of the painter Joseph Kuzkovsky (1902–1969), whose large painting, now entitled *Led to the Slaughter—Babiy Yar*, hangs in a hallway in the Israeli Knesset. In fact, his own title for this work, which had hung on the wall of his drawing room in Riga, was *If I forget this …*, which makes much more sense to me, both because of its Biblical reference *If I forget thee, O Jerusalem!*, which the painter had told me he'd had in mind and, more importantly, because of the self-portrait worked into the painting of the painter as a young man, hands clenched into fists, burning with hatred of the Nazi murderers, desperately looking for a way to overcome them.

Once when I visited him with a girl named Sarah, whom I'd taught to skate when still at school, Kuzkovsky asked her to sit for a portrait. She was an attractive girl. They started discussing arrangements and I felt left out. I must confess I'd half hoped he'd ask me too—if only to confirm that she and I were worthy of intimacy—but he never did.

He died that same year; I'd like to think he'd had the time to paint Sarah (she and I drifted apart, so I have no way of knowing). I am still glad I took the trouble to look up his widow a few times after she'd immigrated to Israel in the early 1970s. She (and their sweet little dog called Nefesh—meaning "soul" in Hebrew) lived near Tel Aviv and, though much saddened by Joseph's death, she maintained the charm and hospitality of their home in Riga, where I'd been a welcome guest.

I was glad to be able to contribute to and be part of that wonderfully selfless group of young Zionist dissidents and to partake of the wisdom and sacrifice of the older generation, but my mind was far too often elsewhere. They were all united by a single idea;

I was thinking restlessly along a number of routes, some pointing one way, others in a diametrically opposed direction.

My main pursuit was literature and, specifically, poetry. To relieve my boredom at work, I took to writing letters to friends and relatives in verse—specifically in dactyl, imitating Homer's *pléon epì oínopa pónton*—"sailing upon the wine-dark sea". (Dactyls, rather common in Russian poetry, were rarely used in English verse until the nineteenth century and almost disappeared again after Swinburne.) My friends took this in their stride, but after a few such letters my sisters and their husbands got worried and wrote to Mother to ask if I was all right.

My friend Itella lent me her English literature textbook. She was a student in her final, diploma year in the English Department of Riga University and doing serious stuff. I looked only at the most modern poetry and still remember that there was a lot of Hardy and some early Yeats—nothing later than that. (When, some dozen years later, I mentioned this to John Heath-Stubbs, he chuckled and said that more or less the same attitude had at the time governed English studies in his *alma mater* Oxford: recent reputations being controversial, one should keep to those already established.) I was puzzled by the English meters: even in recognizably traditional poems they seemed much freer than Russian prosody.

Religion had begun to make inroads into my mind. Apart from accompanying Mother to those Saturday night meetings at various religious homes, I had been urged by her to go to the synagogue on festive days and, little by little, also on Saturday mornings. I didn't pray; instead, I used my time there to analyze the Hebrew with the help of the parallel Russian translation in the prayer book. As always, I approached everything through analysis and through language. It was a sort of scholarly learning, two for the price of one: advancing in Hebrew and researching Judaism. But it was far too remote from my real concerns—literature and psychology—and so both oppressed me and played havoc with my mind. Soon, ever impressionable and probably genetically predisposed to paranoia, I'd be on the threshold of religious delusions—like connecting the sudden appearance of the sun on an overcast day with a promise of light and happiness I'd just read in a prayer book in the synagogue. I was saved from all that by my ever-wakeful libido and my passion—waiting in the wings—for a girl who was to be the greatest love of my youth.

One image has remained in my mind's eye. Having turned off the main thoroughfare and delved into the rabbit warren labyrinth of tiny streets of the old town, I'm about to go into the blind alley of the synagogue to spend the next two or three hours on its lower ground floor, cool and slightly damp, illuminated by electric lighting, listening to prayers. Before I take the final few steps I notice a young woman in a bigger street leading off the alley—leading, in fact, to another thoroughfare and city center. Her beautiful body is sharply outlined by the sun. My whole being yearns to go there, to go up to her and to say something. But I can't. I'm too shy—and my religious duty calls! I turn my back on the girl and enter the synagogue yard. Psychoanalysts would have a field day analyzing what they would surely interpret as a return to the womb.

Gradually a sense of general crisis deepened and depression set in. My poetry was of no interest to anybody. My status had plummeted. I was wasting my life. Most of the time there was nothing to do and my mind was half-empty or occupied with things of little interest at best and at worst hostile to me. Boozing with friends usually made it worse, bringing feelings and expressions of regret mixed with self-pity.

I had no girlfriend; Yevgeniya drank more and more; when inebriated, she became indiscriminately horny. Once I brought Aaron over to have a drink with her; generally ascetic and abstemious, he barely touched the alcohol, but she quickly got drunk and gave him the eye. He, a faithful married man, was aghast and hurried to leave. I left with him.

Mother was ever-vigilant. Anya the Zionist girl rang when I was out; tactful, she wouldn't reveal to me just what she'd been told, but it took her a month to try again. Itella did tell me about her telephone exchange with Mother. She'd had an English book for me and had asked Mother for my telephone number at work, only to be told the following: "I can't give it to you, as too many girls phone him there and distract him from working." Itella fumed: "No one has ever dared talk to me in that way!" Mother was unperturbed: "I did the right thing: it's quite enough those hussies phoning here—they can at least leave you alone at your workplace."

To be honest, the whole thing amused me more than it made me angry. Neither girl measured up to my Moscow women friends, and I didn't have anyone whose phone call would make me face Mother in a serious confrontation. (When one such girl appeared, there were reasons why she never phoned me at home.) So I just laughed heartily together with my friend Vladimir Kosov, who advised me to swear to Mother that I'd marry the very next girl she told off on the phone. But I'd remember that situation when years later I was severely depressed and a psychologist told me: "You need to be among young people, your peers, your own age, boys and girls, you must have lots of friends, meeting them in cafes, joining them at parties. Being with your elder relatives is the same as being alone or even worse. It's contraindicative for you."

Looking back, I think that one of the greatest things my father wanted to do for me was pay my rent, should I decide to move out and live separately from Mother. Now I saw him more often and felt closer to him. When I complained about her, he said: "If you want to live on your own, I'll give you the money. Nothing fancy, of course, just a room, I know one in Maskavas Street."

I considered this briefly and even mentioned it to Mother. "He just wants you away from me. He'll do anything to have you go elsewhere. But you don't know how to cook. Here you always have hot chicken soup on the table."

I should have taken up father's offer. It would have taught me much about independence. Living on my own would have made it possible for me to have a real friend among those girls with whom there was mutual affection but who lived with their parents, ruling out any serious relationship while I still lived with Mother. A girlfriend would have given me much-needed warmth, alleviating my emotional and physical loneliness; she would have allowed me to pour out my own frozen feelings.

I still remember how I hesitated. The idea of getting away from Mother was tempting, but then I imagined living away from the city center and having to take a tram to work or to a get-together with friends: I imagined what it would be like to have to take full care of myself, shopping, cooking, cleaning, washing—and I chickened out. It's easy to blame myself for avoiding life's challenges, but I was already sick at heart and afraid of being totally alone. Paradoxically, the decision to stay where I was would ultimately lead to feeling a hundred times worse. That was my first life lesson on despondency: it has no pity; if you don't make a real effort to fight it, it'll defeat you utterly.

Then Marina said, as we kissed by night in a Riga park in the early autumn of 1970: "It'll be cold soon. What are you going to do when winter comes?"

The chicken soup was to lead to a near-suicidal clinical depression.

Chapter 22: Marina

"I can't go back to yesterday because I was a different person then," says Lewis Carroll's Alice. There's no time in the mind, and I can go back to yesterday, even as a different person. Traumas remain forever ready, their largely subconscious bulk triggered off instantaneously.

I've now been moved from my upstairs perch down to the office to sit with the four other people of our section. (I don't remember why: most likely because somebody left.) I'm lucky: I have the window seat, which has always been (and will always remain) my favorite place. Opposite me sits Ilga, a Latvian woman in her early thirties; to my right is Marina, who's twenty-two and Russian. Ilga and Marina are doing clerical work. Next to Ilga is Aaron, my boss, and after him the head of our planning section, Yevseev. The last two are very often absent from the room. I am twenty.

Along the corridor there's another section, and Vera Nikandrova is sitting there. She's also a clerk, like Marina. She's younger, nineteen, pretty and sweet. Occasionally I come out into the hall to smoke and sit down in an armchair. If she happens to pass by she sits down too and we chat. I like her and can see she likes me. She looks innocent, childlike, I'm sure she's never had a boyfriend. I've seen many like her among first-year students at Moscow University. I hardly pay any attention to Marina, who's over two years my senior and married anyway—to an army lieutenant, of all people. Even though he's a first lieutenant meant shortly to be promoted to a captain, I'm still unimpressed. The fact that she's studying for a degree in Russian at Riga University doesn't particularly sway me either, as she's doing this by taking evening classes or in some extracurricular fashion (I'm not sure which and am not interested in finding out); in my opinion, neither route really counts.

Then something happens. It's tempting to say something indefinable, but the truth is that I simply don't remember. It may have been a phrase she said or the way she moved close to me or a look she gave me or red spots appearing on her pale cheeks while we exchanged a few words. It may have been her quoting a line or two of poetry. Perhaps she even asked me to show her my own work: everybody in our section knew I was writing verse. (Thoughtful and reserved, Ilga had called me "a writer"—making me blush with delight— just because of the way I'd probed into the tragic story of her parents under Stalin and the way I'd listened to her, riveted.)

Anyway, whatever it was, it made me start giving her closer looks.

Marina had chestnut hair, blue eyes, pale skin, and full lips. She looked intelligent and was attractive, even if not perhaps conventionally pretty. Although on the short side—five foot four or thereabouts—she had a really beautiful figure, slim and lithe.

Ilya Ehrenburg wrote in his memoirs *People, Years, Life* that it's impossible to know why one woman attracts you rather than another. Maybe so, when you're older and more cerebral and fall in love. But at the age of twenty, it's quite easy to know—not at that age, of course, but later, when looking back at your young self. It's all to do with an indistinct, an unformed pushing of the raw vernal blood, an attack which brooks no resistance. Youth, though physically the strongest time of your life, can be very vulnerable—sometimes really helpless—that way.

It is difficult to define eroticism in a female colleague who doesn't flirt and is dressed modestly. Everything in Marina—walk, grace, talk, glances—was that of a woman conscious of being a woman. Next to Marina, Vera Nikandrova looked an immature girl.

I would usually go home during the lunch hour—for the chicken soup. Marina also went home. Both of us lived within walking distance, and nobody minded if we were late—as we usually were—coming back. One summer day, as the lunch break was approaching, she said to Ilga—they were not only colleagues at work but good friends: "Today I'm going to stay in for my lunch and have just a sandwich and a soda pop." Her voice was louder than usual and her body moved slightly, almost imperceptibly, toward me as she was saying this. When we were left alone, I suggested we both went out for a coffee to one of the nearby places. "Why not?" she said.

The next day she announced to Ilga that she'd go for a walk in a nearby park instead of lunching. My ears already pricked, I invited myself to be her companion on this walk. In the park, she asked me to recite some of my poetry, and I was only too happy to oblige. "Marina, do inspire me for my next poem!" I suggested. "I'm not planning to inspire you yet," she replied.

"I don't want to go home for lunch this whole month," she said to Ilga after this. "He's at home, on leave."

"Your husband the lieutenant?" asked Ilga.

"Who else?" Marina said and gave a dismissive shrug.

Our next outing was to the Tallinn restaurant, just a few doors away from our institute. In Riga's restaurants you didn't have to have a lavish meal but could just ask for a coffee and a piece of cake. "This place played host to the worst day of my life," she said. "It happened a year and a half ago." I knew she'd got married about then, so I ventured to ask: "Do you mean your marriage banquet?" She didn't answer, but tears welled to her eyes.

"Marina, could we … I wonder if perhaps … if you might have a few free minutes after work," I stammered, nervous as I'd never felt before with a girl. "Perhaps we could walk in the park … for a few minutes … if you have them to spare, that is."

"I've got to get back home after work," she said. My heart sank and I began mumbling: "Of course, of course, I understand …" when she interrupted me and went on: "But tomorrow I'll be returning books to the library, so you can come with me, if you like."

That day we walked from one park to another for two or three hours after the library. When it got dark, I kissed her, and she responded, with her lips and with her whole body.

The next morning there were flowers on her table. "I'm sorry," I said, "It should have been I who bought them."

"You go to work like on a date—and you even get paid for it," Zhenya Konyaev said. He was never envious but always happy for me.

An erotic obsession followed: lips and hands on benches in dark parks. (What she wrote to me later—"I love your hands when they aren't too insistent"—wasn't true: she didn't mind the urgency, just as I loved her nervous caresses.)

All the dykes crumbled and a flood burst in. Psychiatry sees romantic obsession as a mental disorder, and I can attest to this. Looking back on that time, I can't help but reflect on two of my favorite sayings, "Feed the brain to keep it sane!" and "Rest is Rust." My brain had been quite empty, and inertia had set in. Whatever little thought and action there had been was of an even more depressed and mechanical nature than usual, because my chances for Riga University—the only ray of hope on the horizon—had just fallen through.

When our exit visa application was turned down, I had had to begin thinking of other arrangements in order to put my life in the country back on the right track, for who knew how long it might take for me to fulfill my dream of exiting to freedom—if I ever did. University had always been for me a *sine qua non*. There being no Psychology Department at Riga University, I had to settle for the next best—English language and literature. It would never have occurred to me to study Russian, as both that language and literature were a known quantity (or so I thought), whereas other tongues and other poetries kept teasing and tempting me. ("Don't tempt alien speech," warned Mandelstam, himself fixated his whole life on foreign verse and its evasive sounds; my life had made me confront a number of languages and, in the case of English, to go so far as to attempt to make alien cadencies my own, as far as humanly possible.)

Having pulled myself together following the blow of the visa authorities' refusal, I had made my way to the English Department and spoken to its head, Dr. Tsemirauga, about the possibility of taking an external degree—the kind Marina was doing in Russian—while continuing to work. She was nice and friendly and reacted kindly to my story of a parent's illness and the resulting need to come back from Moscow. Of course, she asked the obvious question—why I had quit instead of getting a transfer—but I had some yarn or other (most likely to do with panicking, impulsiveness, and inexperience) at the ready. She made me sit a couple of English tests and then accepted me for the second year in the department. I had to take two or three exams to make up for the first year, at the beginning of autumn. One of them being Latin, I rushed out to buy a Latin textbook (which I still have, after all these years!). My happiness was almost delirious as I realized I wasn't lost and the situation was redeemable. As long as I could carry on studying, I didn't even mind waiting for the exit visa.

At the end of the summer I went to see Dr. Tsemirauga again to fix the date for my exams and to enroll officially as a second-year student in the department.

"Something isn't quite right with you, Comrade Dubnov," she said.

"What can be possibly wrong with me?" I inquired, still in high spirits and feeling very much at home within the walls of higher learning.

"It has come to our attention that you have applied to leave the country for Israel," she said. "As a result, we can't have you as our student. We don't invest in young people whose aim is to get their education here and take advantage of it abroad."

Fair enough, I felt like saying, but in this case let me leave! It's cruelly immoral to do what you're doing—keeping me locked up here while barring me from getting an education. But I held my peace: it had nothing to do with Dr. Tsemirauga, who in fact had been helpful and against whom I bore no grudge whatsoever. She had her instructions from a different authority, which could not be gainsaid.

(It's impossible to know just how the university had found out that I had applied for an exit visa. There were no computers back then. I see three possibilities. Generally open and occasionally a blabbermouth, sharing my happiness over the acceptance by Riga University was the last thing I could hold back. So I must have talked about it to some half a dozen people. Not my closest friends Zhenya Konyaev and Yuri Afremovich, and not Aaron Shlomovich, but somebody or other among the remaining few could have betrayed me. I'd like to hope not. The second possibility is that the Deputy Education Minister wasn't in a hurry to forget how he'd been let down and made a point of checking with Riga's institutions of higher learning to prevent me from enrolling there. But perhaps the likeliest is the third possibility. There were general rumors among young people in my position—those wanting to leave the Soviet Union but worried about their education—that the 1970/71 academic year was the first one for which the KGB arm of Latvia's Ministry of the Interior circulated lists of those who'd applied for their exit visas among all institutes of higher education in the republic. That was done to ensure no one among the would-be émigrés might have a chance to get in.)

No wonder, then, that I took such a leap into the obsession of love: it was about the only thing that could make my position bearable. Having said that, the girl, quintessentially feminine, intelligent and intuitive, sensitive and artistic, with a psyche both strong and tremulous, was a worthy cause.

The first time I dared put my arms around her in our office when we were left alone, red spots showed on her cheeks and she whispered: "Don't—Ilga will be back any moment!" I pressed her against me. Not knowing enough about a woman's sexuality, I still guessed at something when she shivered, almost convulsively, in my arms and rushed out. "Please forgive me," I said when she came back in a few minutes. "I've already forgiven you," she answered at once. That phrase would become a refrain whenever I apologized for real and imaginary wrongs—and I sometimes begged her pardon for hardly any reason at all, just to hear her say it.

Everybody in our section knew what was going on. Yevseyev, our boss, was an amazingly kind and tactful man. Upon coming into his own office and finding Marina and I alone, even just sitting at our respective desks, he would say gingerly, almost guiltily: "I'm just popping out into the hall to have a cigarette."

We'd both burst into laughter simultaneously the moment the door closed behind him; Marina and I had an almost identical sense of humor.

I also admired her audacity. She was a married woman; people who knew her might have seen us on those night-time trysts in gardens and several cinema visits. One colleague at work did in fact see us. She walked into our office under some pretext or other, when we were all at our desks and asked in an innocent tone: "Marina, I saw you last night, quite late, in Strēlnieku Park, with a man—walking so fast, so fast, almost running. Was it your husband?"

"No it wasn't!" she snapped, jumped up, and left the room.

(I enjoyed not only being with her but also the sheer process of walking together: we had the same brisk pace, rare with women.)

There was nowhere for the two of us to go to make love. I briefly thought of trying a hotel but dismissed the idea as both impractical and absurd. I'd never stayed in a hotel before and didn't even know if they'd take anybody in for just a few hours. (They definitely wouldn't, but it never occurred to me that I could book a room for one night and then use it only part of the evening.) I was also afraid of offending the girl: inviting her to a hotel was bound to look like a cheap travesty of love, like a banal extramarital affair of which there must have been thousands around every day. I was too naïve to analyze her question: "What will you do in the winter?"

(My friend John Hunt, an Anglo-Irish writer, once told me about the Dubliners' solution to this kind of problem: in the summer and early autumn they all went to the countryside just out of the city bounds, to do what they needed. Alas, this was impossible in Riga, for a whole host of reasons.)

Now, the question of nature versus nurture is notoriously difficult, but I believe that traits like kindness and warm-heartedness on the one hand and cold cruelty on the other are usually hereditary. The time is the late 1940s, a few years after the end of the Great Patriotic War, the place an orphanage somewhere in Siberia. Menstrual cotton wool falls out of a young woman teacher's clothing. Twelve-year-olds pick it up, put it on a stick and march around, shouting out the name of the teacher at the top of their voices and adding a swear word. Almost all the children participate. Some of them will carry this harshness into their adulthood; in others, their latent genes will come to life and push out shoots.

Aaron Shlomovich, brought up in that orphanage, surprised me with a tactfulness I didn't expect. He spoke deferentially and chastely about the situation Marina and I were in. "It moves and pains me to see you two," he said, "young people so much in love yet unable to consummate it. I wish I could help, but I have no room anywhere outside my own home, with my Cerberus of a wife."

Vitaly's comments presented a sharp contrast—and Vitaly had come not from a post-war orphanage but from an elite, well-to-do family of university professors. In late October he and Grisha came to stay with me for a few days and I showed them around Riga. On the second of November I decided to mark my twenty-first birthday in a modest riverside restaurant and invited Marina and three friends, Vitaly, Grisha, and Zhenya Konyaev. We drank and chatted; she gave me a beautiful smoking pipe for a present (I smoked heavily at the time, both cigarettes and pipes; curiously enough, I'd later give up smoking while fighting drinking). Then Marina and I danced, and the physical contact tormented us both. Pale, her eyes closed, she seemed almost in a trance, pressing her hand painfully into my chest. She couldn't stay too late, so we all left about nine. Marina went her way, and the four of us, ours. As Vitaly, Grisha, and I were climbing the stairs back home, after parting from Zhenya, I said: "I'm crazy with jealousy. I try not to think of her in bed with her husband." Vitaly thought for a few seconds and said: "And you know, everything's allowed in bed between husband and wife—anything, absolutely anything goes!"

I couldn't sleep that night, restlessly tossing and turning.

Ever-trusting—or, better, hopelessly infantile—I didn't hold that remark against him, thinking he was merely stating a fact, with no ulterior motive, no agenda of his own. I thought it was just a comradely scoff, with no trace of malice. I still refused to learn and still knew nothing about the world of ill will and intrigue.

Vitaly left the next day, and in two days so did I, likewise for Moscow.

From Certificate of Attendance and Graduation
USSR State Construction
Higher Engineering Courses

Issued to comrade Dubnov Yevgeny Leonidovich to certify that he has graduated from the courses of raising qualification of senior technicians and engineers specializing in scientific organization of labor and improvement of construction planning processes. The courses commenced on November 3, 1970 and ended on November 18, 1970.

It was Aaron who had to go to Moscow to participate in these courses, but he sent me instead, on the grounds that he was too busy. I was only too glad to travel on the government's dime to look up my friends and see Moscow once more. I also thought of making contingency plans regarding university: since Riga was closed to me, perhaps I might be able to enroll for evening education at the Moscow Institute of Foreign Languages. If we were refused an exit visa again, I'd go to Moscow, find a daytime job and study in the evenings. Nobody in the Riga Visa Office would know where I was and what I was doing, so I could reapply for the exit visa every year while I continued studying. (I don't know how practicable the whole idea was, but I did talk to the dean of the Institute of Foreign Languages that November, and she said she'd enroll me if it came to that—i.e. if my father got better and I came back to Moscow.)

In my eagerness to go, I failed to realize that no one cared about the government's money and, in order to make it easier for Yevseyev to send me (Aaron had already told him he wanted me to go instead of him), I had said that I'd save on the hotel and expenses by staying with my relatives in Moscow. Although my life-list of committed stupidities is quite impressive, this was one of the biggest. Instead of living it up in a decent Moscow hotel and eating out to my heart's content, I had to impose on the Vilensky family once again. This also meant there was hardly any place for me to be alone with a girl, Lena or Sveta—or indeed, somebody new, from the courses or the hotel—a woman who might have taken my mind off Marina. The institute had the money to pay for Aaron and it would have used this money to pay for me. But I wasn't thinking straight: I was totally besotted. So much so in fact that I even stopped writing letters in verse, which hitherto had been one of my chief consolations, proving to myself that I could still "do it."

(I had been using various prosodic forms more complicated than the original five- and six-foot dactyls, which after a while had begun to seem too easy. I had tried every genre and every poetic mold: the acrostic and the villanelle, the sonnet and the Alexandrian, the ballad and the historical epic song, the canzone and the triolet, the terza rima and the ottava rima, the septima and the Russian folk verse. My friends applauded, while Mother, in her letters to her daughters and in-laws, gave an epistolary equivalent of a theatrical sigh: pity a mother who has such a good-for-nothing for a son!)

My parting from her on the eve of my departure is one of my most vivid memories.

"Your Dubnov is being sent on a business trip to Moscow," her mother said to her. (Marina told me about their conversation.) "Yes, I know," she replied. "And you aren't, are you?" asked her mother. "No, I'm not," Marina said. "A pity," the other shrugged.

I'd officially left the day before, but on the day of my departure I came back into the office for the lunch hour to invite the girl out to the basement bar in the Riga Hotel by way of taking my leave. "I knew you'd come to say goodbye—because I was waiting for you," she said.

In the bar we snuggled in the least illuminated little corner, drank coffee and brandy, nibbled at small pieces of cake, and kissed surreptitiously two or three times. We must have looked like newly-weds. Mostly, though, we talked: she was a marvelous conversationalist, quick, witty, both romantic and wry, informed, and with no need to "clear [her] mind of cant" (Dr. Johnson) because, just as I did, she hated platitudes.

At one point I borrowed a pen from a sympathetic waitress and said to Marina: "Write something nice to me on this serviette." She wrote: "I don't know anything nice but your love." Then she hesitated and added: "A joke."

"It isn't a joke, Marina," I said.

"Tell me how you love me," she asked. "Apart from wanting to sleep with me. Because I'm not going to—not here in this bar."

"What a shame—I thought you might, just about," I replied in the same tone—and then said, quite seriously: "The way I love the city's parks and gardens, its streets and vistas. And not only the city—landscape too—together with all their sounds. Yes, I love you the way I love space and its music."

"What about time?" she asked.

"No, I don't love time," I said. "It intimidates me. I think I'll spend my whole life grappling with it."

That lunch break took two and a half hours. ("Two and a half hours to say goodbye to such a girl is nothing," said Aaron, sensitive and sympathetic as ever.) Finally, we left in our different directions: she back to work and I home to pack. On an impulse, a couple of minutes later I ran after her, caught up with her as she was crossing the Bastion Mound park, took her by the shoulders from behind, turned her round to face me and kissed her all over the face. Then I let her go and watched as she walked on, quickly but not very steadily.

I wrote to her, and she wrote back, and once I phoned her in the office, on an agreed day during the lunch hour.

Of those two weeks in Moscow, I best remember the wonderful hospitality of the Vilenskys upon whom I imposed, and, vaguely, meeting old friends and fellow students. As for the courses, apart from the address (Bolshaya Dorogomilovskaya 27, trolleybus 39 or by metro to Kiyevskaya Station—names and numbers which were easy for me to memorize, as they were associated in my mind with specific details and mnemonic devices), I hardly recall anything at all.

As I was leaving Moscow—this time for good—a tenuous white flurry started, now thickening—flake on flake—now disappearing over the horizon, dream-like.

On the train, I kept wiping the mist off the carriage window with a passionate hand to watch the snow-covered ground. The gentle, dimly luminous snow looked to me like a naked girl. I'd never felt so much desire for one particular woman before.

Back in Riga, Boris—the one who'd plagiarized my poem about the caryatids—was to be my savior. He had a small room in Maskavas Street, and after much beseeching from me, agreed to give me the key for a few hours one evening.

Still I didn't have the heart to invite Marina directly for intimacy: I said I wanted to read her my poetry. We fixed it for December 14. The day before, she was a bit tardy leaving at the end of work, so I waited up for her. We often left the building together and then went home in our opposite directions, but that was the first time I actually made a point of it and waited; I also saw her off as far as Riga University, which was about halfway on her journey and then turned back. Next morning, the day of my "poetry reading," we just happened to arrive at the front door at the same time and so went into the office together, meriting the comment from Ilga: "Going out together, and coming in together, and so together throughout your lives."

We were to meet in the city center, by the Bastion Mound. It was raining, now hesitantly, now restlessly. The tram didn't come, and I walked. I was about half an hour late. When I got there, rain-drunk, she was waiting under the tram stop shelter.

"I'm sorry I'm late," I said. "Please forgive me."

"I've already forgiven you," she said.

At last we got to Boris's flat. Nervous, I recited my verses for quite a while before daring to approach her. I kissed her and made to take off her clothes, but she said: "Please, don't. Please. I'll do it myself." She got undressed, with her back to me, as though embarrassed to face me. "Don't touch me there, please," she said when I attempted to caress her. (She'd always say "please"—even in intimate moments—and I was invariably moved by this girlish, exaggeratedly helpless pleading.) Then I undressed and turned her around, and she began to stroke me all over with her most sensitive and most gentle fingers.

Of our intimacy I remember only that it was beautiful and hypnotic and that at one point she raised herself above me and looked at me for some time.

I think we only had about half an hour naked together before there was a knock at the door. It was some friend of Boris's. I told him Boris should be back in an hour, and he said he'd wait for him outside in the corridor. A quarter of an hour after that Boris himself knocked. I was angry: we'd agreed he'd return later, but there was nothing I could do. She wanted to leave. She must have felt embarrassed passing by two men ogling her hungrily, like a cheap tart; looking down, she slipped out quickly.

We stepped into quivering puddles. The air was damp but the wind was weak and the rain seemed to have stopped. As we stood and waited at the tram stop, strengthening gusts of wind swayed the branches of nearby trees and sprinkled us with raindrops—and then the rain started again and came down really hard. There was, as there always is, something mesmerizing about multiple strings and drops of descending water tossed about. We watched the downpour and stayed silent.

Seeing her home on the bus, I joked about my poetry being evidently so marvelous as to persuade her to succumb to my courtship. She gave a tiny little smile and said: "Of course I knew what I was coming for."

"Oh, Marina," I mumbled in bliss and kissed her there and then.

"Don't," she said, "I've already made myself up for the homecoming."

Yes, in Zhora's immortal words, she was a woman, and I was a boy, but somehow it didn't matter in this case, because she never tried to manipulate me.

Earlier that day Aaron had told me about something that had happened when Marina and I had been out of the room. Zina from the Planning Section had come in and said: "That girl of yours, Marina, I so often see her and this Dubnov together. But she's older than him, isn't she? And isn't she married? Is she going to apply for a divorce, then, or what?" And Ilga, Aaron said, had answered: "Things happen in life, you know."

"Marina," I said, just before she had to get off, "divorce your husband and marry me." That was the only time in my life I proposed.

The whole idea was, of course, totally impractical, for a number of reasons, the main ones being my intense and controlling mother and, more crucially, the fact that such a change in circumstances would have dramatically reduced our chances of obtaining an exit visa. My mother and I would be quite unexpectedly granted a permission to leave the country in three months, during a very brief period of relaxation, after which few people got out, until the late 1980s. If Marina had divorced, that and getting married would have taken far longer than three months, passing over that window of opportunity. Also, marriage would have altered the situation in yet another way: instead of letting go an elderly woman and her son, a university dropout, both without any qualifications, of no use to the state, the latter would have been asked to release from its clutches a newly established young family, one member of which was an ethnic Russian, with a Russian mother who might very well apply later to join her daughter abroad under the clause of the "humanitarian reunification of families." The state would have thought twice before issuing exit visas to people it rather wouldn't see leave. No sooner was Mother summoned to the Visa Office and told we'd be allowed to go than two or three very pretty Jewish girls bent on Israel came over and hinted they'd like to marry me. That could well have been their best opportunity to fulfill their dream there and then, but Mother was quite right to shrug it off. Too much had already been sacrificed—for me especially—to follow that novel and most risky path at this point. None of this was in my thoughts at that moment—and I wasn't to know we'd be let go so soon.

"Divorce your husband and marry me," I said.

"No," she said. "I'm older than you. You'll get tired of me in a couple of months."

"You're only two years older, and it doesn't matter," I protested. "I'll never be tired of you!"

"Two and a half years older," she said and repeated: "You'll get tired of me in a couple of months."

We got off at her stop. Raindrops splashed on her hair, forehead, neck. She gave me a little wave of her hand without looking back. The bus that had become so dear to me closed its doors and moved on and out of my life. I went back home on foot. It was a three-quarters-of-an-hour walk. The rain drenched my hair, ran down the nape of my neck, and gripped every step I took.

Next morning there were flowers on her desk.

"What a beautiful bouquet!" said Ilga.

"It's to mark an occasion," said Marina.

"I see. I understand everything," said Ilga.

I had to apologize to Marina again—and, indeed, I was to buy her flowers exactly a month after our lovemaking, but even so it pained me then that I hadn't thought of it in time.

And then something happened, rather tragicomic.

"Don't touch me," Marina said. "It's all over!" When I pressed her as to why, she qualified her statement: "Finished at least for the time being." When I pressed her further, she said: "I've got a husband at home celebrating his promotion to the rank of captain, each night with a different set of people. I'm meant to be joining in the drinking and the toasting."

A few days went by without me being able to touch her. Having to see her every day and not feel her body close to mine and her lips against my lips was painful. One evening I got drunk and phoned her. I knew she was still living in her mother's flat; her husband had moved in after the marriage. So I just looked up her mother's surname in the telephone directory and dialed the number.

"Do you want the big Marina or the little one?" asked a woman's voice.

I hesitated. "Little Marina" sounded like a child, and I hazarded: "The big one."

"Speaking," said the same voice.

"Oh, Marina," I started, "It's me, I'm sorry for phoning you at home, but I simply wanted to talk to you."

"Yes," she said. "Go on."

"I see," I chuckled in my drunken state. "You can't talk because the others are listening. Am I right?"

"What is it you wanted to say to me?" she asked.

"OK, OK," I hurried on, "Marina, do you remember that tomorrow's Yevseev's birthday and we'll be all celebrating? So perhaps you and I could slip out at some point and …"

"Is that all?" she inquired, rather curtly.

"Why … yes …" I was taken aback by her tone.

"Well, hang up then," she said—and she hung up.

Next morning I was sent out, as the youngest in our section, to get the drinks to celebrate the boss's birthday. We made a contribution of a few rubles each; it was meant to be a surprise for him, but of course he knew. Marina wasn't there (Ilga contributed her share): I thought that she might just be late, but still I was on tenterhooks.

Angry with her for the way she spoke to me on the phone, I decided to visit Irene, who meanwhile had had the time to get both married and divorced—or so she said. Anyway, the birthday celebrations wouldn't start for another three or four hours. The trip by bus to the outlying and quite rundown part of the city where Irene was living now—a far cry from her parents' well-appointed apartment in the city center bordering the Park of Peter the Great—took an hour. Her communal flat was likewise rundown; she led me through an untidy kitchen to her own room. I was almost shocked by the way she'd changed since I last saw her a year before. Her face looked unhealthy, pale and haggard; nothing in it reminded me of the pert and flirtatious girl I had been so fond of at school and even after.

Her room was half in darkness, and she was wearing a thin white cloak that looked like a nightgown. She produced a bottle of fortified wine. Two things occurred to me: that she might be turning into an alcoholic, like Yevgeniya, and that she might be seducing me.

But perhaps love does have its span—at least when not consummated. Fashions also shift—and modify attitudes and even feelings. Apparently our generation was not destined to suffer the sort of Platonic love that had inspired Dante and Petrarch. I had no more interest in this girl—the one I'd dreamt about night after night and written my very first love poem to.

We chatted for an hour or so, and then I got worried about being expected back in the office with the drinks. There was also nothing really left to discuss with Irene. Her adolescent exuberance, perky coquetry, and, perhaps most importantly, beauty were all gone. I saw before me a girl with whom I had little in common. She wasn't interested in art and literature, and read no books. She worked now as an ordinary secretary with no special qualifications, but most secretaries I knew then—and would meet later in life—were much more intellectually alive, knowledge-seeking, and curious about life. Irene's informed gossip about our former classmates—who'd got engaged, married, divorced, had a child in or out of wedlock, and so on—which I used to find charmingly amusing, now irritated me. I apologized for having to go so soon, explained the reasons and promised to come again. That was the last I saw of her.

The first thing to greet me as I was coming up to the front door of our institute—with a heavy load of bottles—was a formidable backside walking away in the opposite direction. I identified it as belonging to Marina's mother, our personnel officer. But it wasn't the backside or its size that held my attention, but the man the woman was escorting. He looked drunk. Although taller than her, he was half her girth, and she almost walked him, holding him tight, like a mother taking a sick child to the doctor.

Following this, other, still weirder scenes presented themselves to me in quick succession. As I was climbing the stairs to our office, I bumped into Lena, the graphics artist from the neighboring room. Seeing me, she began to giggle uncontrollably, covering her mouth, and just about managed to say in between the giggles: "Quick go in, they're waiting for you!"

"Having fun, are you?" I asked and added, shaking my bag so that the bottles clanked: "You'll have even more fun now that you've been invited to the booze. We're celebrating Yevseev's birthday."

In our office, Aaron was laughing, rather wildly, I thought; Ilga was smiling in her reserved Baltic way, and Yevseev was shaking his head, seemingly in disbelief. Marina was still absent.

I took the bottle of brandy and three bottles of wine (we were going to invite a few important people from other sections; Ilga was meant to get a big cake and some sandwiches) out of my bag, put them on the table, and addressed Yevseev ceremoniously: "Happy birthday, Ivan Alexandrovich, many happy returns! This is a modest appreciation from all the members of our section who'd be grateful if you'd join us in a small celebration."

"Well, thank you all kindly," said Yevseev, "but for the moment I must apologize because I've got to go to a meeting. I'll be back in half an hour."

"Aren't you lucky to be alive," Aaron said to me after he left.

"Why? Is this meant to be April first, All Fools Day?"

"Marina's husband was here only a couple of minutes ago," explained Ilga. "He was looking for you. He was drunk."

"And he was brandishing his brand new revolver," Aaron elaborated. "It would have been an honor for you to die by a bullet from such a lovely glistening thing. Too late though. Amazing you two didn't come across one another on the staircase."

"I have no idea what you're on about," I said with as much dignity as I could muster. "I know—didn't Marina tell us—that he's been promoted and issued with a personal gun, so he must have had a bit extra to drink, lost his head, and come here to show off."

"All right, all right," said Aaron. "The important thing is that you are you and not your ghost—something up there must love you—and that the incident will be hushed up—for his and Marina's sake. Only we and Lena witnessed it. She immediately summoned his mother-in-law, who took him home. The moment he saw her, he gave her his gun, burst into tears, and let her lead him away."

"Where did she put the gun?" I asked, because I couldn't think of anything else to say.

"Marina Vasilyevna came with her handbag," explained Ilga. "Lena had told her what was going on, so she must have equipped herself in advance."

The penny dropped. The "big Marina" I'd spoken with on the phone was my Marina's mother.

Yevseev came back as he'd promised (I had a strong suspicion he'd had no meeting but, with his usual tact, wanted to be away while my colleagues updated me on recent events); we had three or four guests from other sections, plus Lena—and spent the two or three hours still left of the working day most pleasantly, in moderate boozing and chatting, avoiding the topics of religion, politics, sex, and guns.

CHAPTER 23: THE SPRING OF '71

M other was summoned to the Visa Office to explain to its head, one Kaija (meaning seagull in Latvian—an amusingly incongruous surname for a high-ranking Interior Ministry apparatchik with KGB connections), why, how, and when she'd signed a letter of protest to the international community against being refused to leave the country. Such letters, organized by *refusenik* leaders, had been finding their way to anti-Soviet Russian émigré publications, like the *Possev* in Germany. From what she told me, she'd remained true to form under the questioning. The authorities aimed to find and isolate the instigators who were posing a threat to their rule; the "little people" like Mother were of interest to them only insofar as they could provide information.

Kaija tried both the soft approach—gently berating her like an erring schoolgirl—and the hard—raising his voice and threatening that she'd never be allowed to leave the country unless she cooperated—but in Mother he'd picked the wrong person. "Somebody approached me in the street," she shrugged. "I've no idea who those people were, I'd never seen them before, and I signed because I've always considered—as you well know—your refusal to let me be reunited with my dear elder brother to be unlawful and in violation of our country's nobly stated policy of 'Humanitarian Reunification of Families.'"

The growing volume of protests, at home and abroad, became particularly unwelcome as the Soviet leadership decided that to be economically solvent while continuing to re-arm, it needed to play the game of détente and also prepare for Nixon's visit, which was to take place a year later. (According to Kissinger, Nixon suggested a summit to Brezhnev as early as 1970.) For *refuseniks* like us, 1971 was to be a propitious year, with détente bearing fruit in just a few weeks.

Against this background of lofty global politics (most of which would be shown as either misjudged or misapplied—see, for example, Kissinger's admission, in 1978, of the failure of his approach to the Soviet Union), in my humble microcosm my young man's love life proceeded independently.

Marina told me what had happened when I'd phoned and talked to her mother. "That was your Yevgeny," said the "big Marina" after hanging up. It was the weekend; they'd been celebrating her husband's promotion; no one was exactly sober. The freshly minted captain inquired, and she panicked, thinking I was about to spill the beans—if I hadn't spilled them already to her mother. So she confessed and told him about our kissing and corresponding. Fortunately, she hadn't told him we'd been intimate, although, as our subsequent meeting showed, he had his suspicions.

"How could you think I'd betray you?" I asked.

"I was drunk, and you'd spoken to my mother, and I thought you might've wanted to punish me for treating you coldly. So when he asked, I decided to pre-empt your revelations."

"Silly girl," I said. "But it's my fault, really. Please forgive me."

"I've already forgiven you," she said.

The revolver episode swept under the carpet, the man was supposed to come again, sober this time, to confront me.

He appeared the very next day. Marina came up to me in the office and said: "My husband is here, in the hall, and wants to talk to you."

I was very nervous, but acquitted myself well. I denied almost everything, admitting to only one friendly kiss. I said his wife had a fertile imagination—it wasn't for nothing, after all, that she was studying literature—and things had got inflated in her mind. As for our walks together, I explained that we were talking about poetry.

I didn't know how much he actually believed, but he impressed me favorably—for a military man. (My own knowledge of them, though meager, included our military course lecturer at Moscow University, a high-ranking fool.) I thought Marina's husband would be an asinine martinet, but he was quite civil and bore himself with honor. "There were letters my wife wrote to you," he said. "I'd like to have them back."

"Letters? Did you say letters?" I laughed—quite convincingly, I thought. "I wouldn't call them that. A couple of short notes, really, quite Platonic and romantic in a very conventional literary way, that's all. They were of no interest to me, so I burned them."

"You burned them?" he asked. His tone showed hesitation.

"Of course—what else could I have done with them do you think?" I summoned the most puzzled face I was capable of, as if to say, "How can anyone apparently so reasonable doubt this most obvious course of action?"

"Wait, I want to bring Marina here so you can tell both of us you'll never pester her again," he half-asked, half-ordered.

When she appeared, she was white as alabaster. "Yevgeny will never pester you again," he said. "From now on, he'll keep away from you."

"Of course," I nodded. "I always have, really. The whole thing's a figment of Marina's imagination. She's the literary kind, you know what they are like."

She withdrew without raising her eyes or saying a word.

"So I suppose this episode's over," I said to the man, "and there isn't any need to further …"

I couldn't think how to finish the sentence and let it trail off. He left, and I followed Marina into the office.

The institute was having its annual New Year Party (on the 25th of December, to allow its employees to celebrate the 31st at home with their families) in a restaurant at the top of the Sports Palace, also called the Daugava Stadium, far out of the center but well known to all city dwellers. There was to be a jazz band and dancing.

"Marina, please come," I said.

"What's the point?" she replied, saddened. "If I come, it'll have to be with my husband. So I'd better not."

"I'll feel lonely there without you," I complained.

"I have one request to make of you. Don't dance with Nikandrova."

"I won't dance with anybody," I promised.

"No need for that, dance with whomever you like, just not with her."

It was an unreasonable request, as I realized the moment I saw Vera Nikandrova at her table in the restaurant. She looked fresh and lovely. There seemed to me to be something vaguely wrong too, almost unethical, about Marina's request: I'd done all I could by asking her to marry me. She'd refused; why did she think she had the right to ask me to avoid another girl?

But I did keep my promise, technically. I danced with about a dozen female colleagues, including—twice—Mrs. Nartysh, the wife of the institute's director. (In a bit of fun and tomfoolery, I later boasted to my friends Zhenya Konyaev and Yuri Afremovich about pressing her against myself in full view of everybody, including Mr. Nartysh himself. Zhenya quipped that I should expect to be fired any day now, whereas Yuri, half-Latvian himself, wasn't fooled and said that no Latvian wife would dance with her husband's employee in public in a manner suggesting even a tiny bit of intimacy.) Vera, evidently the most popular girl at the party, was invited non-stop, with hardly a pause for breath. She and I would occasionally exchange a glance and a smile.

At last I decided that enough was enough, went up to her table, and invited her for a walk around the huge building.

We wandered at random through great dark halls and winding corridors, feeling both like fairy-tale characters and explorers of yet unknown regions, until suddenly we emerged from the darkness into the edge of the blaze of the stadium's playing area. We found ourselves on the uppermost terrace. Far, unimaginably far below, in the bright light of the ice-covered arena, a game of hockey was in progress—or perhaps a practice. We sat down, and she gave me the pink balloon some admirer had presented her with, to hold. It was wonderfully romantic, one of my life's treasured images, a girl's face in a particular place, a portrait interacting with the background.

"Let me take the confetti out of your hair," I said, and she closed her eyes. From the action beneath us came excited exclamations and shouts from the hockey players, the referee's whistles and the screeching of skates against the ice. We were alone on the crepuscular terraces. "I'm cold," she said and put her head against my chest. I hugged her.

At last we went back. The party was finishing, our colleagues crowding by the cloakroom to collect their coats.

"Give that balloon back to her!" one young man shouted to me.

"I blew it up for you, Vera," his friend said to her accusingly.

"And we both gave it to you as a New Year's gift," the first one chimed in again.

"You're a traitor!" the second man said, only half-joking, I thought. My pride, badly battered in the last few days, revived.

"Here you are," I said, giving the wretched thing back to the girl and excusing myself: "I must go to the loo."

When I came back, the crowd was rolling noisily out of the building. I retrieved my coat and waited. She came back a minute later. "All right, let's go."

"What did you tell them?" I asked.

"That you'll see me home."

I was glad she'd got rid of that silly balloon. People outside were sharing taxis. We stood in the foyer for a few minutes until most of them had gone, and then walked all the way to her house on the crunching snow, holding hands and talking. It must have taken about an hour. She lived with her aunt; I don't remember why not with her parents or even if they were alive. The aunt happened to be away, so I stayed the rest of the night at her place, having rung up my mother to say Aaron had kindly offered to put me up and that in the morning I'd go straight to work with him. There was an old-fashioned stove in the flat instead of central heating; frozen after the long walk, we fed the stove with a few logs, lit them, and enjoyed the warm blaze.

"Are they to your liking, my lord?" she asked, as though in jest, and gave a nervous little laugh.

"Very much, Vera," I answered in all seriousness and honesty, and kissed her beautiful breasts. We slept separately.

Meanwhile, things on the exit visa front were livening up. Mother was summoned again to the Visa Office and told to apply again. We couldn't, though: in order to do so she, the principal applicant, had to submit a renewed request, certified by a notary, from the close relative abroad she was asking to rejoin in the framework of the "Humanitarian Reunification of Families."

Her brother and my uncle Meir, however, had recently died in Israel. Mother had already become worried by the absence of letters from him, but it was I who'd had to be the bearer of the bad news. When in Moscow in November, I'd been told about his death by the Vilenskys, who were closely related to his wife—now his widow. (She and their children could not inform us directly, as the KGB read letters from abroad and listened in to international telephone calls.)

And so there was nothing Mother could do but play the wronged citizen card.

"I'm not going to reapply," she said in the Visa Office, "on principle. Your rejection of my original application was unjustified. I stand on my right to have that application reconsidered and honored."

After two or three attempts to convince her to apply anew, they relented and said, all right, but how do we know your brother still wants you—or if he's still there and not in another country—or, indeed, if he's still alive?

She wrote a carefully worded letter to Uncle Meir's family asking them to confirm they still wanted us, and they replied with a telegram which said they all were eagerly waiting for us and hoped to be reunited soon. The Visa Office accepted this telegram in lieu of a formal request; this was most unusual, but as I've already said, we were lucky with the timing. Soviet interests needed détente with the west and so the top brass had cleverly decided to kill two birds with one stone: get rid of troublemakers useless to the state, while presenting this to the west as a gesture of good will, humanity, and democracy.

Now we had to wait again. The institute organized a weekend trip to Tallinn, very cheap, as all such workplace outings were, and I eagerly joined. Vera also came along; we slept in the same tent in our sleeping bags, but she wanted no lovemaking. "Your 'male compulsion' is the only thing that interests you," she said. That was unfair: there, in the night tent, I recited to her Alexander Blok's whole "Carmen" cycle of poems by heart—no mean feat, clearly showing I had other interests and compulsions. For that matter, it's clear to me that it was Blok's own eros which had given birth to those poems, so charged are they with a throbbing, barely controllable desire. Later, when, on the eve of my departure from the country, the girl offered belated and impracticable intimacy, she cited that night as the turning point in her growing love for me. It wasn't, of course, my feat of memory, although the cycle is quite long, but my choice of love poems and my heartfelt, passionate way of reciting them that had particularly moved her. As for memorizing poetry, we all took it for granted that if you liked a poem you learnt it by heart. Needless to say, it would be really puzzling—and off-putting—if poets at poetry readings had to read their own verses from an open book. I never saw such a sight in Russia. All the poets I saw read—Evtushenko, Voznesensky, Vinokurov, as well as several lesser known ones—recited their work from memory. Even though I may have had an exceptional memory for poetry—remembering not only my own verses along with their whole history of revisions and variants but hundreds of my favorite poems by others—still I attribute the whole phenomenon of verse memory to this Russian tradition into which I was born. Later, when studying English literature, the first thing I did was memorize poems I liked by Yeats, Eliot, and others—and I was taken aback by our professor's request to jot down, as a kind of quiz, a line or a few words we students might be able to recall from the poems studied two days before. I wrote down the whole "Eros Turannos" by Edwin Arlington Robinson and was just embarking on Sylvia Plath's "Daddy" when our time was up. "Wow!" exclaimed the professor looking at my pages. I got his meaning only after I glanced at other students' sheets, with only a few words—or, at best, lines—on them.

In Tallinn I revisited the block of flats where I'd been raised and was greatly bemused by the shrinking of its back yard. I remembered it as huge, but now it looked really small. I also visited Grandpa Prizant's grave. It looked terribly neglected. I had a strong suspicion no one had visited it for years, ever since my mother had come from Riga just in time for his funeral. He wasn't really our grandfather—just a family friend—but we all called him Grandpa. I remembered him visiting us on weekends for dinner from a very young age. He'd stay for a while, and then we all walked with him to the tram stop to see him off. I'd grown up under his admonishments: "Boy, don't be naughty!" which I never took seriously (I don't think I was naughty: that was just something his generation was probably meant to say to a child). He was a lonely old man, most likely in his late seventies or early eighties, whom his son and daughter-in-law had tried to throw out of his own flat. Hearing this at the age of eight or nine, I could hardly understand it: how could a son do this to his own father? (Growing up with this image of a wicked son made it easier for me, years later, to understand the realism in Shakespeare's depiction of wicked daughters in *King Lear*.) The old man's words that ours was the only place in the whole world where he felt totally at home was a testimony to my parents' righteous hospitality, kindness, and human warmth. They also went to stand up for him in court when his son initiated legal proceedings to rid himself of his own parent, and it was thanks to them that he won the case and the son had to back off. Two or three years after we left, Mother dreamt of Grandpa Prizant knocking on her door with his stick. She immediately went to Tallinn and had been in time to bury him (his son wasn't present at the funeral).

In my sleeping bag in the tent, I also had a dream of him. Half-blind, with his impenetrably thick spectacles, he was standing on the platform of a railway station, while I was on the train, waving at him behind the carriage window. When I woke up, I said to Vera that I had to find the grave of one of my grandfathers. I telephoned Mother and got directions from her. The only person at the cemetery in the morning, I swept the rotten leaves off his cracked tombstone, picked up a few pebbles to put on it, as custom required, and left.

To the average Soviet citizen, the whole Baltic corner of the country looked uniformly—and temptingly—western, but we from Riga could see right away that Tallinn was freer in the European sense. (It must have been at least partly due to tourists from Finland just across the Bay of Tallinn.) The night bar with a show we went to, although modest by western standards, would not have been tolerated in Riga. A scantily dressed girl danced and ran round the stage, teasingly close to the nearest tables at which men were sitting, craning their necks toward her, their hungry eyes bulging. I was one of them, and my starved self-esteem fancied that the lady, who'd occasionally stop for a few moments opposite some table or other, lingered longer at ours and granted me a particularly sweet smile.

Back in Riga, Marina treated all us members of the section to a story of a military marriage and divorce. A student in a military academy lived with a girl. She complained, why wasn't he marrying her? He was told to marry her and threatened with expulsion if he didn't—and that in his final diploma year! So he married and lived with that woman for many years, rose to the rank of colonel, and finally divorced her. While the divorce proceedings were in motion, a military order came through promoting him to the rank of general with a concomitant move to a high appointment in Moscow. Within twenty-four hours that order was rescinded and the man was told to resign. He found out about the would-be promotion only after he got his divorce and resigned his commission.

The story was most likely authentic: in the Soviet Union there was a strict moral code both in the army and the Party, rather Victorian (and, just as in the Victorian era, lots of malodorous affairs were taking place away from the public gaze). I've already mentioned the reaction in the Communist Party headquarters to my mother's complaint about having been refused the exit visa. She claimed that she was a victim of her communist ex-husband, who'd been unfaithful to her and then had left the family without even minimal provision for her (according to her, that was meant to persuade them to let her out of the country as one who'd suffered from a perverted communist, but I strongly suspect that her primary motive was revenge on my father and the chance to poison his life). The Party man was apparently most sympathetic—which doesn't surprise me, given Mother's rhetorical powers—and begged her to abandon her plan to leave the country. "We'll bring your ex-husband to book, we'll teach him to pervert communist morality!" he promised solemnly.

But though I tended to believe Marina's story about the hapless army officer, I still wondered if the very act of telling it wasn't linked to my offer to marry her. She might have wanted to hint at her unwillingness to harm her husband's military career: a divorced officer would have little chance of further promotion, at least according to that story.

Later that same day, she was looking for a pair of scissors to cut a piece of paper, and I remembered I had a razor blade in my bag (sometimes, not wanting to overdo my morning lateness at work, I'd take my shaving things with me and, having shown up in our office for everybody to see I was there, go to the gents to shave). I gave her the razor blade—I had brought a few packets of those high-quality Wilkinson blades from the Vilenskys in Moscow, who'd been getting them from their relatives in the west—and she did her cutting with it. Then she examined it closely and said: "That's foreign: you must have relatives in the west."

Only she, Ilga, and I were in the room.

"Yes, I do," I said, with emphasis. I was certain that was enough for her to understand I was thinking of emigrating: such were the times.

She took the blade and started stroking it flatways gently against her face.

"You'll cut yourself like that," said Ilga.

"No I won't," Marina answered and went on with the blade. "Please keep it—if you like," I said.

She wrapped it up—carefully, not to say lovingly—and put it in her handbag. I think she was torn between her husband and me. The former offered long-term security; the latter, love and poetry, at least short-term. I was torn apart by my desire for her.

In the words of Aristotle, "We cannot learn without pain."

March came with its thaw. She wouldn't walk with me after work, repeating her refrain about everything being over between us, so I wandered in the parks alone, occasionally exchanging greetings and a few words with people walking their dogs. The quadrupeds' noses and eyes seemed to me restless with new ideas, beside which I myself looked stale. Struggling to work out Shakespeare's *Othello* in the original, I began to wonder if I was similar to his "sick fool Roderigo, / Whom love hath turn'd almost the wrong side out." The thought horrified me, and, unaware that what I really needed was a psychiatrist to deal with my state of mind, I dived headlong into Nature in an attempt to escape the depression—definitely clinical, requiring medication if not hospitalization.

Early in my life I'd come across the words of Vasily Sukhomlinsky (1918–1970), a Soviet educator who stressed humanistic values and sensitivity to the natural world and was one of the very first real environmentalists in the world: "A genuine amazement before the mystery of nature opening itself to us is a powerful impulse for an impetuous stream of thoughts." (Later, I'd study Henry David Thoreau and remember with warmth Sukhomlinsky's quote when encountering Thoreau's words on "a subtle magnetism in Nature.") I'm certain that Riga's beautiful well-tended gardens (with which, among the cities of my life, I can only compare those of London) and leafy streets played an important, positive role in my precarious mental state.

Ever since the signs from the Visa Office had turned favorable, I began walking those streets and gardens with a much older man who wanted to teach me Hebrew. I wish I could remember his name. He'd learned the language as a pupil at Riga's Hebrew school before World War Two and now volunteered to pass his knowledge to young people who'd applied for their exit visa to Israel. (I tried to probe into his own situation—why wasn't he thinking of leaving himself—but he said it wasn't realistic, never explaining the reasons.) His Hebrew must have been good but a bit rusty: when arriving in Israel and quoting him on the word *yofi* (cool), a variant of *yafe* (nice, beautiful), supposedly spoken only in Haifa, people shrugged and said it was a most common word, spoken all over Israel.

There was deep sadness in the man; perhaps that was why I confided in him about my feelings for a girl, and he reciprocated, telling me about his great love many years before—a love that had nearly driven him out of his mind.

I sometimes stood in front of the mirror in our flat and observed my eyes widening as though independently of me. Reading Irving Stone's *Lust for Life* in English wasn't helping either: the language wasn't easy, and the life of Van Gogh seemed frighteningly, grossly tortured even for a great artist. There's no doubt now in my mind that the giddily romantic love of a young man is nothing more than a sexual obsession; when blocked and combined with a generally upsetting situation and a hereditary tendency to depression, it easily develops first into a reactive and then a clinical depression. Still, that love moved me to write some half dozen poems, three of which I kept, publishing them in my first book.

Indeed, poetry was my comrade-in-arms in fighting on—both composing it and getting feedback on it. Marina was always forthcoming in her support ("I love your poems very much," she'd say), and so was Vera, but they were concerned parties, so to speak, and it was Bein's opinion that really helped me endure the multifaceted poignancy of the very end of my stay in the Soviet Union.

Although frowned upon by the authorities for his refusal (or rather congenital inability: he was too unruly) to toe the line and as a result was not published, his poems were known to Riga's cognoscenti. His work, in my opinion, greatly suffered from an almost total lack of critical faculty, an inability to revise and cut an ever-increasing outpouring of raw emotion (in that, he was an antipode to Vladislav Khodasevich, whose small output was crafted to perfection)—but I consider Joseph Bein (1934–2011) a notable poet and chronicler of the time. I definitely benefited from exposure to the musicality and spontaneity of his verse, qualities I would have to learn to temper and balance with judgment and reserve.

Despairing, I confessed to him my doubts about the value of poetry in general and my own gift in particular. I'll never forget his response: "Stop this nonsense! How many young people in this city write poems worth reading and remembering, like yours? Five? Ten? Twenty?"

I knew the parsimony of his praise—and was greatly cheered up.

Equally valuable—though perhaps more so in later years—was his criticism.

"Dubnov," he'd say, "one can't breathe in your lines, so packed are they." That taught me how to deploy space in verse, how to de-clutter it so that the sounds feel free inside—and helped pinpoint a major reason for the merit of a number of Russian poets. It also came in very handy much later, when John Heath-Stubbs and I translated Russian poetry into English. "Pushkin's genius lies to a large extent in his spaciousness," I'd say to John. "In that respect, he's a bit like Tennyson: both had a remarkable ear for sound." (I loved Tennyson's cadences, as in his "Tithonus," one of my favorites, but John also alerted me to what he considered his "cloying" excesses of sonority.)

Here's one of our translations of Pushkin (it first appeared in the British magazine *Agenda*); reading it out loud now, I still feel grateful to Joseph Bein for his advice, all those years ago.

From "Autumn"

O mournful season that enchants the eyes,
Pleasing to me, as beauty bids adieu
And sumptuously all nature fades and dies,
With forests clad in gold and purple hue.
In their high canopy the fresh wind sighs,
And waves of drifting mist the heavens bedew—
With first keen frost, the sun's infrequent ray
And hoary winter's frosts, still far away.

Presently Mother was called again to the Visa Office to be told we had permission to leave the country. I submitted my resignation, effective from March 25, 1971.

CHAPTER 24: ENVOI

I was to leave the country with a number of send-offs, some amusing, some threatening, some almost unbearably painful.

On a bus a drunk said to Aaron: "You'll be a surgeon." And to me: "And you, a general practitioner."

"Why can't I be a surgeon?" I asked.

"You wouldn't be able to cut," he said and showed the way I'd touch patients when examining them—ever so gently. Then he took my hand, turned it round and over and gestured despairingly.

Having fastidiously avoided expletives, I was regaled with quite a number of them in quick succession at my friend Yevgeniya's birthday. (Like Vera, she either had no parents, or they were away; perhaps one of them was an alcoholic; I seem to have paid little attention to such significant details in my close friends' lives—a measure, I now see, of my essential egocentricity at the time.) Her aunt Klavdia—her only relative around—and a few other middle-aged women gathered in the room next to us, and the aunt announced: "Let's sing with our Soviet voices!" And presently they sang several bawdy songs in which parts of the male and female anatomy worked in harmony with verbs that described their interaction.

Then the other women left and the three of us chatted. "How come you know people so well?" Klavdia asked me. "You've seen neither hunger nor death on a mass scale but you understand everybody."

It's easy now to laugh at how I must have felt flattered and probably showed it, but in my totally insecure state at the time, every good word, no matter how meager, was a blessing. Anyway, I think she mistook one thing for another. I didn't "know people" at all, let alone "so well," but I liked them and I was open to them—and was also interested in the recent past of the country. Deserved or not, in a few weeks I'd gratefully take her compliment with me to a new land where new challenges were lying in ambush.

We also discussed love. She must have had her niece and me in mind, but I'm certain she was also expressing her own deeply held belief when she said: "If you ask me, I'd say, 'Love's all there is, I wouldn't swap it for any diamond rings or any worldly treasures.'" Many, perhaps most, Russian women would have subscribed to that.

Some two weeks before quitting my job, I wrote a letter to Marina—while she was sitting next to me in our office. It was a love letter of farewell; I said that very soon I'd be leaving the country. She read it, said it wasn't so much a letter as "a work of art"—and left, although it was still early in the day. Perhaps the letter made her feel wistful. It was a kind of shamanic word pour of tenderness.

The next day I asked her to go to a good photographer's studio to have a color portrait taken. (In 1971, most photographs in the country were still black and white.) I gave her the money. The pictures arrived by post shortly after I quit: she looked very beautiful and very sad. I confided in my father, for the first time, man to man, very sheepishly, and even showed him the photo. His older man's understanding and empathy moved me and made me regret not having had his paternal guidance or at least occasional pieces of advice throughout those crucial years of negotiating adolescence and emerging into youth.

I was taking with me the regret of having missed a father.

And, of course, the KGB—how could one leave the Soviet Union without it?

Two days before quitting I approached Dmitry, the young man in charge of all photocopying for the institute. I asked him if we could photocopy my diaries together, in return for a bottle of vodka. This needs explaining.

Manuscripts, letters, anything handwritten or typed, was not allowed to be taken out of the country. I was desperate to smuggle my diaries out. Having a xeroxed copy made and trying to send it abroad through *samizdat* channels, while taking the original with me on the off-chance I might not be searched, was the most promising way to do it. The risk in making photocopies, though, was in their being prohibited. Indeed, the very name of the Xerox machine—*the Era*—was swaddled in layers of ominous secrecy. (A parallel with this today would be a government controlling everything appearing on the web and prosecuting authors of dissident posts.) There were dark stories circulating of people caught photocopying dissident *samizdat* material.

We locked the door and started working. I'd taken apart my four pocket-size diaries and fed them to the young fellow—quite amiable, especially with help of my vodka—who did the photocopying. About an hour later, when we had nearly finished—the original pages, dropped by the primitive Xerox machine, were strewn all over the floor—the door opened and Mysina, the head of the section, walked in. Dmitry had made the mistake of taking the key out of the lock; Mysina had another key and had unlocked the door from the outside.

With dexterity unexpected in a woman of such substance, she moved to pick up the pages from the floor. But I was quicker: in two swift movements I swept them into a corner away from her, gathered the heap up and stuffed it in my pockets. Still, she managed to grab a few pages.

"Please give those back to me," I said. "They're mine, pages from my literary diaries."

"First I'll have to look at them and then we'll see," she said, clutching her trophies.

Yevseev, the head of our section, shook his head sadly: "I thought you were an intelligent and educated young man, but you've behaved like a country bumpkin. All you had to do was to ask me, and I'd have arranged it for you in no time, quietly and safely."

I felt terrible, letting him down like that. Unauthorized use of photocopying machines was a grave offense, pregnant with trouble, the degree of which depended on the nature of the xeroxed material. And that, indeed, was the next stage in the saga.

Explanation

From: Yevgeny Dubnov
To: Comrade Uldis Janovich Nartysh, Director, State Latvian Institute of Urban Construction Planning

One of my most admired writers, Konstantin Simonov, writes in his memoirs about a suitcase he once lost on the train. The suitcase contained a manuscript of his novel. He never reconstructed it. Trying my own talent as a writer in my own small way (I've already had a few poems published, in, among others, the newspaper *Lenin's Path*), I became terrified that I too might lose something which would be indispensable for me when writing prose (whereas poetry can be memorized, prose can't)—my youthful diaries. I didn't realize I needed a special permission, as my diaries are no more than a young person's observations of life and people around him—often childishly silly, but sometimes, I venture to hope, astute and sharp. I explained my fears of losing those notes to my friend Dmitry in the printing and copying section: he thought them exaggerated but was kind enough to agree to help. Finally, we made those photocopies (there wasn't much, just a small number of diary pages) in the lunch break rather than working hours. I am sincerely sorry if it caused any misunderstanding. If somebody is at fault, it is I and not Dmitry, who only innocently wanted to help a friend and a budding writer.

I submitted this letter on the day of my resignation; all further news had to come from Aaron, who came several times to visit me during the day when he could get away from work (my mother, true to form, treated him to her renowned chicken soup).

According to his reports, Yevseev and even Nartysh himself were all for ignoring the incident, but Mysina had already brought it to the attention of the head of the fire safety department (throughout the country, these were the watchful eyes of the KGB) who, in turn, wasn't prepared to hush it up but instead insisted that Nartysh forward the information to the central KGB headquarters of the Latvian Republic. Aaron also said that I was a fool—which I already knew—because only recently two Latvian chaps had been caught xeroxing the Bible—a terrible crime, promoting religion with the use of the atheist state machinery! So the issue was sensitive—and who knew if the secret police would let it go or decide to put our exit visas on hold while they looked deeper into the matter. They might well decide to investigate my writings, views, connections, and even—should they come to the conclusion that I was a young dissident writer—prefer to keep me in the country rather than have me besmirch it from abroad. That outcome was probably unlikely—or so I hoped—but who knew if they wouldn't find it safest and easiest to defer our departure until they had examined my case—"until further notice"? Then the propitious political moment may be gone and our lives return to the limbo of uncertainty. Nothing was ever certain in that country with no real laws.

Presently I was summoned to the office of Nartysh himself. "It'll most likely be for a sort of 'explanatory conversation,'" said Aaron. "Do you know what was written in those pages Mysina managed to grab?" "I've gone through all the pages," I said, "and although I'm not entirely sure, it seems there are four missing, from my first year at Moscow University. This is good news. I was even more of a nincompoop then than I am now, and the things I jotted down were mostly adolescent fun rather than dissident observations. But who knows? Even one short entry harshly critical of—or just laughing at—the state …" I trailed off, withering under Mother's pitying gaze. "If it comes to that," she said, "you can stay here and nurture your idiocy—I won't become a hostage to it. I'll be leaving."

She'd have never left without me—for one thing, it would have been a victory for my father. I'd have stayed with him if she'd gone.

Entering Nartysh's room, I was relieved to see that there was no one else there, no "plainclothes men"—not even the head of our fire safety! That meant the situation was still salvageable. On his table lay four pages from my diary—the handwriting was childish! So I'd been right: they were early notes.

"I read your explanation," he said, "and it does make some sense, however limited. I also tried to read these pages from your diaries. Could you please help me decipher your handwriting in a couple of places?"

Hungrily I grabbed the page he was offering me and glued my eyes to it. Most of it was indeed nonsense from my first university year, but in the middle of the page there were a few lines about a Young Communist League outing we'd had outside of Moscow on some red calendar day or other. I'd sarcastically described the way the majority of our fellow students (Vitaly, Grisha, myself, and two or three others had remained on the perimeter) had gathered around the bonfire and sung Young Communist songs. Thinking back, I'm not proud of the supercilious and snide tone of that entry, but it might have been a kind of psychological defense. It was difficult at the age of seventeen to be different from dozens and dozens of your peers, and something in my subconscious mind must have yearned to join in and be like everybody else, arms round each other's shoulders, boys and girls singing together. These were basically nice brainwashed kids—but I'm glad I never took part in their ideologically inspired gatherings, even if the price was certain alienation and, worse perhaps, that defensively assumed sense of superiority.

I decided to read out loud the previous entry instead, which described a drunken fight in the dorm: "And so he kicked him in his—I beg your pardon, comrade director—in his very bum!"

"Now please read the one underneath," he pointed his finger at the Young Communist gathering. It was clear to me that he or somebody else had done their homework.

"'Fire … blaze … singing … songs … students … arms round one another …' I'm unable to decipher my own childish handwriting from over three years ago, Uldis Janovich, but it seems to be a description of some sort of faculty excursion outside Moscow, lighting the fire and all of us singing together."

He picked up another page: "Would you mind reading this?" Once more it was a problematic entry, a mockery of an ideological event. And once more I did the same trick: first I readily read out something surrealistically absurd before or after the offending entry, like the inability of a drunk to urinate into the bowl and instead pissing all over his own long winter coat; then I slowed down to puzzle out the script.

Nartysh was closely watching my performance; I thought he looked bemused: was I really the infantile and frivolous young man I appeared to be or was there more to this than met the eye? To my surprise, he let me have my pages back—but, of course, they would have been xeroxed for the KGB.

That night I had a frightening dream: I was passing by a never-ending wall covered with huge photographs of the country's leaders, each of whom followed me with his eyes. I recalled the dream years later when, working for the BBC Monitoring Service and having to watch Soviet television, I wrote this poem:

All My Russia

In the film I was watching there were flying cranes;
Men for the front were leaving their girls grief-numbed
In that part of earth—most memorable—that remains
The motherland where I was born and named.

My eyes kept shifting from the TV screen
To the photo-portraits hanging over it,
That row of leaders' faces with obscene
Scowling jowls, all seeming to connect

In one clenched tragedy of terror and misery,
Cynicism and submission. And suddenly
It became for the first time clear to me:
This picture was all my Russia, locked in me.

(Reading, 1984, translated with Anne Stevenson)

Ultimately, there was no follow up. From what I knew first-hand and from what I heard and read, then and later, the Soviet Secret Police people were far from obtuse. Their selection and training were tough and the remuneration and respect from their superiors, in the Service and the Party, high. They must have decided not to waste their time on a youngster who was merely a nuisance when there were real threats around. Various political trials were coming up later in 1971, and juggling the détente abroad and repression at home required the KGB's undivided attention. With my irrepressible—incurable, really—sense of comic abandonment, hilarity, and fun, I imagine the KGB man—most likely low-ranking, to fit the case—looking at my file in front of him and saying disgustedly: "Fuck you, why are you fucking wasting my fucking precious time on this fucking little shithead?" (Or something to that effect, I won't stand on the exact wording.)

I sent the xerox copy of my diaries abroad through clandestine channels (it would arrive safely) and took the original with me on the train to Brest-Litovsk on the border. I put it in my pocket. I wasn't searched.

That was still to come.

In late April I had two vivid dreams, respectively—and quite appropriately, I think, for the times and my personal life—political and lyrical. In one, theaters and concert halls were being turned in front of my very eyes into secret police headquarters and a voice said: "Pay attention, remember! There's a Japanese saying: 'The nail that sticks out will be hammered down!'" In the other, it was snowing in mid-spring in a Riga park and there was Marina, looking very sad.

I couldn't very well do much about the first dream, but I decided to act on the second when it began to snow on the first or second of May—something unheard of in Riga's climate. Just before five, the end of the working day at our institute, I hid myself in the entrance hall of a block of flats across the street and when Marina came out, I followed her—not crossing and slightly behind, until I was certain none of our colleagues was around. I didn't want to embarrass her. I caught up with her just before the University of Riga.

"Marina," I said, "I wanted to talk to you. Soon I'll be leaving the country."

"Please," she said. "Please. Let me be."

"One last conversation," I begged.

"This isn't like you," she said. "This asking and pleading doesn't become you. Your future is before you—it is poetry."

That was the last time I saw her. It was the most painful of my farewells or, as I've called them, send-offs from the country.

I was leaving Riga with terrible feelings of guilt for the pain I'd apparently caused Marina. I realized much later that there was no logical reason for me to have such feelings, which are prominent in the three poems inspired by my love for her published in my first volume of poetry. I never imposed myself on her and I offered to marry her. She chose to stay with her husband, and that was that.

But guilt had been deeply implanted in me by my mother. Wherever I lived, I was to go on blaming myself for absolutely everything, including situations not of my own making and even other people's mistreatment of me. I now think that if there is to be any self-reproach at all in such cases, it should be confined to a sense of regret for coming too close to immoral manipulators and intriguers, having missed the tell-tale signs. In general, it's a real conundrum, because to some extent you're so often really at fault, to some degree, while on the other hand it's quite arrogant to think you can prevent so much in life, as if it is all under your control. Throughout the vicissitudes of my life, I've learnt that in order to remain sane it's essential to measure and establish, as rationally and precisely as possible, one's own degree of guilt and remorse. (And in general, the therapeutic process is not only the Freudian precept "Where id was, ego shall be," but also the journey from the vague to the defined.)

I was fortunate to leave my father—until our reunion twenty years later—with a positive image of him. Although still very much against my leaving and hardly on good terms with Mother, he kept helping us with all practical and physical matters, like ordering containers and packing our old furniture for shipping. I remember that in our last days in the country he was always around, worrying and assisting. I, in my depressed state, wasn't of much use.

Vera Nikandrova telephoned amidst the preparations; we met in Petrovsky Park at the bottom of my street. I still remember the beautiful black-and-white neckerchief she was wearing. "I've made up my mind to ... lose my ... to become intimate with you," she said, "and I'll put my aunt before the accomplished fact. I want us to become lovers—even though you're leaving!"

It was less than a week before my departure; I was about to part from Father, friends, the cocoon of my mother tongue, everything—and go into a totally unknown world. She'd left it too late. I told her I loved her and gently persuaded her to abandon her resolution as impractical. She was the sweetest girl I've ever met.

The farewell at Riga's Central Railway Station was one of the most poignant events in my whole life, generally not short of hurt. I didn't know (and I still don't) if I'd ever see again my beloved cityscape and the landscape that had nourished my childhood and early youth: the gigantic squares of Moscow, Riga's fair gardens, the Baltic's sloping dunes, and that visionary and evanescent beauty of the snowflake, which was present in my life for up to six months each and every year. (Nor did I have any inkling I was lugging myself along with myself: all my only half guessed-at complexes, obsessions, compulsions, and a tendency to depression; on the positive side, I'd also take with me Language and Poetry.)

More immediately, on the platform stood my father and the closest friends from my adolescence and early youth, privy to my innermost thoughts and secrets, Zhenya Konyaev and Yuri Afremovich. My father looked sorrowful, my friends were encouragingly optimistic, perhaps only for my sake.

That morning's telephone conversation with Vera had also made me ache. She wanted to come to the station to see me off. "I'd like to give you my neckerchief as a parting present," she said. "You liked it." I had to persuade her against coming. It was a given that there'd be secret police cadres on the platform, to photograph those seeing off people emigrating to the west (a.k.a. "traitors of their Socialist Motherland"). Now, Zhenya and Yuri (who, still a soldier, managed to get two days' leave from the army) were surely known to them as my friends of many years and not suspect politically. Aaron Shlomovitch was known as my boss and in good standing in the institute as an engineer; being Jewish, it would have been better for him not to attend my departure (and I appreciated his dauntlessness: few in his position would have come), but still, there was nothing so terribly egregious about his seeing off his young employee. It would have most likely merited a marginal footnote in the KGB's ledgers, but no more. For Vera, though, I felt it was inadvisable. Let her not have even that marginal footnote, I thought. Let her be totally clean in their eyes, let her have a normal Soviet life with no KGB shadow at all, no matter how small.

Altogether, there must have been some two dozen people on the platform, a few of them young members of Riga's clandestine Zionist community, the people I'd gone to Rumbula with to clear the place for the hoped-for monument to the fallen in the Holocaust. Having said goodbye to everybody and standing now at the carriage window, the train's heavy shudder a long-familiar harbinger of immediate departure, all at once my glance fell on my father's figure, looking hunched and miserable on the edge of the crowd. I had already taken my leave of him, but something prompted me at that last moment to shout out to him: "Farewell, Father! Dad! Farewell!"

As a child, I'd often go to Tallinn's Central Railway Station after school to listen to the tracks, holding my ear close to the steel rails. Now, on my most fateful ever rail journey, I kept imagining all the voices of my life till then—of my twenty-one and a half years—reaching me simultaneously with the sounds made by the train, the two mixing and interweaving and depending on each other—and, finally, becoming fused together.

The train followed the purpose of the rails; it rumbled, switching to other tracks that were burnished white under the sun; it carried me into the enigmatic distance and undiscovered, unexplored languages yet to be mastered.

We arrived at Brest-Litovsk, a Belorussian town and a major railway junction on the border with Poland. There we were to be searched and transferred to a train to Warsaw and ultimately Vienna.

The young man—most likely an employee of the Ministry of the Interior, perhaps even its KGB branch—who searched our luggage turned out to be unexpectedly decent. He let me keep all my correspondence—something not allowed by protocol, according to which no handwritten documents were to be taken out of the country. Browsing through the letters, he came across my correspondence with David Burliuk (1882–1967), an avant-garde painter, "the father of Russian Futurism" and Vladimir Mayakovsky's close friend. (Burliuk left Soviet Russia after the Revolution and, when I corresponded with him in my early adolescence, had been living in the USA—where Mayakovsky had actually visited him—for many years; at the time of my teenage infatuation with Mayakovsky and Russian Futurist Movement, I had been in touch with the Mayakovsky Museum in Moscow, and they had kindly provided Burliuk's address in America. My correspondence with Burliuk is now in the Bakhmeteff archive of Russian and East European culture at Columbia University in New York).

The man took his time reading Burliuk's letters to me carefully. Then he came across a postcard from the celebrated Soviet critic Korney Chukovsky, with whom, encouraged by Burliuk's positive response, I had corresponded two years later, when I was sixteen (I had complained to him that the critics had been consistently underestimating the influence of Futurism on Mayakovsky—and, lo and behold!—he had wholeheartedly agreed with my point.)

I see this Interior Ministry official facing me tall and lean, probably in his early to mid-thirties. He stuck in my mind because he didn't search me and also because of the following episode. My jacket pockets held all the pages of my diaries from 1967 to 1971. Later I asked many other émigrés about their exit from the country: almost all said they'd been searched mercilessly, including their persons.

The signature on the postcard was almost illegible. "This is from Korney Chukovsky, isn't it?" he asked. "Yes, it is," I said. And then he asked Mother to come with him: he wanted a word with her.

I was on tenterhooks. What if, in addition to everything else, they had got to know about my blunder with the photocopying in Riga and my file had been passed on to the local KGB? After about a quarter of an hour Mother came back, stony-faced. "What was it all about?" I asked her in a whisper, while a few yards away the man was busy looking at the green-bound dog-eared notebook containing all the poems I'd written up to then. She said, almost inaudibly: "This foul regime—a curse upon it!" (Later, in the train, when we had crossed the frontier, she told me about her conversation with the customs official. "Leave your son behind," he'd said, trying to make her change her mind. "Leave on your own, you're an elderly woman, another few years and you'll be a pensioner, but he's young, he writes poetry and criticism, and it looks as if he's beginning to be noticed. Who knows what awaits him in exile, while here in his motherland he could make a name for himself?")

"I'm afraid you can't take this out of the country," said the man, putting my notebook aside on a table, "it's against the rules."

I'm still grateful to him for having confiscated my poems and I hope by now the KGB has got rid of them once and for all (even if in a couple of years' time they were to use an immature and over-romantic poem from that notebook in what I thought was a tongue-in-cheek warning to stop translating anti-Soviet articles—something I did as a student in Israel to supplement my grant; I hope to describe how the KGB did this in a later volume). I don't think one's juvenilia—a period of apprenticeship—should be of interest to anybody. By May 25, 1971—the date of my departure from the Soviet Union—I must have written down in that notebook about three or four dozen poems, half of them at least the exercises of a trainee. I'd reconstruct from memory those I wanted to keep—and, unafraid that anything might slip my mind, in no particular rush, I'd actually do so only a few months later, by which time I'd have decided to keep only about a third.

Over the border, on a train to Warsaw, Polish policemen (in green, like my confiscated poetry notebook) checked our documents. Upon reaching Warsaw, we found out that we'd have to wait for two or three hours for our connection to Vienna. I decided to take a stroll rather than sit and wait in the claustrophobic compartment.

An incorrigible photographer, I took my camera with me for possible snapshots. Having changed a ruble to zlotys to buy a couple of postcards with rather drab views of Warsaw at a station kiosk, I happened to see a breathtaking sight. There was a tall tree growing further down next to the railway tracks, reaching as high as a narrow little bridge hanging low over them. The bridge looked old and rickety. Against the background of that tree stood a young man and a girl, locked in a kiss. That was a God-sent photo opportunity, not to be missed. I chose the best spot to take the picture and clicked the shutter.

Just as I was looking for another position (the young people were still motionlessly in love), a green-clad Polish policeman came for me at an agitated trot. He shepherded me into a small room inside the station, where I was interrogated by another green fellow. The latter spoke passable, if heavily accented Russian. They surely thought I was a spy photographing their military readiness. Explaining myself, I went on and on enthusiastically and romantically about the two lovers on the bridge and my passion for photography, until the man dismissed me with a wave of his hand. The first chap escorted me back to my carriage and told me not to get off the train again. Imagine my mother's reaction when a Polish policeman delivered me straight to our compartment and into her hands!

In the night, as the train sped through Poland, I had a dream. In it appeared many of those who'd come to see me off in Riga. My father was speaking to me didactically—it sounded like a paternal pep talk—and after his address, somebody whose face I couldn't see made a strange announcement: "Upon your arrival, we give you our farewell gifts."

On waking, I wrote it down immediately. A few minutes later the train pulled up at Vienna's central station. We were beyond Soviet reach.

Ahead lay *metanoia*, the journey of fundamental shift, the ordeal of deep change.